THE THEORY OF PROTECTION

THE
THEORY OF
PROTECTION

BY

W. M. CORDEN

OXFORD UNIVERSITY PRESS

Oxford University Press, Walton Street, Oxford OX2 6DP

OXFORD LONDON GLASGOW NEW YORK
TORONTO MELBOURNE WELLINGTON CAPE TOWN
IBADAN NAIROBI DAR ES SALAAM LUSAKA ADDIS ABABA
KUALA LUMPUR SINGAPORE JAKARTA HONG KONG TOKYO
DELHI BOMBAY CALCUTTA MADRAS KARACHI

© OXFORD UNIVERSITY PRESS 1971

First published 1971
First issued as paperback 1977

Casebound ISBN 0 19 828171
Paperback ISBN 0 19 828413

Reproduced and printed by photolithography and bound
in Great Britain at The Pitman Press, Bath

To Dorothy

PREFACE

THE essentials of the new positive theory of effective protection and tariff structure are presented in the core of this book, Chapters 3 to 7. These chapters expand, elaborate and revise my article 'The Structure of a Tariff System and the Effective Protective Rate'[1] and take into account recent developments in this branch of theory. The key chapters are Chapter 3, which sets out the theory of effective protection in partial equilibrium terms, and Chapters 4 and 5, which similarly develop the theory of tariff structure in general equilibrium terms.

While this book can be read right through, some readers may wish to read only the more original or advanced sections, so here is a guide. Chapter 2 is elementary, unsophisticated *grammar*. Such static partial equilibrium analysis is very useful for handling many practical problems and is a necessary foundation for the more difficult analysis of later chapters, but the reader familiar with trade theory or impatient with Marshallian manipulations should certainly pass it by. This also applies to Chapter 9. The other chapters, notably the five core chapters, are not at the same elementary level, though readers familiar with trade theory could pass over section I of Chapter 3 and of Chapter 4. Chapter 8 is a brief excursion into second-best welfare economics. I intend to deal with the welfare aspects of protection more thoroughly in another book, *Tariffs, Welfare and Growth*, the present book being the first instalment in a review of all the main aspects of the theory of protection, designed to make this theory more realistic while maintaining rigorous methods of analysis. Finally, Chapters 9 and 10, on the theory of quantitative import restrictions, are not crucial to the main lines of the argument.

In general, the level of analysis is rather simple. I have kept mathematics to the bare minimum, mainly because I have a personal preference for diagrammatic reasoning and exposition. Chapter 6, section VII of Chapter 4 and section VI of Chapter 7 call for more background in economic theory than the rest of the book, and some readers may be advised just to skim over these.

[1] *Journal of Political Economy*, 74, June 1966, 221–37.

At this stage I should mention one difficulty I encountered, namely the choice of a suitable title for the book. It will be evident that the actual title chosen is broader than the coverage of the book, since I deal only with a part—perhaps a half—of the theory of protection. The rest—welfare, growth, monopoly, and so on—is to come in the other book. I hope that too many readers will not be disappointed. Plausible titles that were reasonably precise in describing the contents appeared too clumsy, and all the brief titles, other than the one chosen, too narrow. The final choice of title rested on an unscientific, small-sample public opinion poll.

I am grateful to the University of Chicago Press for permission to incorporate in this book some passages from my article in the *Journal of Political Economy*.

The main ideas of this book were conceived, and some of the book was written, while I was at the Australian National University from 1962 to 1967. Much of the theory in the book is a by-product of my work on Australian tariffs and import restrictions; the practical importance of tariffs in Australia and the hot controversy surrounding tariff policy have been constant stimulants. More recently I have been interested in the protectionist policies of some less developed countries.

A centre-piece of this book is the new, but very simple, concept of *effective protection*. I have put down in Appendix I some notes on its origin; this takes the place of acknowledgments here to the many others who have worked on this subject. In addition, there is a comprehensive bibliography in Appendix III. Here I must refer particularly to Harry Johnson, who is one of the pioneers, as well as popularizers, of the modern theory of effective protection and whose perceptive criticisms as editor of the *Journal of Political Economy* of the first draft of my 1966 article, as well as general encouragement over many years, have been quite invaluable.

I owe a great deal first to the Australian National University and then to Nuffield College for providing excellent facilities and stimulating environments. Some of the work was also done while I was a visitor at Monash University in 1969. John Flemming, Harry Johnson, Maurice Scott and Richard Snape have all read drafts of various chapters and given me valuable comments which have, I hope, made the final result less imperfect. Stanley Engerman also commented on several chapters and was a constant adviser at the last stages. I owe a particular debt to John Black who read the whole book in draft, and again in proof, and saved me from many slips and confusions. The development of my ideas and my methods of approach have been much influenced by James Meade, my teacher at the London School of Economics, and by Heinz Arndt, my close colleague at the Australian National University for five years. Miss Penny Sylvester of Nuffield College very competently typed several drafts of much of the book. Finally, my greatest debt is owed to my wife and daughter who, in two continents, have put up cheerfully with a husband and father endlessly drawing diagrams and dreaming about theories.

W. M. C.

Nuffield College, Oxford
November 1970

CONTENTS

8. On the Uniformity of Tariff Structures   **180**

9. Import Quotas: Partial Equilibrium Analysis   **199**

10. Import Quotas: General Equilibrium Analysis   **221**

11. Conclusion   **239**

Appendices   **245**

Author Index   **259**

Subject Index   **261**

1

INTRODUCTION

THIS book presents a systematic restatement of the positive, static theory of protection. The term *protection* is interpreted very broadly. Traditionally the policy instrument of the tariff has been identified with the target of protection, but this is just one possible assignment of instrument to target. Here we are concerned with the whole range of trade taxes and subsidies, direct subsidies and taxes on the consumption or production of traded goods, multiple exchange rates, and indeed all interventions affecting trade, including quantitative restrictions. We are concerned mainly with their effects on resource allocation—that is, protection—but do not ignore other effects, notably on the pattern of consumption and on the balance of payments, and also on the prices of the factors of production.

The type of question the analysis should help to answer is the following. Consider a country with a complicated set of tariffs and other trade interventions. What are the net effects of the whole structure on resource allocation, on the consumption pattern, and so on? Which industries have been expanded by the structure and which contracted? We are not concerned with assessing the desirability of the protective structure or with defining the properties of an optimum structure. Hence the task is limited to *positive* analysis; but this is an essential foundation for welfare analysis.[1]

The theory of protection has recently made considerable advances on both the welfare and the positive side. The welfare theory of protection is concerned with 'arguments' for protection and free trade and with assessing the social benefits or costs from systems of protection. It is as old as modern economics itself, and the free trade versus protection issue dominated much of the literature of British economic thought in the nineteenth century. The debates and issues have been revived

---

[1] Chapter 8 is a diversion into second-best welfare analysis.

in recent years as a by-product of the reaction against colonial-
ism and the desire for industrialization by less developed
countries. The recent advances in the theory of trade and
welfare stem mainly from the work of James Meade,[2] have
been carried forward by various writers, notably Harry
Johnson,[3] and have led to considerable clarification of the
issues. The net result of the new trade-and-welfare analysis
is the view that tariffs and other interventions in trade are
hardly ever first-best devices. For example, the infant-industry
argument for protection rests on some kind of externality or
'distortion' connected with the domestic production or use of
particular factors, or some failure in a particular market,
possibly the capital market, and this requires not a tariff,
but an intervention as close to the point of the distortion or
market failure as possible. This approach hinges on various
assumptions which are by no means always realistic, but these
matters we need not pursue further here. The essential problem
is to define realistically the relevant constraints and then
determine the optimum structure in the light of them.

Until recently one would hardly have thought that one could
devote a whole book almost solely to the *positive* theory of
protection. The positive theory consisted of not much more
than the sort of simple analysis which makes up Chapter 2
of this book, section I of Chapter 4, and the earlier parts of
Chapter 9. It is in the positive theory that the most rapid
advances have been made since 1965, mainly through the
development of the new concept of *effective protection*. The
stimulus to the application and elaboration of the new ideas
has come from the need to understand the workings of those
less developed economies which have been using many complicated types of trade intervention. While the subject matter
of this book should be of special interest to students of less
developed countries, we are not concerned here with particular
countries or cases, nor is this book a guide to practical problems
of measurement. It presents, rather, the fundamental tools of
analysis. To appreciate the full significance of the issues

[2] J. E. Meade, *Trade and Welfare* (Oxford University Press, London, 1955).
[3] The best exposition is in H. G. Johnson, 'Optimal Trade Intervention in
the Presence of Domestic Distortions', in R. E. Baldwin et al., *Trade, Growth
and the Balance of Payments* (Rand McNally, Chicago, 1965).

discussed in this book and the importance of the tools, the reader is referred to the new book by Little, Scitovsky and Scott, *Industry and Trade in Some Developing Countries*,[4] while a book which applies the new tools for actual measurement, and discusses many of the practical measurement problems, is Balassa's *The Structure of Protection in Developing Countries*.[5]

We shall make all sorts of simplifying assumptions. The analysis is static. There is perfect competition, and hence also absence of increasing returns. Tariffs and other devices do not discriminate between foreign countries of supply or demand. The levels of economic activity and the tariffs and trade interventions of foreign countries are given, so that there are no international repercussions through multiplier effects, nor any retaliatory tariffs or reciprocal tariff reductions. Some of these assumptions are not as limiting as might seem. The extension to a growing economy may not be very difficult, and in any case static analysis is the essential foundation for the analysis of protection and growth. The assumption of perfect competition is generally not crucial at all, and is removed at various points, notably in Chapters 9 and 10. Increasing returns could also be allowed for rather easily. But one need hardly justify the making of simplifying assumptions; justification is needed only for the choice of particular simplifying assumptions rather than others. Here a very important characteristic of our approach must be noted. We are mainly concerned with the small country—the country which not only faces given world demand and supply conditions in the form of given demand and supply *curves* but which is a price-taker rather than a price-maker in world markets. World prices can of course alter for exogenous reasons; the point is that the policies of 'our' country cannot alter them. The assumption is removed at various points, but it is a key assumption in much of the book. So one must certainly ask oneself whether it is a reasonable assumption. There is hardly a country which cannot influence at all the prices at which it trades. But many countries, notably most of the less developed

[4] I. Little, T. Scitovsky, M. Scott, *Industry and Trade in Some Developing Countries* (Oxford University Press, London, 1970).

[5] B. Balassa (ed.), *The Structure of Protection in Developing Countries* (Johns Hopkins Press, Baltimore, 1971).

countries, cannot influence their trading prices very much, especially import prices. The analysis in this book is really meant mainly for the study of these countries. The art of economic theory is to select sensible strategic simplifications, and the assumption of given world prices seems to meet this need; it is a convenient first approximation for the study of many economies, making possible the introduction of numerous complications in other directions.

The plan of the book is as follows. Chapter 2 presents the partial equilibrium theory of protection on the assumption that the protected industry is vertically integrated. Chapter 3 introduces the concept of effective protection but still adheres to partial equilibrium analysis. Chapters 4 and 5 develop the theory of tariff or 'protective' structure in general equilibrium terms: Chapter 4 is *real* analysis, with the exchange rate or money factor prices assumed to maintain balance of payments equilibrium, while Chapter 5 is concerned with the balance of payments effects of a protective structure and the appropriate exchange rate adjustment. Chapters 6 and 7 deal with important difficulties in the theory of effective protection and tariff structure. The general approach is first to tackle a problem with partial equilibrium analysis and then, where possible, to expand to general equilibrium. Chapter 8 applies some of the preceding analysis to an issue of tariff policy, namely whether a tariff structure should be uniform or at least whether the optimum structure should have uniformity as a reference point and depart from it in a systematic way. Finally, Chapter 9 presents the theory of import quotas in partial equilibrium terms while Chapter 10 puts import quotas into a general equilibrium framework, the aim of these two chapters being to integrate the theory of quotas with the theory of trade taxes and subsidies advanced in earlier chapters.

2

THE PARTIAL EQUILIBRIUM
FOUNDATIONS

WE begin with the partial equilibrium, static analysis of
tariffs and other taxes and subsidies affecting trade. Production
at home is perfectly competitive and in this chapter is assumed
to be vertically integrated. Until section V the elasticity of
foreign supply is infinite, the country playing only a small
part as a buyer in the world market. Together with the parallel
assumption for exports—that the elasticity of foreign demand
is infinite—this may be called the *small country assumption*
and will be maintained also in the four subsequent chapters.[1]

I. *The Partial Equilibrium Analysis of Tariffs*

We consider a single homogeneous product which is both
imported and produced at home. This will be called an *importable* product. In Fig. 2.1 the supply curve of imports is SS' so
that OS is the free trade price of imports. It is drawn for a
given exchange rate. It will be defined here as the price of
imports at the importing country's frontiers and thus includes
costs of transporting the good to the country; it is thus the
c.i.f. ('cost, insurance, freight') price. If the cost of transport
were excluded it would be the f.o.b. ('free on board') price.
The supply curve of domestic import-competing production is
HH'. It traces out the marginal cost of domestic production.
The domestic product is assumed to be a perfect substitute for
the import. The domestic demand curve for the product is DD'.
It represents the demand for imports and domestic production
combined. Neither HH' nor DD' need be a straight line. Free
trade domestic production is OA and consumption OB. The

---

[1] *Small country assumption* is a convenient shorthand to be used throughout
this book. Many small economies are of course significant suppliers in the
world market for their main exports, and hence face less than perfectly elastic
export demand schedules. But it is rarer for a small economy to be able to
affect significantly the prices of most of its imports.

assumption is made that when the price of domestic output is identical to the price of imports the consumers first take up all domestic production at that price, imports being the residual. Alternatively it might be assumed that the domestic product is marginally of better quality or more conveniently available than imports, so that it is this marginal difference which creates a preference for the former when the prices of the two are the same.

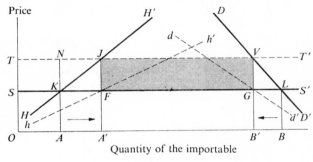

Fig. 2.1

The precise assumptions underlying the partial equilibrium supply and demand curves HH' and DD' need not be set out because a variety of assumptions are compatible with such curves. All sorts of reactions affecting prices of other goods or of factors, or indeed government policies, can be supposed to be associated with movements along these curves. The essence of the partial equilibrium method is that we blinker ourselves to look only at the product or industry concerned and ignore any reactions outside the immediate field of vision. It is normal, but not essential, to assume that money income stays constant. We must assume only that movements along one of the curves do not shift the position of the other curve; there must be no relationships between them other than those indicated in the diagram.

Now a tariff is imposed at the rate ST/OS. This is its *ad valorem rate*, namely the proportion by which the tariff raises the value or price of the import to the buyers in the domestic market. The rate per physical unit of the import—the *specific rate*—is ST. The tariff could be fixed in either form. If the import price stayed at OS a specific tariff of ST would have exactly the same effect as an *ad valorem* tariff of ST/OS. But if the import price fell the *ad valorem* equivalent of a given specific tariff of ST would rise and if the price rose the *ad valorem* equivalent would fall. We shall assume that the tariff applies to all imports whatever the source; it is thus *non-discriminatory*.

The tariff raises the price received by domestic producers and paid by domestic consumers from OS to OT. This in turn raises domestic output to OA', reduces consumption of the product to OB', and reduces imports to $A'B'$. Thus there is a squeeze on imports both from the production and the consumption side, as indicated by the arrows. The value of imports falls by $AKFA'$ plus $B'GLB$. Customs revenue raised on the imports which remain after the tariff is imposed is $FJVG$ (the shaded area). We shall assume until section VI that the tariff is not so high that it completely eliminates imports. Instead of the tariff we might have had an import subsidy, which is simply a negative tariff. It would have reduced the domestic price below OS and all the preceding and following conclusions referring to a tariff would be reversed.

The following effects of the tariff can be distinguished. (1) *Production* or *protection effect*. Domestic output rises by AA'. The protected output, measured at its import equivalent value, is worth $AKFA'$ and at the new domestic prices established by the tariff, $ANJA'$. An import subsidy would have yielded *anti-protection*. (2) *Consumption effect*. Consumption falls by BB'. (3) *Import* or balance of payments *effect*. As already mentioned, imports fall by the sum of the production and the consumption effect. (4) *Revenue effect*. Customs revenue is raised. (5) *Redistribution effect*. Since the price to domestic producers has risen at the expense of domestic consumers there is a redistribution of income. On the original domestic output of OA this redistribution is $STNK$.

The consumer is in fact subsidizing the output of the domestic product by ST per unit. On the total amount of output this subsidy is $STJF$. This is the *subsidy-equivalent* of the tariff. If there had been no tariff but instead output had been subsidized directly from the Treasury to an extent designed to result in the same amount of protection, the cost of this subsidy would have been equal to this subsidy-equivalent.[2] The consumer not only finances the subsidy-equivalent but also is taxed to yield customs revenue, indicated by the shaded area. Thus the *consumer tax equivalent* is the sum of the subsidy-equivalent and the customs revenue, namely $STVG$. If instead of the tariff, a consumption tax had been imposed designed to yield the same reduction in consumption as the tariff, the tax would have yielded a revenue equal to this consumer tax equivalent. In fact the tariff ST/OS has the same effect as a consumer tax ST/OS which is used partly to finance a subsidy to producers at this rate and partly to yield net revenue.

All these references to the *consumption effect*, 'the consumer' and the *consumer tax equivalent* may give the impression that this analysis does not apply to goods used for investment purposes. But this is not so. The words 'consumption' and 'consumer' should be interpreted very broadly here to mean 'usage' or 'purchases', and by 'consumer' we mean anyone who buys the product, for whatever purpose.

The tariff rate might be fixed neither in specific nor in *ad valorem* terms, but might be variable. There are two main types of variable tariff. One is the *sliding-scale tariff*, the rate of tariff, whether specific or *ad valorem*, varying with the price of imports (for example, '10 per cent plus 2 per cent for every cent that the price of a unit of the particular imports falls below one dollar.').[3] The other is the *equalizing tariff*. Broadly this means that a 'target' is fixed for the domestic price of the importable concerned, and the tariff is then set so that the price of imports *including duty* will reach this target price whatever the cost of imports. A fall in the duty-free price of imports leads then automatically to an 'equalizing' rise in the

---

[2] The subsidy-equivalent of the whole tariff system has been measured in Canada and Australia. See J. H. Young, *Canadian Commercial Policy* (Royal Commission on Canada's Economic Prospects, Ottawa, 1957) (where it is called the *cash cost* of the tariff), and J. Vernon et al., *Report of the Committee of Economic Enquiry* (Commonwealth of Australia, Canberra, 1965) Vol. II, Appendix L (iv). It bears some relationship to the monetary value of the welfare cost (if any) of protection, but is not necessarily equal to it.

[3] The most celebrated—or notorious—sliding-scale duties in history have been the British duties on grain—the Corn Laws—that operated in one form or another from 1463 to their repeal in 1846. At times the Corn Laws consisted of a simple equalizing duty. For a discussion of sliding-scale duties, see G. v. Haberler, *The Theory of International Trade* (William Hodge & Co., London, 1936) pp. 343–345.

tariff.[4] The 'target price' may be determined arbitrarily, or may be set so as to be equal to the marginal cost of production of a given ('target') amount of domestic import-competing production. In the latter case it will vary if the domestic supply curve shifts, falling if the supply curve shifts to the right. In fact, if the domestic 'target' price is fixed, the equalizing tariff is a special and extreme case of the *sliding-scale tariff*. When the duty-free import price falls the tariff rate rises so much that the price including duty stays constant.

A distinction must be made between a *formal* and a *nominal* tariff rate. The *formal* rate will be defined here as the rate that is stated in the tariff schedule, while the *nominal* rate will be defined as the *ad valorem* equivalent of this rate expressed in relation to the c.i.f. price of imports.[5] In the rest of this book—as in the preceding discussion—we shall generally refer to nominal and not formal rates. The formal rate may be a specific one, say $1 per square yard, or one which adds, or perhaps subtracts, a specific from an *ad valorem* c.i.f. rate, or is expressed in alternative form, such as 20 per cent or $3 per square yard, whichever is the higher (or lower), or it could be a sliding-scale or an equalizing tariff. In all these cases, if one has information on the c.i.f. price of the product one can calculate the *ad valorem* equivalent to obtain the nominal rate. Furthermore, some countries, such as the United States, Canada and Australia, value their imports for tariff purposes at f.o.b. prices, hence excluding transport costs. This leads to the result that *ad valorem* nominal rates will be lower than the *ad valorem* formal rates. For example, if transport costs account for 15 per cent of the c.i.f. price, a formal tariff rate of 20 per cent will convert into a nominal rate of 17 per cent. It means that even if the formal rate is the same for all imports of a product

---

[4] The European Economic Community protects its agriculture with equalizing tariffs ('variable levies'), the target prices being reviewed annually. In addition there are export subsidies.

[5] The term *apparent* is really preferable to *nominal*, since the truly nominal rate is what I have called the *formal* rate. *Apparent* was used in two of the earliest contributions on effective protection (C. L. Barber, 'Canadian Tariff Policy', *Canadian Journal of Economics and Political Science*, 21 Nov. 1955, 513–530, and W. M. Corden, 'The Tariff', in A. Hunter (ed.), *The Economics of Australian Industry* (Melbourne University Press, Melbourne, 1963)). But the usage *nominal* was established by B. Balassa and H. G. Johnson, and has been followed since in my own work and that of others.

irrespective of source the nominal rate will be relatively lower for goods coming from more distant sources, where transport costs are higher. A change in transport costs will alter the nominal rate resulting from a given formal rate. Finally, some customs authorities value some imports for duty purposes at the domestic prices of the exporting or the importing country.[6] If there is some element of price discrimination or dumping in the exporting country the domestic price in the exporting country may be higher, so that if it is used as a basis for valuation the nominal rate will exceed the formal rate (apart from any f.o.b.–c.i.f. complication). If the price in the importing country is used, and if this price is determined by the import price plus tariff—that is OT in Fig. 2.1—then the nominal rate (ST/OS) will also exceed the formal rate (ST/OT).

An indirect way of imposing what is in fact a tariff is to require *advance deposits* on imports. This technique of reducing imports has been very common, and has been used in recent years not only by less developed countries but also by Britain and France.[7] Some proportion of the value of imports (usually c.i.f.) has to be deposited some time in advance of the required payment (perhaps when permission to buy the necessary foreign exchange is obtained). Assuming funds are freely available at a given rate of interest the equivalent nominal tariff rate is then $z.q.r.$ where z is the proportion of the c.i.f. import value to be deposited, q is the time-period, (expressed as a proportion of a year) for which the deposit has to be made, and r is the rate of interest. If there is some quantitative credit

---

[6] The best-known example of the latter is the *American Selling Price* procedure for valuing U.S. imports of benzenoid chemicals. See H. G. Grubel and H. G. Johnson, 'Nominal Tariff Rates and United States Valuation Practices: Two Case Studies', *Review of Economics and Statistics*, 49, May 1967, 138–142, where it is shown that an average of the relevant formal tariff rates 23·9 per cent to 26·4 per cent converts into a 'true' average in the range 40·2 per cent to 53·2 per cent.

[7] See E. A. Birnbaum and M. A. Qureshi, 'Advance Deposit Requirements for Imports', *IMF Staff Papers*, 8, Nov. 1960, 115–125, and L. B. Yeager, *International Monetary Relations* (Harper and Row, New York, 1966) p. 117 and p. 398. Import prepayments have been very important in Indonesia; see W. M. Corden and J. A. C. Mackie, 'The Development of the Indonesian Exchange Rate System', *Malayan Economic Review*, 7, April 1962, 37–60, where the many permutations of this system, all of which have been used in Indonesia, are listed.

control there will in effect also be an element of quantitative import restriction.

II. *Production Subsidy and Consumption Tax*

The tariff can now be compared with alternative devices for protecting domestic production of the importable or reducing domestic consumption of it. First it is compared with a production subsidy, then with a consumption tax, and (in the next section) with a *linking scheme*.

A production subsidy per unit of output would shift the domestic producer's supply curve downwards. In Fig. 2.1 it has shifted it down to hh', the vertical distance between HH' and hh' being the subsidy per unit. If the subsidy were a constant specific rate per unit then hh' would be parallel to HH' while if it were constant *ad valorem* it would be a constant percentage below HH'. If the subsidy is designed to protect to the same extent as the tariff it will raise output to OA', the protection effect thus being identical. The cost of the subsidy will be $STJF$ ($=$ subsidy-equivalent). The price to consumers will remain OS. Thus the protection effect will be identical with that of the tariff but there will be no consumption effect. As a result the import effect will be less, the squeeze on imports being only from the production side. Instead of a revenue effect, there is a charge on the revenue equal to the subsidy. Finally, there is a redistribution to producers, but it comes not from consumers but from the Treasury.[8]

A consumption tax will shift the demand curve to the left, to dd'. If it is designed to have the same consumption effect as the tariff, it will reduce consumption to OB', and will raise revenue of $STVG$ ($=$ consumer tax equivalent). The price to producers will remain OS so that there will be no protection effect. The squeeze on imports will be from the consumption side only. The revenue effect will be greater than in the case of the tariff by the subsidy-equivalent $STJF$ and there will be no redistribution to producers. In fact, the consumption tax

---

[8] Up to 1970 Britain protected much of its agriculture with 'deficiency payments', which were production subsidies varied annually. The comparison between a tariff and a production subsidy thus indicates the main distinction between the European Economic Community's method of agricultural protection and that recently prevalent in Britain (though the E.E.C. equalizing levies are varied continually and only the target price is altered annually).

is the equivalent of combining a tax on imports (a tariff) with a tax on production at an equal rate, the combination of the two avoiding any production effect. The tariff would raise revenue of $KNVG$ while the production tax would raise $STNK$. This type of tax on consumption of a particular product is often called an *excise tax*. Sometimes the term excise tax is confined to the production tax element while the tax on imports at an equal rate that necessarily goes with it is called a *border tax* or *border tax adjustment*.

There are three prices in our simple diagram, the duty-free price of imports, the price facing producers, which determines production, and the price facing consumers, which determines consumption. With a tariff the import price is OS and the other two prices are OT. With a production subsidy the import price and the consumer price are OS and the price facing producers is OT. With a consumption tax, the import price and the price facing producers are OS and the consumer price is OT. Thus in each case two prices are identical and one differs.

III. *Linking Schemes*

Protection can be provided by a *linking scheme*. This can take either of two forms, though the effects of both are

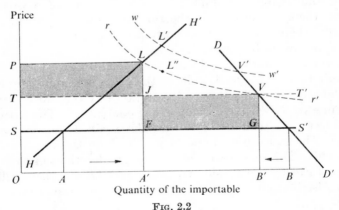

Fig. 2.2

essentially the same. Consider first a *self-financing subsidy* scheme. A tariff is imposed, the revenue from which is then used to finance a production subsidy. In Fig. 2.2 the rate of tariff is ST/OS; it determines the price OT facing consumers. The revenue from the tariff is the shaded area $FJVG$ and is then used to finance a production subsidy. Producers receive the price OP; the tariff raised their price from OS to OT and the subsidy raised it further to OP, the production subsidy per unit being TP. Alternatively one could say that the production subsidy shifted the producers' supply curve down by TP. The total production subsidy is the shaded area $TPLJ$ and must be equal to the tariff revenue, also shaded. Note that the production point L and the consumption point V are both on the rectangular hyperbola rr' which is drawn in the space with origin at the point S. Equilibrium may be thought of as obtained in the following way. First a tariff is imposed, yielding consumption point V. Then the rectangular hyperbola rr' is drawn through V, and its intersection with the domestic supply curve yields the production point L. If the supply curve shifted to the right imports for a given rate of tariff would fall and so revenue and hence the rate of production subsidy would fall. The new production point would be some point such as L'' on rr' between L and V. If, with a given domestic supply curve HH', it were desired to increase the rate of protection it would be necessary to raise the tariff rate and move to a higher rectangular hyperbola, such as ww', yielding consumption point V' and production point L'.

This scheme differs from a tariff, a production subsidy, and a consumption tax in two ways. Firstly, there is no revenue effect. Secondly, it leads to three prices, not two, namely the price of imports OS, the price facing consumers OT and the even higher price facing producers, OP. It is simply the equivalent of a tariff linked with a production subsidy, the two revenue effects cancelling out.

The same result can be brought about by a *quantity-linking scheme* of the kind that requires a trader or consumer to purchase at least Y units of domestically-produced product for every X units that he imports. This is sometimes called a *mixing scheme*.[9] Thus the fixed ratio of domestic purchases to

[9] These are very common, especially in less developed countries. For example, Brazil has operated such schemes for coal, lead, aluminium and asbestos. See J. Bergsman and P. S. Malan, 'The Structure of Protection in Brazil', in B. Balassa (ed.), *The Structure of Protection in Developing Countries*, 1971.

imports may be $OA'/A'B'$. This particular ratio would lead to the equilibrium shown in Fig. 2.2. The domestic purchases would cost OP per unit and the imports OS. The average cost for the two combined would be OT. Thus the price facing consumers is OT and the effect is the same as that of the previous scheme. If the ratio of minimum domestic purchases to imports were raised there would have to be a movement to a higher rectangular hyperbola, such as ww', with consumption point V' and production point L'. If the ratio stayed fixed but the supply curve shifted to the right the movement would have to be to a lower rectangular hyperbola, involving an increase in domestic production and consumption in the same proportion, so that the ratio of production to imports stays at the required level.

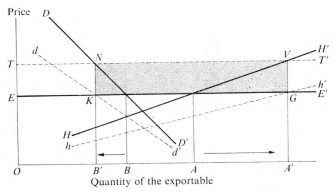

Fig. 2.3

IV. *Protection of Exportables*

The simple analysis of sections I, II and III can be applied to *exportables*, namely goods which are both exported and sold at home. It can be shown that in certain crucial respects an export subsidy has the same effect on exportables as an import tariff has on importables. Production subsidies and consumption taxes on exportables also have similar effects as they have when applied to importables. Indeed the analysis is so similar that we can be very brief here.

In Fig. 2.3 the quantity of the exportable is shown along the horizontal axis. The foreign demand curve, EE', is assumed to be infinitely elastic. Thus the country plays only a small part in the world market for its exports. The supply curve of domestic production is HH' and the domestic demand curve for the exportable is DD'. This time production is greater than consumption, and exports are the residual. With free trade, production is OA of which OB is sold to domestic consumers and BA is exported. An export subsidy of ET/OE (or ET in specific terms) is then imposed. Now assume for the moment that the c.i.f. import price is above OT, the excess of this import price over the f.o.b. export price being explained by transport costs or by foreign tariffs. The export subsidy will then not only raise the price received by producers for that part of their output which is exported but will also raise the price they receive from domestic consumers. For if domestic consumers did not raise their purchase price by the amount of the subsidy the whole of domestic production would be exported. Consumers would then have to meet their needs with even more expensive imports. The export subsidy has thus a production effect in raising domestic output to OA', a consumption effect in reducing domestic consumption to OB' and a two-pronged export effect, raising exports to $B'A'$. The revenue effect is of course negative; the cost to the Treasury is $KNVG$ (the shaded area). There is a redistribution from consumers to producers which on the new, lower amount consumed domestically is $ETNK$, this being the consumer-tax equivalent of the export subsidy. The production subsidy equivalent is $ETVG$, namely the sum of the export subsidy cost and the consumer tax equivalent. If the c.i.f. import price were below OT it would be necessary to impose a tariff sufficient to bring the duty-paid price to OT so that domestic consumers would continue to buy the domestic product instead of imports. If the c.i.f. import price is equal to the f.o.b. export price the rate of tariff that needs to accompany an export subsidy must thus be at least equal to the rate of subsidy, while in the usual case, where the c.i.f. import price exceeds the f.o.b. export price, the required rate of tariff could be less.

An export tax clearly will have an effect the opposite to that of an export subsidy. In particular, it will be *anti-protective* for the domestic industry concerned and will lower the price to domestic consumers, hence leading to increased consumption. It will not require any concurrent tariff or import subsidy.[10] It might also be noted that export subsidies can be provided in various indirect forms. The main form of export subsidization in advanced countries results from special export credit arrangements—providing financing or refinancing facilities at rates of interest below the market rate and favourable export credit insurance and guarantee facilities. This form of subsidization has certain special effects (in particular it encourages more export credit provision and more exporting to risky markets than otherwise), but to some extent can be analysed in the same way as straightforward export subsidization.

The rate of export subsidy of ET/OE in Fig. 2.3 is the *nominal*, and not necessarily the *formal* rate of subsidy. The distinction between a formal and a nominal rate can be made just as in the case of tariffs. But care must be taken about the definition of the nominal rate in this case. It was explained above that to calculate nominal tariff rates imports should be valued at c.i.f. prices, which are the prices at which they arrive in the country. Hence it is consistent with this approach that for the calculation of nominal export subsidy or tax rates exports should be valued at the prices at which they leave the country, which are the f.o.b., not the c.i.f., prices. Thus in the case of export subsidies or taxes the nominal rate expresses the subsidy per unit as a proportion of the f.o.b. price. The relevant prices for both imports and exports might be called *frontier prices*.

Instead of the export subsidy a production subsidy per unit of output might have been given. The price to the consumer would have stayed then at OE, there would have been no consumption effect and the cost to the Treasury would have been $ETVG$ (= production subsidy equivalent). If a consumption tax at the same rate had been imposed, the price to the producer would have stayed at OE, there would have been no production effect, and revenue of $ETNK$ (= consumer tax

<hr>

[10] Export taxes are only referred to briefly here, being just negative export subsidies. In practice they are common and important in less developed countries, especially as sources of revenue. The tax rates are often sliding-scale. For a full description, see R. Goode, G. E. Lent, and P. D. Ojha, 'Role of Export Taxes in Developing Countries', *IMF Staff Papers*, 13, Nov. 1966, 453–501.

equivalent) would have been raised. In fact the export subsidy is the equivalent of combining a production subsidy with a consumption tax, the production subsidy being partly financed by the tax on consumers and partly by a contribution from the Treasury. The consumption tax can be seen as the equivalent of a production tax combined with an export subsidy at the same rate. This is the same as taxing domestic production by means of an *excise tax* but exempting production for export from this tax, this exemption being a *border tax adjustment*. As in the case of importables, the border tax adjustment converts the excise tax from a tax on production into a tax on consumption. In the absence of the border tax adjustment the products are being taxed if their origin is domestic, while with the adjustment they are taxed if their destination is domestic. Thus a tax on the so-called *origin principle* taxes domestic production while a tax on the *destination principle* taxes domestic consumption.

Finally, there is the possibility of a *linking scheme* applied to exportables. This could be analysed in the same way as in the case of importables. Such a scheme might take the form of a *home-price scheme*; this is a self-financing subsidy scheme for exportable production and means that domestic consumption of the exportables is taxed and the proceeds are then used to subsidize exports.[11] The price to consumers will then be higher than the price to producers, which in turn will be above the export price. Such a scheme may require a tariff, to ensure that consumers buy the domestic product instead of imports.[12]

v. *Foreign Elasticities Not Infinite*

So far the *small country assumption* has been maintained. We now remove this assumption, hence introducing the terms

[11] The term comes from Australia, where *home-price schemes* apply to butter, wheat, sugar and some other minor agricultural exports; hence Australian butter is cheaper in London than in Melbourne. This is sometimes described (though not in Australia) as 'dumping'.

[12] There is a self-financing element in the European Economic Community's export subsidization of agriculture, but it is *not* a home-price scheme. Export subsidies ('restitution' payments) are partly financed from tariff revenue on imports, which should normally be different products from the subsidized exports. The prices to consumers and to producers are equal in this case (allowing for distribution costs, etc.), as is true of any ordinary export subsidy.

of trade effects of a tariff or an export subsidy or tax. The small country assumption will be restored again in the next chapter and maintained also in Chapters 4, 5 and 6.

If the elasticity of the foreign supply of imports is positive, extra imports can only be obtained at a higher price and a reduced demand for imports will lower the price. This case is represented in Fig. 2.4. This diagram shows on the horizontal axis the quantity of *imports*, not importables as in Fig. 2.1. The foreign supply curve of imports is SS'. The domestic demand curve for imports is NN'. It is obtained by subtracting at each price the domestic supply of importables (as shown by HH' in Fig. 2.1) from the domestic demand for importables (DD' in Fig. 2.1), the demand for imports being the residual. The elasticity of NN' at any price depends on the elasticities of HH' and DD', and on the ratio, at the relevant price, of domestic production to domestic consumption of importables. At the price of OS (Fig. 2.1), this ratio is OA/OB.[13] In Fig. 2.4 the free trade price of imports is OP, the quantity of imports OR and the value $OPGR$.

An *ad valorem* tariff PL/OP is imposed, the tariff-inclusive foreign supply curve being TT'. In the first instance, before the foreign duty-free price falls, this raises the domestic duty-inclusive price to OL. But the reduced quantity demanded which results from the higher domestic price causes the foreign price and hence the duty-inclusive price to fall. The new equilibrium yields a duty-free foreign price of OW, a duty-inclusive domestic price of OV ($WV/OW = PL/OP$), an import quantity of OQ, and customs revenue indicated by the shaded area $WVJH$. Assuming that export prices and prices of all other imports are constant, the fall in the foreign price represents a terms of trade improvement. The tariff revenue is obtained partly at the expense of domestic consumers—the domestic price having risen by PV—and partly at the expense of foreign suppliers—the foreign price having fallen by PW—

---

[13] If e_c = elasticity of DD', e_h = elasticity of HH' and e_n = elasticity of NN', and if H/C = ratio of domestic production to consumption, then

$$e_n = \frac{e_c + \dfrac{H}{C} e_h}{1 - \dfrac{H}{C}}$$

the sum of the two price changes yielding the tariff revenue of WV per unit. Compared with the case of Fig. 2.1, the same *ad valorem* tariff rate (WV/OW in Fig. 2.4 $= ST/OS$ in Fig. 2.1) yields a lesser rise in the domestic price and hence lesser domestic production, consumption and redistribution effects, and a lesser fall in the quantity of imports. It could be shown that if the elasticity of the NN' curve over the relevant range were unity the fall in the value of imports and the amount of customs revenue raised would be the same as when the import

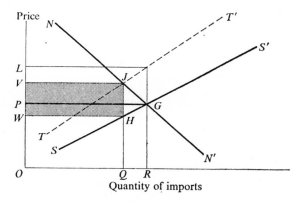

FIG. 2.4

supply elasticity is infinite. If the elasticity were greater than unity, the value of imports would fall by less and revenue would be greater than when the import supply elasticity is infinite, while if the elasticity were less than unity the import value would fall by more and revenue would be less. Finally, a domestic production subsidy at the rate WV/OW or a domestic consumption tax at that rate would cause imports to fall, and there would be a favourable terms of trade effect, but the foreign price would not fall as far as OW.

Next we consider the terms of trade effect on the side of exports. When the foreign elasticity of demand for exports is not infinite, an export subsidy or tax will have a terms of trade effect. The argument is illustrated in Fig. 2.5 which shows the quantity of *exports*, not exportables, along the horizontal axis. The foreign demand curve for exports is EE'.

The supply curve of exports is NN', being derived by subtracting at each price domestic demand for exportables (as shown by DD' in Fig. 2.3) from domestic production (as shown by HH' in Fig. 2.3). With free trade the export quantity is OR and the price is OP. An export subsidy at the rate PL/OP establishes the subsidy-inclusive export demand curve TT'. In the new equilibrium, the quantity of exports has risen to OQ, the foreign price has fallen to OW, and the domestic price facing producers and consumers has risen to OV. The cost of the

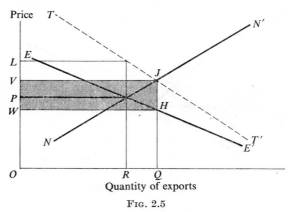

FIG. 2.5

subsidy is the shaded area $WVJH$, and the new value of exports, excluding the subsidy, is $OWHQ$. The price of exports has fallen, so on this account the terms of trade have worsened. The value of exports may have increased or decreased, for the quantity is higher while the price is lower. If the elasticity of demand were unity the value of exports (always excluding the subsidy) would have stayed constant, if greater than unity it would have risen and if less than unity would have fallen. The extent of the domestic price rise and hence the protection afforded by a given rate of export subsidy, as well as the increase in the quantity of exports, will be less when there is a terms of trade effect than when there is not. Since the price of exports has now fallen while the quantity has risen less than before, the value of exports must have risen less than when there was no terms of trade effect and—as we have seen—if the elasticity of demand is less than unity—will actually decline.

A subsidy on domestic production of the exportable or a tax on its domestic consumption at the same rate as the export subsidy would have the same qualitative effect as the export subsidy, but to a lesser extent; the export quantity would rise, price would fall, and value would rise or fall depending on whether the demand elasticity is greater or less than unity.

VI. *The Rate of Protection*

Let us now explore the concept of the rate of protection so as to note some complications that will become significant later. In the simple cases of sections I to IV the concept is quite clear and indeed obvious. In these cases the foreign elasticities are infinite and there are imports of the importable and exports of the exportable both before and after the taxes and subsidies have been imposed. As Fig. 2.1 shows, a tariff or a production subsidy leads to a rate of protection which is the same as the rate of tariff or production subsidy, namely ST/OS. One can give four meanings to this rate. It is (i) the proportional divergence at the margin between the domestic supply price and the foreign supply price, (ii) the proportional increase in the domestic price facing the producers that finally results, (iii) the proportional increase in the price received by the domestic producers before they respond to the higher price by increasing supply, and (iv) the maximum rise in the price to the domestic producers allowed by the tariff or production subsidy. But this rate of protection is clearly not the sole determinant of the increase in domestic production that results from the tariff or subsidy. It is important to stress that by *rate of protection* we do *not* mean the protective effect—that is, the proportionate domestic supply increase AA'/OA. This supply increase depends also on the elasticity of supply over the relevant range.[14] The higher the elasticity the greater the protective effect of a given rate of protection. Of course, if the elasticity were zero there would be no supply effect irrespective of how high the rate of protection was. It is also possible that the supply curve starts on the vertical axis between S and T, so that there is no domestic production

---

[14] This is an obvious point, but not always understood, as borne out in recent writings, published and unpublished (and comments in seminars) on effective protection. It should be read in red print here.

under free trade but production starts as a result of the tariff or subsidy. The supply response is then zero up to a certain price, so that a tariff somewhat lower than ST/OS would not have any production effect.

Complications arise when we depart from the simple assumptions of sections I to III. Suppose now that the foreign elasticity of supply of imports is less than infinite, as illustrated in Fig. 2.4. We could then mean by the rate of protection (i) the proportional divergence at the margin between the domestic supply price and the foreign supply price; this is the rate of tariff WV/OW. Alternatively, we could mean (ii) the proportional increase in the domestic price that finally results; this is PV/OP and is lower than the previous measure. It depends not just on the rate of tariff but also on the elasticities of the foreign supply and the domestic demand curves, the latter depending in turn on the elasticities of the domestic demand and supply surves for importables.

Finally, we could mean (iii), the proportional increase in the price received by the domestic producers before they respond to the higher price by increasing supply. This is a more complex concept. If one subtracted the foreign supply of importables at each price from the domestic demand for them one would obtain the demand curve that faces the domestic producers. The third measure yields the proportional upward shift of this demand curve at the original quantity of domestic output. It depends on the elasticities of the foreign supply of imports and the domestic demand for importables but not on the elasticity of supply of domestic production.

Returning to the assumption of an infinitely elastic foreign supply curve of importables, yet another complication, illustrated in Fig. 2.6 (page 24), can be introduced. The free trade price is OS and a tariff of ST/OS is imposed. This is so high that all imports cease. Indeed a tariff of SP/OS would have been sufficient to end all imports. Thus the tariff has converted a traded good into a non-traded good. We might now say that part of the tariff, namely PT, is redundant; there is 'water' in the tariff. The *utilized* rate of protection, SP/OS, might be distinguished from the *available* rate of protection, ST/OS. The *utilized* rate gives the rate of protection in the sense of (i) and (ii) above, while the *available* rate gives it in the senses of (iii) and (iv). One might argue that the redundant element or 'water' in the tariff is of no relevance. It affects neither domestic production, nor consumption or income distribution. It can thus be contrasted with a tariff that does not affect domestic production because the supply elasticity is zero but which still affects consumption and income distribution. So it seems that one should always refer to the *utilized* rate. But this must be qualified. We depart here from the assumption of perfect competition generally maintained in this chapter and Chapters 3 to 8.[15] It could be shown that when domestic production is monopolized an apparently 'redundant' tariff may indeed affect production, consumption and income distribution. The c.i.f. import price plus tariff sets the upper limit to the price the potential monopolist can charge; as the tariff is raised, at first a profit-maximizing monopolist will increase his output to replace imports, but once all imports are eliminated, further increases in the tariff will lead him to reduce output, until the point is reached where the monopolist has equated his marginal cost with the marginal revenue derived from the domestic demand curve. Any further increases in the tariff would not lead him to raise his price or reduce his output further. Thus there is an intermediate stage where an increase in the tariff does not affect imports, these having been eliminated, but leads to a reduction in output and consumption. The tariff is indeed *import-redundant* but is not *output-redundant*. Furthermore, even when there is domestic competition, the redundant element in the tariff may represent a safeguard or insurance for the domestic producers in case the foreign import price falls. Hence there may be as much significance in the rate of protection *available* to be used as in that actually used. In any case, at this stage the distinction should be noted.

This discussion is also relevant to exportables. If the foreign elasticity of demand is less than infinite there will also be three possible concepts of the rate of protection. Furthermore,

---

[15] It is on the whole not a crucial assumption for our purposes, since the assumptions generally maintained in this book of given world prices and that some trade remains in each traded product ensure perfectly competitive behaviour even when there is a sole domestic import-competing (or export) producer in a particular product.

an export tax may be so high that exports are completely eliminated, a part of the tax possibly being redundant. One could then distinguish the *utilized* from the *available* rate of export tax.

A combination of tariff and export subsidy may convert an imported good into an exported one, hence leading to *trade reversal*.[16] This presents a problem for the meaning of tariff redundancy and—when the free trade export price is below the free trade import price—for the concept of *rate of protection*. We refer again to Fig. 2.6. The free trade import price of the

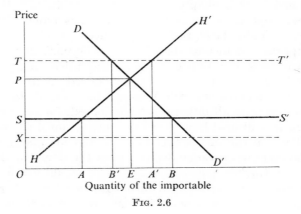

Fig. 2.6

product, *OS*, is assumed for the moment to be equal to the free trade export price. As drawn, in free trade there would be imports of *AB*. A tariff of *SP/OS* would eliminate imports, and any further increase beyond that—if unaccompanied by an export subsidy (as assumed in our earlier discussion)—would be redundant. Production and consumption would be *OE*. Now suppose that an export subsidy at the rate of *ST/OS* is provided, the aim being to increase domestic production to *OA'*. Thus the price to domestic producers rises to *OT*. In all four possible meanings of the term, the rate of protection is now equal to the rate of export subsidy *ST/OS*. Is then the whole of the tariff redundant? In one sense it is. Irrespective of the level of the tariff, the rate of protection and hence the amount

---

[16] As in the case of European Economic Community wheat and butter, and also Australian butter.

of domestic output is given by the rate of export subsidy. But in another sense, the region of tariff redundancy is reduced. If the price which the domestic producer receives on the home market is less than OT he will choose to export all his product and the whole of domestic demand will be met from imports. It is necessary to bring the tariff up to the rate of export subsidy ST/OS if domestic consumption is to be supplied from domestic production, so leaving $B'A'$ of exports. If the tariff were SP/OS imports would be OE (with exports OA'). If the tariff is raised above this, imports will fall, and if it is raised to the level of the export subsidy rate imports will disappear. Only beyond this does an increase in the tariff make no difference. Thus, while in the absence of the export subsidy any tariff above SP/OS is redundant, *with* the export subsidy any tariff at all is redundant from the point of view of domestic production but only a tariff above the export subsidy rate is redundant from the point of view of domestic consumption.

Next consider the more complicated case where the free trade export price is below the free trade import price, namely at OX in Fig. 2.6. The margin between the import and the export price might be explained by transport costs or foreign tariffs. To raise the domestic price to OT the rate of export subsidy needs to be XT/OX; hence the rate of tariff which is required to ensure that all domestic consumption is met from domestic production is now less than the rate of export subsidy. But what is the rate of protection? The proportional divergence at the margin between domestic supply price and foreign demand price is equal to the rate of export subsidy XT/OS; this gives the rate of protection in the first meaning of the term, as applied to an exported good. But the proportional increase in the domestic price that finally results is equal to the rate of tariff, namely ST/OS; this gives the rate of protection in the other three meanings of the term. Clearly, which concept one uses depends on one's purpose, but it is at least worth noting that the term *rate of protection* in this case is not unambiguous. Generally the second meaning of the term is the one we shall have in mind when considering resource allocation effects of tariffs, export subsidies, and so on. But for *marginal* welfare analysis the first meaning is the relevant one.

Finally, the concepts of *protection* and the *rate of protection* might be given much wider meanings than they have been given so far. Suppose that the foreign supply price of importables shifts upwards, perhaps because foreign costs have increased. This has an effect very similar to that of a tariff. The domestic price of importables rises, import-competing production increases, consumption falls and income distribution shifts towards producers of import-competing goods. So it appears that a rise in the cost of imports is a form of 'protection'. But there are two differences. Firstly, the revenue that would have gone to the Treasury goes instead to the foreign suppliers. Secondly—and this is the crucial difference—the foreign supply curve is generally a constraint given to the home country while the tariff is a policy variable. In a theory concerned with instruments of economic policy it is important to distinguish a constraint from a policy variable even though changes in them may have certain effects in common, and some of the analysis of tariffs can certainly be used to analyse the effects of a change in foreign prices. The same applies to a change in the foreign price of exports. A rise in the export price has an effect similar to that of an export subsidy: production of exportables will increase and domestic consumption will decline; but there will be no subsidy cost to the Treasury.

Furthermore, the foreign supply and demand curves incorporate the costs of transporting imports and exports. A rise in transport costs will shift the supply curve of imports (defined in c.i.f. terms) upwards—and so have a protective effect for import-competing industry—and will shift the demand curve for exports (defined in f.o.b. terms) downwards—and so have an anti-protective effect for exportable production.[17] Hence the analysis of protection can certainly be applied directly to analysing the effects of changes in transport costs. But again, transport costs are not the same as the home country's tariffs. The former are in general constraints while tariffs and export subsidies are policy variables.

The same argument might be applied to tariffs and export

[17] If the transporting is done by the home country's ships one might either treat transport services as invisible exports, or measure imports f.o.b. and exports c.i.f. and regard transport as services, possibly non-traded services, which are jointly demanded with imports and are inputs in production for export.

subsidies or taxes imposed by the foreign country. A foreign tariff shifts the demand curve for exports (the foreigner's imports) downwards and so has an effect similar to that of an export tax by the home country. A foreign export tax raises the foreign supply curve of imports (the foreigner's exports) and so has an effect akin to a tariff by the home country. Thus our analysis can be used to analyse the effects in the home country of trade taxes and subsidies—and indeed production and consumption taxes and subsidies—imposed by the foreign country, bearing in mind that the revenue effects will affect the foreign Treasury and not the home Treasury. Notwithstanding this, in general we shall take the foreign demand and supply curves as given, treating not only foreign demands, costs and transport costs, but also foreign tariffs, taxes and subsidies, as constraints. When we refer to 'free trade' we shall mean generally the absence of trade taxes and subsidies in the home country; it will not necessarily mean the absence of such devices in other countries. Our primary concern is with economic policy in one country from the point of view of that one country, with the policies of other countries given.

3

TARIFFS ON INPUTS AND THE
EFFECTIVE PROTECTIVE RATE

So far we have assumed that the domestic production of the protected product is vertically integrated. Now let us remove this assumption and allow for purchased produced inputs into this product, inputs which are themselves traded, and which may be subject to tariffs, taxes or subsidies. One question then is whether a tariff, for example, on the product concerned protects only the value-added in the production of this product or whether it protects also the production of its inputs. And if it protects only the former, to what extent does it do so? Another question is how the protection of the value-added in this product is affected by tariffs, taxes or subsidies on its inputs. To deal with these questions we introduce the new concept of the *effective protective rate*— namely the rate of protection provided to the economic activity which produces the value-added in the product concerned.[1] This must be distinguished from 'protection' of factors of production. The relationship between effective protection and factor prices will be discussed in Chapters 4 and 7.

Consider now an importable product, to be called cloth, which is produced by two factors of production, namely a produced product, to be called yarn, and another factor, to be called the *value-added product*, which is the value-added by the cloth industry—the product of the *activity* of weaving. The *value-added product* is in turn produced by primary factors of production, that is by various kinds of labour, capital and natural resources. The *value-added product* is literally the 'product' of the primary factors, though it could be thought of, for the moment, as simply a bundle of primary factors. The

[1] See Appendix I on the origin of the concept and the literature.

concept will be further examined in Chapters 4, 6 and 7.[2] We shall assume at this stage that the produced input, yarn, is also an importable and that domestic production of it is vertically integrated. There are at this stage no other inputs. Later in this chapter we shall allow for exportable inputs. Non-traded produced inputs—which complicate the theory considerably—will only be introduced in Chapter 7.

Now we make three crucial assumptions:

(1) *Fixed coefficients*. There is a fixed physical input coefficient in domestic production of yarn into cloth. This coefficient is the same for all firms. Since production functions can differ between countries this assumption does not mean that the relevant input coefficient must be the same as in foreign countries. Units of the *value-added product* can be so defined that the physical input coefficient of this product into cloth is also fixed, but this is just a convenient definition, not a separate assumption. One unit of value-added product is simply the value-added that goes with one unit of cloth. This fixed coefficient assumption does not mean that there must be fixed coefficients in the production of the value-added products; the proportions in which labour, capital and so on are employed can vary.

(2) *Small country assumption*. The foreign elasticities of supply of imports of cloth and yarn are both infinite.

(3) *Trade remains*. There are actual imports of cloth and yarn and such imports remain after tariffs have been imposed. These assumptions rule out terms of trade effects as well as trade reversal.

Assumptions (2) and (3) eliminate difficulties discussed in the last section of the previous chapter. The assumption that the fixed input coefficient is the same for all domestic firms will be reconsidered briefly in section VIII. Apart from that, assumptions (1) and (2) will be maintained throughout this and the following two chapters and reconsidered respectively in Chapters 6 and 7, while assumption (3) will be generally maintained, but removed briefly in section VII.

---

[2] An alternative term is *net output* (used, for example, in P. A. David, 'Measuring Real Net Output: A Proposed Index', *Review of Economics and Statistics*, 48, Nov. 1966, 419–425) but the distinction between gross and net is probably best reserved to refer to the inclusion or not of depreciation. (We ignore depreciation in this chapter; see section VI of Chapter 7). The term *net* is also used in another sense in Chapter 5.

Finally, the approach in this chapter will continue to be partial equilibrium. The big step to general equilibrium will be taken in the next chapter.

I. *The Effective Rate in a Partial Equilibrium Model*

In Fig. 3.1 quantities of both cloth and yarn are shown along the horizontal axis, the units being so chosen that one

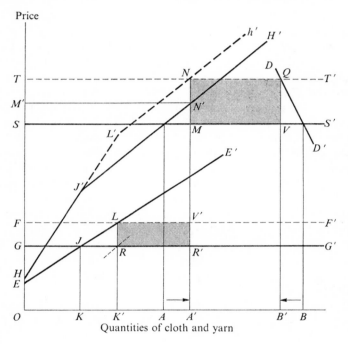

FIG. 3.1

unit of yarn is required by domestic producers to make one unit of cloth, as indicated by the fixed input coefficient derived from their production function. The foreign supply curve of yarn is GG' and of cloth SS', so that OG and OS are the free trade c.i.f. import prices of the two products. It can be seen immediately—before drawing in any domestic demand and supply curves—that, provided domestic prices are set by foreign trade prices, the price which will be charged for a unit of value-added by the cloth industry—that is, for the *value-added product*—is GS. We shall call this the *effective price* of cloth, as distinct from OS, the price for the whole cloth product, which can be called the *nominal price*. Suppose a nominal tariff on cloth of ST/OS is imposed, with no tariff on yarn. The *effective price* of cloth then rises from GS to GT. This yields the *effective protective rate* for cloth, ST/GS—simply the proportional increase in the effective price resulting from the nominal tariff. If, instead of the nominal tariff on cloth, there had been a tariff on yarn of GF/OG, the effective price of cloth would have fallen from GS to FS; the effective protective rate for cloth would then be negative, namely, $-GF/GS$. If a nominal tariff on cloth of ST/OS had been combined with a nominal tariff on yarn of GF/OG, the effective price of cloth would have changed from GS to FT, the effective protective rate being $(ST-GF)/GS$. Whether the effective price rose or fell and hence whether the effective rate were positive or negative would then depend on whether ST were greater or less than GF.

Now let us draw in the domestic demand and supply curves. The demand curve for cloth is DD' and the free trade consumption of cloth is OB. The domestic supply curve of yarn is EE', the free trade domestic production of yarn being OK. The supply curve of cloth, HH', is not so straightforwardly drawn. It is the vertical addition of the supply curve of yarn facing cloth producers and the supply curve of the cloth value-added product. The former is identical with the yarn supply curve of domestic producers only up to an amount of yarn demanded of OK. In the absence of a tariff on yarn any extra yarn beyond OK demanded by cloth producers will be obtained by them from imports, not from extra domestic supplies. Thus the yarn supply curve facing cloth producers is EJG', with a kink at J. The supply curve of the cloth-value-added product is then added vertically to the curve EJG' in Fig. 3.1 to yield the supply curve of cloth $HJ'H'$. The important point to note is that the supply of the cloth value-added product depends not on the nominal price of cloth, but rather on the *effective* price, which is literally the price of the value-added product. It depends not on the price of the product but on the price of the activity. Under free trade, domestic production of cloth is then OA. This domestic output of cloth also yields the demand for yarn. It follows that free trade imports of yarn are KA and of cloth AB.

The tariff on cloth of ST/OS reduced domestic consumption of cloth to OB'. As in our discussion in Chapter 2 (Fig. 2.1) this consumption effect depends on the nominal tariff on cloth. If there were no tariff on yarn the new domestic output of cloth would be given by the intersection of $HJ'H'$ with TT'. But we assume now that a cloth and a yarn tariff are imposed at the same time. The latter raises domestic output of yarn to OK'. In addition it shifts the supply curve of yarn facing producers of cloth upwards from EJG' to ELF'. From the point of view of cloth producers (who are the yarn consumers), the tariff on yarn represents a tax on their input which raises their costs of production. The new supply curve of cloth is then $HL'h'$; from the kink at L' it is vertically above the previous supply curve by the amount of the tariff on yarn, GF. The new output of cloth is OA'. In the diagram the output of cloth has increased, which implies that the effective price of cloth must have risen, so that the tariff on cloth per unit, ST, must have been greater than the tariff on yarn per unit, GF. Imports of cloth have fallen from AB to $A'B'$, there being the usual two-pronged squeeze on imports as indicated by the arrows. Imports of yarn have changed from KA to $K'A'$, and could have risen or fallen, since both domestic supply of and demand for yarn have gone up. If the cloth tariff per unit had been less than the yarn tariff per unit so that the effective protective rate was negative, domestic output of cloth would have fallen, imports of cloth might have increased or decreased, demand for yarn would have fallen, and imports of yarn would definitely have decreased.

Revenues raised from imports of cloth and yarn are the shaded areas $MNQV$ and $RLV'R'$ respectively. The subsidy equivalent for yarn is derived as before and is $GFLR$. The sum of this subsidy equivalent and the revenue from the tariff on yarn is the consumer tax equivalent of the yarn tariff. If we take this consumer tax as given and thus the cloth supply curve of $HL'h'$ as given, then the subsidy equivalent of cloth is derived as before (in Fig. 2.1) and is the area $STNM$. But this extent of subsidy to producers would not be necessary to raise cloth output to OA' if there had not been a tariff on yarn. The cloth subsidy equivalent in fact pays partly for the yarn consumer tax equivalent. This yarn consumer tax equivalent accounts for $M'TNN'$ of the cloth subsidy equivalent, and the remainder of the latter, namely $SM'N'M$, is the *net* subsidy equivalent for cloth, the amount of production subsidy that would be required to raise cloth output to OA' if there had been no tariff on yarn. SM' is the excess of the cloth tariff ST over the yarn tariff GF.

What is the significance of the effective protective rate for cloth? First, we notice that, given our assumptions, it affects only the *output of cloth*. It is not relevant for the consumption of cloth or for the production of yarn. Cloth consumption depends on the nominal tariff rate for cloth, and yarn production on the tariff on yarn. At this stage we are assuming that, whatever happens, imports of yarn remain, so the tariff on cloth, while it reduces demand for yarn, has no effect on domestic output of yarn. The cloth tariff therefore protects only value-added in the cloth industry. Secondly, the increase in cloth output depends not only on the effective protective rate but also on the elasticity of supply of the value-added product. The effective rate for cloth is distinguished from the nominal rate in two respects: first it takes into account the tariff on yarn, and secondly it expresses the change in the domestic price in relation to the effective, not the nominal price. The importance of the first distinction is obvious; in particular it allows for the possibility that in spite of a positive tariff on cloth, the tariffs can cause output of cloth to fall. The purpose of the second distinction is not so obvious and indeed does not become evident in the partial equilibrium model. One could conceivably take the excess of the absolute cloth tariff over the yarn tariff, namely SM' $(= ST - GF)$ and express this as a proportion of the nominal cloth price OS. The resultant tariff rate (which might be called the *adjusted nominal rate*) could then be related to the elasticity of the free trade supply curve of cloth, $HJ'H'$, the result yielding the same rise in domestic output as when the effective rate is related to the supply curve of the value-added product. The point of preferring the effective protective rate concept to this alternative approach of the adjusted nominal rate will emerge from the general equilibrium model to be developed in the next chapter.[3]

It has been assumed so far that domestic yarn production is vertically integrated. This assumption can be removed without creating any complications. Suppose that raw cotton is a produced importable input into yarn, and is also in infinitely elastic supply. One can then calculate an effective protective rate for yarn which may differ from the nominal rate. It will depend on the nominal rates for raw cotton and for yarn and the input coefficient of raw cotton into yarn. A tariff on raw cotton will shift the yarn supply curve upwards just as the tariff on yarn has done this to the cloth supply curve, and the change in the output of yarn will depend on its effective rate and on the elasticity of the supply of the yarn value-added product. Similarly, if there were produced importable inputs into domestic raw cotton production an effective rate for raw cotton could be calculated which, together with the supply curve of the cotton value-added product, would determine the change in output of cotton resulting from the set of tariffs. But the important point is that, *given the small country assumption*, the effective protective rate for a product is not influenced by tariffs on inputs into its inputs. One need go only one step downward in the input-output structure. A tariff on raw cotton, while it reduces effective protection for the yarn producers, has no effect on the effective rate for the cloth producers. To the latter only the cost of yarn matters, and that is determined by the given world yarn price plus tariff.

Another assumption has been that there is only a single produced input into cloth, namely the importable, yarn. We shall continue to assume that all produced inputs are importables, but we can allow for many such inputs—various kinds of yarn, dye-stuff, and so on, all used in fixed physical proportions in the cloth industry, and each with its own tariff. The effective tariff on each and the value-added supply elasticity of each will determine the change in output of each resulting from the set of tariffs. The question is how the effective protective rate of cloth is affected by the multiplicity of produced

---

[3] The adjusted nominal rate is not a new concept, and is sometimes described as the *net* protective rate or the *net* tariff rate; but in this book (Chapter 5) we have preempted this term for another purpose.

inputs. This matter is better handled algebraically in the next section but the main point is that the equivalent of the single input tariff rate GF/OG (Fig. 3.1) is now a weighted average of the various input tariffs, the weights being the shares of the various inputs in the cost of cloth production assuming free trade prices, the equivalent of OG/OS.

II. *The Algebra of Effective Protective Rates*

The relationships between the nominal tariff rate on a product, its effective rate, the nominal tariff rates on its inputs, and the shares of the inputs in the cost of the product at free trade prices can be brought out clearly algebraically. Initially it will be assumed that there is only one produced input, again an importable. By share in cost at free trade prices is simply meant the ratio OG/OS in Fig. 3.1. (Hence 'cost' can either refer to marginal cost, including in this the normal profits that are embodied in the supply curve, or alternatively one can mean the industry's total revenues). With the assumptions listed earlier, this share is determined by the given foreign prices and the fixed input coefficient. The final product, j, can be thought of as cloth and the input, i, as yarn. There are (as shown in Fig. 3.1), no taxes or subsidies affecting j and i other than the import tariffs.

The formula for the effective protective rate for the activity producing j—that is, for the j value-added product—can be derived as follows:

Let

p_v = value-added per unit of j in activity j in absence of tariffs, in other words, the free trade effective price;

p_v' = value-added per unit of j in activity j made possible by the tariff structure; in other words, the effective price after tariffs have been imposed;

g_j = effective protective rate for activity j; in other words, the proportional increase in the effective price resulting from the tariffs;

p_j = nominal price of a unit of j in free trade;

a_{ij} = share of i in cost of j at free trade prices;

a_{ij}' = share of i in cost of j after tariffs have been imposed;

4

t_j = nominal tariff rate on j;

t_i = nominal tariff rate on i.

Then

$$p_v = p_j(1-a_{ij}) \tag{1}$$

$$p_v{}' = p_j[(1+t_j)-a_{ij}(1+t_i)] \tag{2}$$

$$g_j = \frac{p_v{}'-p_v}{p_v} \tag{3}$$

From (1), (2), and (3),

$$g_j = \frac{t_j-a_{ij}t_i}{1-a_{ij}} \tag{4}$$

This is the key formula, the implications of which can really be summarized as follows:

If $t_j = t_i$, then $g_j = t_j = t_i$. (i)

If $t_j > t_i$, then $g_j > t_j > t_i$. (ii)

If $t_j < t_i$, then $g_j < t_j < t_i$. (iii)

If $t_j < a_{ij}t_i$, then $g_j < 0$. (iv)

If $t_j = 0$, then $g_j = -\left(t_i\dfrac{a_{ij}}{1-a_{ij}}\right)$ (v)

If $t_i = 0$, then $g_j = \dfrac{t_j}{1-a_{ij}}$ (vi)

$$\frac{\partial g_j}{\partial t_j} = \frac{1}{1-a_{ij}} \tag{vii}$$

$$\frac{\partial g_j}{\partial t_i} = \frac{-a_{ij}}{1-a_{ij}} \tag{viii}$$

$$\frac{\partial g_j}{\partial a_{ij}} = \frac{t_j-t_i}{(1-a_{ij})^2} \tag{ix}$$

Furthermore, equation (4) can be written as

$$g_j = \frac{t_j}{1-a_{ij}} - \frac{a_{ij}t_i}{1-a_{ij}} \tag{4.1}$$

or as

$$g_j = t_j + \frac{a_{ij}}{1-a_{ij}}(t_j - t_i) \tag{4.2}$$

or as

$$t_j = (1-a_{ij})g_j + a_{ij}t_i \tag{4.3}$$

In addition

$$a_{ij}' = a_{ij}\frac{1+t_i}{1+t_j} \tag{5}$$

Substituting (5) in (4) we have

$$g_j = \frac{1-a_{ij}'}{\dfrac{1}{1+t_j} - \dfrac{a_{ij}'}{1+t_i}} - 1 \tag{6}$$

Or alternatively

$$g_j = \frac{\dfrac{t_j}{1+t_j} - \dfrac{a_{ij}'t_i}{1+t_i}}{\dfrac{1}{1+t_j} - \dfrac{a_{ij}'}{1+t_i}} \tag{6.1}$$

What does all this mean? The key equation (4) tells us that the effective rate g_j depends on the nominal cloth tariff (t_j), the nominal yarn tariff (t_i), and the free trade input share (a_{ij}), which is the ratio OG/OS of Fig. 3.1. To take an example, if the cloth nominal tariff rate is 22 per cent, the yarn tariff is 10 per cent and the input share is 40 per cent, the effective rate would be 30 per cent. Implication (i) tells us that if the yarn nominal tariff rate is equal to the cloth nominal rate, then the cloth effective rate will also be equal to the cloth nominal rate; there is no divergence between the nominal and the effective rate. Note that this refers to tariff *rates*, and not to the absolute tariffs per unit; if these were equal the effective rate would be zero. Implications (ii) and (iii) tell us that whether the cloth effective rate is greater or less than the cloth nominal rate depends on whether the yarn rate is greater or less than the cloth nominal rate. Implication (iv) sets out the condition for the effective rate to be negative. Note that the effective rate can be negative even though the nominal rate is positive.

It also shows that if $t_j = a_{ij}t_i$ the effective rate will be zero. Thus, if the yarn rate is 30 per cent and the input share is 40 per cent the nominal cloth rate of 12 per cent will just be sufficient to avoid negative effective protection for cloth. Hence 12 per cent is the *compensating* tariff for cloth, and any nominal tariff above 12 per cent gives cloth positive effective protection. Implication (v) shows that if there is no nominal tariff on cloth but there is a tariff on yarn, the effective protection for cloth must be negative. Implication (vi) gives the formula for the effective rate when there is no tariff on yarn. It shows that in this case the effective rate must be above the nominal rate. Implications (vii) and (viii) show how the effective rate varies in response to changes in the cloth and the yarn nominal rates. Note that if the input share a_{ij} is high, the effective rate will be quite sensitive to changes in the cloth nominal rate. For example, if $a_{ij} = 80$ per cent, so that the value-added by the cloth industry is proportionally very low, and if $t_i = 10$ per cent, then a rise in t_j from 20 per cent to 30 per cent will raise the effective rate from 60 per cent to 110 per cent. Implication (ix) shows that whether a rise in the input share raises or lowers the effective rate depends on whether the cloth or the yarn nominal rate is higher. In equation (4.1) the effective rate has been broken down into two elements: the first, $t_j/(1-a_{ij})$, is the subsidy element, namely the proportional increase in the effective price of cloth resulting from the nominal tariff on cloth; the second, $a_{ij}t_i/(1-a_{ij})$, is the tax element, namely the proportional fall in the effective price of cloth resulting from the tariff on yarn. Equation (4.2) shows that the effective rate on cloth is equal to its nominal rate plus or minus an amount which depends on the input share and on the excess of the cloth nominal rate over the yarn nominal rate (or the extent to which the cloth nominal rate falls below the yarn rate). Equation (4.3) shows significantly that the nominal tariff rate on cloth is a weighted average of its own effective rate and the nominal tariff rate on yarn. Equation (5) is an expression for the input share as it results after the tariffs have raised both the domestic cloth and the domestic yarn price. In Fig. 3.1 this share is OF/OT. It is this share which input-output statistics normally reveal, not the share that would exist if there were free trade.

Equations (6) and (6.1) rewrite the effective rate-formula in terms of this share, yielding the formulae which should normally be used for empirical studies when the input-output data are derived from the country which actually has the tariffs. Equation (6) is simpler and yields the formula which has been used by many researchers,[4] while (6.1) is analytically more meaningful since it brings out clearly the 'deflated' nature of this relation compared with (4).

Now allow for more than one input. Suppose there are two importable inputs, 1 and 2, with input shares a_{1j} and a_{2j} and tariffs t_1 and t_2; then (4) has to be rewritten:

$$g_j = \frac{t_j - (a_{1j}t_1 + a_{2j}t_2)}{1 - (a_{1j} + a_{2j})} \tag{4.4}$$

Furthermore, let $\bar{t}_i$ be the weighted average of the two input tariffs, i.e.

$$\bar{t}_i = \frac{t_1 a_{1j} + t_2 a_{2j}}{a_{1j} + a_{2j}} \tag{7}$$

Then, from (4.4) and (7)

$$g_j = \frac{t_j - (a_{1j} + a_{2j})\bar{t}_i}{1 - (a_{1j} + a_{2j})} \tag{8}$$

All the earlier implications, (i) to (ix), follow if in place of the single input tariff t_i we write the weighted average of the two input tariffs $\bar{t}_i$, and in place of the single input share a_{ij} we write the sum of the two input shares $(a_{1j} + a_{2j})$.

This can obviously be extended to any number of inputs n, in which case

$$g_j = \frac{t_j - \sum_i a_{ij} t_i}{1 - \sum_i a_{ij}} \qquad (4.5) \quad i = 1, \quad 2 \, .. \, n$$

$$\bar{t}_i = \frac{\sum_i a_{ij} t_i}{\sum_i a_{ij}} \qquad (7.1) \quad i = 1, \quad 2 \, .. \, n$$

---

[4] W. M. Corden, 'The Tariff' in A. Hunter (ed.), *The Economics of Australian Industry* (Melbourne University Press, Melbourne, 1963); G. Basevi, 'The United States Tariff Structure: Estimates of Effective Rates of Protection of United States Industries and Industrial Labor', *Review of Economics and Statistics*, 48, May 1966, 147–160, and many others later, notably the studies in B. Balassa (ed.), *The Structure of Protection in Developing Countries*, 1971.

From (4.5) and (7.1)

$$g_j = \frac{t_j - \sum_i a_{ij} \bar{t}_i}{1 - \sum_i a_{ij}} \qquad (8.1) \ i = 1, \quad 2 \ .. \ n$$

In our implications (i) to (ix) we write again $\bar{t}_i$ for t_i and this time $\sum_i a_{ij}$ for a_{ij}.

III. *Production and Consumption Taxes and Subsidies*

It is easy to incorporate production and consumption taxes and subsidies on importables into our analysis of the effective protective rate. It is important here to distinguish taxes and subsidies imposed on the product the effective rate of which we are calculating from taxes and subsidies imposed on its inputs. Consider first such taxes and subsidies on the final good j. It was pointed out in the previous chapter that a consumption tax is the same as a production tax combined with a nominal tariff at the same rate. It affects only the pattern of consumption, not of production. It does not affect the degree of protection and hence does not affect the effective protective rate. On the other hand a production subsidy on the final good has the same effect on production as a nominal tariff at the same rate, while a production tax would have the same effect as an import subsidy. Since both have production effects they both affect the effective rate. It follows that in our formulae (4) and (8.1), t_j should be redefined to represent not just the nominal tariff rate but rather the nominal rate plus any production subsidy or minus any production tax on j.

Next allow for production and consumption taxes and subsidies on the inputs into product j. If we were concerned with the protection of the inputs themselves, then, in line with what has just been said, only *production* taxes and subsidies would be relevant since taxes on consumption of the inputs by the using industry j have no effect on protection of the inputs. But when we are concerned with the effective protection of the using industry j, then only *consumption* taxes and subsidies on the inputs, and not production taxes and subsidies, are relevant. A consumption tax, like a tariff on an input, raises the price to the using industry and so reduces its effective rate. By contrast, a production tax or a production subsidy on an input does not affect the price paid by the using industry. It follows that in our formula (4), t_i should be redefined to represent not just the nominal tariff on the input but rather the nominal tariff plus any consumption tax or minus any consumption subsidy. Similarly, in (8.1), $\bar{t}_i$ needs to be redefined. Furthermore, a_{ij} in (4) and $\sum_i a_{ij}$ in (8.1) need to be redefined to represent the input shares in cost of j not just at free trade prices but at free trade prices that exclude the effects of any production or consumption taxes or subsidies.

What are the implications of production subsidies and consumption taxes on the formula which has to be used for actual measurements of effective rates, namely equation (6)? The main point is that, while a consumption tax on the final good does not affect the effective protective rate for this good (as just explained), it does affect the post-tariff and post-tax share of the input in the cost of the final good if cost is assumed to include the consumption tax. As explained in section III, the input shares available from statistics are based on prices as they are after tariffs have been imposed, so that (taking into account only tariffs), for empirical work equation (6), in which a_{ij}' is an ingredient, needs to be used. Now the question is how production and consumption taxes and subsidies affect a_{ij}' and hence whether equation (6) has to be reconsidered. We shall now redefine a_{ij}' as the share of input i in the domestic value of j, when both i and j are valued at domestic market prices facing consumers, these prices being influenced not only by tariffs but also by consumption taxes and subsidies. We shall introduce consumption taxes on j and i and a production subsidy on j explicitly, letting t_j and t_i refer for the moment only to the nominal tariff rates. The consumption tax and production subsidy rates will be defined realistically as rates calculated on after-tariff prices.

Let

t_j = nominal tariff rate on j, defined now not to include any production taxes or subsidies;

t_i = nominal tariff rate on i, defined now not to include any production or consumption taxes or subsidies;

c_j = consumption tax rate on j (which may be a production tax combined with a border tax at an equal rate); it is expressed as a proportion of the price including tariff;

c_i = consumption tax rate on i, defined as for c_j;

s_j = production subsidy rate on j;

a_{ij} = share of i in cost of j at free trade prices and with no consumption taxes or subsidies;

$a_{ij}{}'$ = share of i in cost of j, valuing both at domestic market prices after tariffs and consumption taxes have been imposed, that is at consumer prices, *not* producer prices.

From (4), allowing for the protective effect on j of s_j and for the tax effect on j of c_i,

$$g_j = \frac{t_j + s_j(1+t_j) - a_{ij}[t_i + c_i(1+t_i)]}{1 - a_{ij}} \qquad (9)$$

From (5), allowing for the effect of c_i in raising the domestic price of i and of c_j in raising the domestic price of j,

$$a_{ij}{}' = a_{ij}\frac{(1+t_i)(1+c_i)}{(1+t_j)(1+c_j)} \qquad (10)$$

From (9) and (10)

$$g_j = \frac{\dfrac{1+s_j}{1+c_j} - a_{ij}{}'}{\dfrac{1}{(1+t_j)(1+c_j)} - \dfrac{a_{ij}{}'}{(1+t_i)(1+c_i)}} - 1 \qquad (11)$$

Note that in (9) the consumption tax on j plays no role, since, as pointed out above, it does not influence effective protection for j, but the production subsidy on j appears, since this raises the nominal protection for j. On the other hand, in (10) it is the consumption tax on j, not the production subsidy, which has a role, since the market price of j (on which the input share $a_{ij}{}'$ is assumed to be based here) is affected by the consumption tax but not by the production subsidy.[5]

[5] Excise and other indirect taxes are taken into account in the various studies in Balassa (ed.), op. cit., and in certain of the countries studied (notably Pakistan) are significant. The first study which systematically introduced excise (consumption) taxes into effective protection theory and calculations was H. G. Grubel and H. G. Johnson, 'Nominal Tariffs, Indirect Taxes and Effective Rates of Protection: The Common Market Countries 1959', *Economic Journal*, 77, Dec. 1967, 761–776. Note that the formula given in that article was confusing, and was corrected in *Economic Journal*, 79, Sept. 1969, 674–675; the revised formula is the same as that given here, except that Grubel and Johnson did not allow for production subsidies or taxes.

IV. *Introducing Exportables*

So far we have been concerned with the effective protection for an importable where the only produced inputs are other importables. It is easy to encompass the discussion to include exportables. In line with the assumptions already made we assume (i) fixed physical input coefficients of exportable inputs into other exportables, exportable inputs into importables or importable inputs into exportables, (ii) that the foreign elasticity of demand for the exports concerned is infinite (small country assumption), and (iii) that after taxes and subsidies have been imposed some exports of these exportables nevertheless remain; hence the tradeable goods remain traded. We also assume that an export subsidy is always accompanied by an appropriate tariff, sufficient to ensure the whole market to domestic producers of exportables and to prevent re-entry of exports for home consumption.

We can calculate the effective protective rate for an importable where some or all inputs are exportables, or for an exportable where the inputs are importables or other exportables. It needs only to be remembered that an export subsidy raises the internal price of an exportable and thus is, from this point of view, the equivalent of a tariff, while an export tax is the equivalent of an import subsidy. An export tax on an exportable input reduces its domestic price and so raises the effective protection for the using industry, irrespective of whether the latter produces an exportable or an importable. Thus a country which exports raw cotton and imposes an export tax on it reduces the costs of its textile industry and hence protects the latter. Exports of the textile industry are indirectly subsidized at the expense of exports of raw cotton. In our formulae (4) and (8.1) g_j can now be redefined as the effective protective rate for any traded good, whether an importable or an exportable, and the i's can include all produced traded inputs, whether importables or exportables.

Three examples can be given of how this method works. In each case we assume that there is only a single produced input. Suppose we have an importable with a 22 per cent tariff where the input is an exportable benefiting from a 10 per cent export subsidy. If the free trade share of the exportable in the cost of the importable is 40 per cent then the latter's effective rate is 30 per cent. This result is exactly the same as if the input had been an importable benefiting from a 10 per cent tariff; an export subsidy raises the domestic price of an exportable input just as a tariff raises the domestic price of an importable input. Next, consider an exportable obtaining an export subsidy of 10 per cent, using as input another exportable on which there is a 25 per cent export tax (expressed as a percentage of the tax-free price). If the free-trade share of the input in the cost of the final good is 50 per cent, the latter's effective protective rate is 45 per cent. Finally, consider a very common situation. We have an exportable not subject to an export tax or subsidy. Its input is an importable paying a 30 per cent tariff. If the free trade share of this input in the exportable's cost is 40 per cent, then effective protection of the exportable is negative, namely —20 per cent.[6]

There are two ways of avoiding negative effective protection for the exportable when the tariff on the input is given. One is to provide a compensating export subsidy (the equivalent of the *compensating tariff* mentioned earlier); in the example above this would have to be at the rate of 12 per cent to yield zero effective protection for the exportable. The other is to have an *export drawback system*, a system widely used in many countries. This means that exportable producers do not pay the tariff on those imports which are inputs into goods that will actually be exported, or if they pay the tariff in the first place, it is refunded once exports take place. Hence negative effective protection for actual exports is avoided, though there is still negative effective protection for exportable goods sold domestically. The system means that export producers will use actual imports, and not domestically produced goods, as inputs for the goods that they will export. But the aim of the tariff may have been to protect domestic production of the input and if the domestic market for the input is limited the failure to use it as input in goods to be exported may negate the purpose of the tariff. Thus the drawback system cannot always be used. In addition there are difficulties in administering

---

[6] Many examples from all over the world could be cited for such a case. See, for example, J. H. Power, 'The Structure of Protection in the Philippines', in Balassa (ed.), op. cit. Power found negative protection (averaging —20 per cent) for all the main categories of manufactured and processed exports, except sugar.

drawback and similar schemes. If tariffs on inputs into goods that are to be exported are not to be paid in the first place it is necessary to ensure that goods which manufacturers say will be exported will actually be exported. They may be required to deposit securities or officials may need to visit factories or inspect consignments. If the tariff is paid initially but is then refunded—the exporters being able to 'draw back' their original payments—an interest-free loan will have been given by the exporters to the Treasury, so that the tariff on the input has not really been zero. Furthermore, there may be forms to fill in and officials to be visited before the drawback can be obtained; all this raises the costs to the exporters and, in the case of small amounts, may discourage them from even applying for a drawback.

To complete the story production and consumption taxes and subsidies on exportables can be introduced. A production subsidy raises nominal protection of the good concerned (raises t_j), while a consumption tax on an exportable which is an input reduces the effective protection for the using industries (raises t_i). The analysis is in fact the same as for importables. Our formulae (4) and (8.1) can be interpreted to take into account not only tariffs and import subsidies, and export subsidies and taxes, but also production and consumption taxes and subsidies on importables and exportables. In principle, for each tradeable good, whether an importable or an exportable, and given all our assumptions, there is an effective protective rate which takes into account all these tariffs, taxes and subsidies on the good itself and on its inputs.

v. *Contents-Protection Scheme*

The governments of a number of countries operate or have operated schemes to make the protection of the domestic motor-car industry conditional on the use by the industry of a certain proportion of domestically produced components and materials. This proportion is often treated as a variable, and in some cases the proportion is gradually raised over time, the aim being to reach 100 per cent domestic content. Such a *contents-protection scheme* has two effects: it influences the effective protection for the producers of the final good and it protects the producers of the inputs. As this type of scheme, in some form or other, is quite common, it is worth analysing in some detail.[7] It need not, of course, be limited to the motor-car industry. It can be shown to be a version of the *quantity-linking scheme* discussed in Chapter 2.

Following is an example of a simple scheme of this kind. There is a given tariff on finished cars and no tariff on components. But the quantity-linking rule is enforced that 60 per cent of all components must be purchased domestically. The sanction is that domestic production of cars will not be permitted unless this minimum proportion is attained. The car manufacturers must then pay a high price for the domestically produced components and the free trade price for the imported components. The average cost of the components will be a weighted average of the two prices, the weights being 60 per cent and 40 per cent. If this average cost exceeds the free trade price of imports by 20 per cent we can say that the *implicit user tax* on components paid by car producers is 20 per cent. The *implicit user tax* is the rate that is relevant for calculating the effective protection on cars. The rate relevant for the protection of components is higher, being the proportion by which the price of domestically produced components exceeds the price of imports. We shall call this the *implicit tariff* on components.

The price of the domestic components is not fixed but rises the more of them are purchased, the quantity purchased being a constant proportion of the total demand for components. This total demand depends on the amount of domestic production of cars; this in turn depends on the effective protective rate for cars. And the effective rate for cars depends on the given nominal tariff rate for cars and on the implicit user tax on the components to which the linking scheme has given rise. But this implicit user tax depends, as we have seen, on the demand for components, which depends on car production. Essentially the scheme has the same effect as a tariff on inputs

---

[7] Brazil, Chile, Canada and Australia are some of the countries that have operated such schemes at various times. See L. J. Johnson, 'Problems of Import Substitution: The Chilean Automobile Industry', *Economic Development and Cultural Change*, 15, Jan. 1967, 202–216; R. J. and P. Wonnacott, *Free Trade Between the United States and Canada: The Potential Economic Effects* (Harvard University Press, Cambridge, 1967), Appendix A; W. M. Corden, 'Australian Tariff Policy', *Australian Economic Papers*, 6, Dec. 1967, 131–153.

when the revenue from the input tariff is used to provide a production subsidy for the domestic producers of the inputs. It reduces the effective protection for the final good and the rate of protection to the input producers (the implicit tariff) exceeds the implicit user tax. The complication is that the rates of implicit tariff and tax depend on the amount of production of the final good.[8]

The scheme is represented in Fig. 3.2, a version of Fig. 3.1. It shows quantities of cars and components along the horizontal axis. The free trade price of cars is OS and of components OG. The nominal tariff on cars is ST. When the supply curve of the car value-added product is subtracted from TT' we obtain LL', the car producers' demand curve for components; it indicates what is left over to pay for components given the domestic tariff-inclusive price of cars OT and the amounts per unit that have to be paid to the value-added product. The supply curve of domestic components producers is EE'. The curve EN is derived by adding on to EE' horizontally the imports of components that are permitted given various amounts of domestic components produced and bought by the car producers; thus GE'' is 60 per cent of GN''. The average cost of components to car producers is traced out by $EE''N''Q$. This is the supply curve of components facing them. Equilibrium is determined at the intersection of the demand curve for components LL' with this supply curve, yielding car production and total components purchases of OA, of which OB are domestically produced components and BA are imports ($OB/OA = GE''/GN'' = 60$ per cent). The cost of domestic production per unit is AD; hence the rate of protection for components (the implicit tariff) is $A'D/AA'$. The cost of

---

[8] The problem could be formulated mathematically. Let the c.i.f. import prices of cars and components be constants. Given the parameters of the two supply curves (the car value-added supply curve and the components supply curve), and with the nominal price of cars ruling domestically and the contents ratio of component to car production as additional parameters, one can (1) solve for car output, for components output, for the effective price of cars, for the price of domestically produced components, and for the average cost of components to car producers, and (2) one can show the effects of changes in any of the parameters (shifts in the two supply curves, nominal tariff on cars, change in the contents ratio) on the unknowns, the change in the effective price of cars being the effective rate, the change in the price of domestic components being the implicit components tariff, and the change in the average cost of components to car producers the implicit user tax.

imported components is AA' and the average cost to the motor-car producers is AC; hence the *implicit user tax rate* is $A'C/AA'$. The two shaded areas are equal. The effective rate for cars is $(ST-A'C)/GS$.

The diagram can be manipulated in various ways to bring out the implications of a contents protection scheme. (a) Suppose

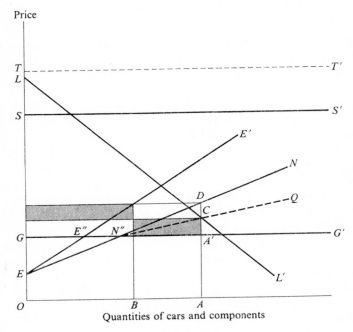

Fig. 3.2

that the nominal tariff on cars is raised; so LL' shifts to the right and hence the demand for components increases, equilibrium shifting upwards and to the right. The implicit user tax and tariff on components rise. It follows (i) that the effective rate on cars does not rise as much as a result of the increase in the nominal tariff as it would have if there had been a fixed component tariff, and (ii) the extra protection for cars yields extra protection for domestic components producers. This last result should be contrasted with our earlier models where the tariff on the input was exogenously determined and not influenced by the nominal tariff for the final good. Provided imports of the input remained, a rise in protection of the final good did not lead to extra protection for the input. (b) If the minimum contents ratio is raised, EN and hence the supply curve segment $N''Q$ shift to the left. The implicit tax and tariff on components rise, the effective rate for cars falls and output of cars declines. (c) If the supply curve of the value-added product of car producers shifts down, LL' shifts to the right, this raising the price of domestic components and hence the implicit tax on components. The effective rate for cars will therefore fall. This is a contrast with our earlier analysis where a shift in the value-added supply curve does not alter the effective rate. (d) If the supply curve of domestic components producers shifts to the right $N''Q$ also shifts to the right, hence the implicit components tax falls, the effective rate for cars increases and car production will increase. Again, this can be contrasted with the earlier analysis where a shift in the input supply curve does not affect the effective rate.

We have assumed so far that car producers are induced to adhere to the minimum contents ratio through some direct sanction, such as licencing of production. Let us now look at two alternative sanctions or inducements which are in practice common. (a) There might be a high tariff on components, say 100 per cent, and the scheme might provide that producers who adhere to the minimum contents ratio will be exempted from paying this duty. There will then be a ceiling of 100 per cent on the implicit user tax which a producer pays as a result of the scheme. If the implicit tax did come out higher it would be to his advantage to pay the 100 per cent tariff on imports and to purchase only those components domestically which are no dearer than duty-paid imports. (b) An alternative inducement to car producers to maintain the minimum contents ratio is to make their own nominal tariff conditional on their adherence to the ratio. If they did not adhere to it but were able to purchase components free of duty they would obtain zero effective protection. It follows that it will only pay them to stay in the scheme if the net result of their own nominal tariff and the implicit tax resulting from the contents scheme yields positive effective protection. If this sanction were combined with sanction (a) above, then if they did not adhere to the minimum contents ratio they would obtain a given rate of negative protection, and it would pay them to stay in the scheme provided the effective protection it provided was not lower than this negative rate. Finally, it might be noted that a sufficient sanction for such a contents scheme may be the threat that failure to attain the minimum ratio would lead to tariffs or import controls on components, or would lead to withdrawal of the nominal tariff on cars or of other forms of assistance.

VI. *Negative Effective Prices*

An effective price might be negative. It might be positive under free trade but made negative by tariffs or consumption taxes on inputs. Alternatively it might be negative under free trade but made positive by a tariff or production subsidy on the final good itself. A negative effective price must be distinguished from a negative effective protective *rate*. It was shown above that the effective *rate* will be negative if $t_j < a_{ij}t_i$. This means only that the tariff system has reduced the effective price. But now we are concerned with the case where either the effective price has been reduced so much that it becomes negative, or where it is negative in the first place, before tariffs are imposed.

An effective price becomes negative as a result of the tariff structure if the tariff on the input is so high that it not only offsets the tariff on the final good but that it more than eliminates the whole of the margin between the free trade price of the final good (the nominal price) and the price of the input, this margin being the free trade effective price. For example, if in free trade the input accounts for 75 per cent of the cost of the final good ($a_{ij} = 75$ per cent), if the tariff on the input is 80 per cent and if the nominal tariff on the final good is only 20 per cent, then the effective price of a unit of the final good which is $100 in free trade would become $-$60. The cost of the input, including the tariff on it, would exceed the after-tariff price of the final good.[9] But this case is just a curiosum.

---

[9] The condition for obtaining such a negative effective price as a result of tariffs is derived from equation (2):

$$p_v' < 0 \quad \text{if} \quad \frac{1+t_j}{1+t_i} < a_{ij} \tag{2.1}$$

There can be no continuing domestic production of a product when its effective price is negative—or indeed when it is zero. Domestic production is likely to cease once the effective price falls below some positive floor. Furthermore, if the input is used only for this product there can be no imports of the input once domestic production has stopped. Hence the *utilized* part of the input tariff cannot bring the effective price lower than the floor at which domestic production of the final good stops.

Next consider the interesting case where the effective price is negative under free trade. This case has been given much attention in the literature on effective protection because empirical work has suggested that it occurs quite frequently.[10] It is generally described as *negative value-added* (or *value subtracted*). The case arises when the free trade price of a unit of the final good is, say $100 but the free trade price of a unit of the input required to produce that unit of the final product is more, say, $120. In that case the effective price is − $20. There would then be no production of the final good under free trade. But a sufficiently high tariff on the final good, associated with no tariff, a low tariff or an import subsidy on the input, could convert the negative effective price into a

---

[10] The pioneering article is R. Soligo and J. J. Stern, 'Tariff Protection, Import Substitution and Investment Efficiency', *Pakistan Development Review*, 5, Summer 1965, 249–269. The authors appeared to uncover twenty-three Pakistani industries with negative value-added, including some very large industries. Subsequent work by Lewis and Guisinger taking into account quantitative restrictions and various other considerations suggests that there may be only five industries in Pakistan (including sugar refining and motor-car assembly) that have zero or negative value-added. See S. R. Lewis and S. E. Guisinger, 'The Structure of Protection in Pakistan', in Balassa (ed.), op. cit. Negative value-added cases have also been found for the United States, India, Philippines and Brazil. See Basevi, op. cit., J. Bhagwati and P. Desai, *India, Planning for Industrialisation*, 1970, Ch. 17, esp. its Appendix; J. Power (on Philippines), and J. Bergsman and P. S. Malan (on Brazil) in Balassa (ed.), op. cit. Also, P. T. Ellsworth, 'Import Substitution in Pakistan—Some Comments', *Pakistan Development Review*, 6, Autumn 1966, 395–407; J. H. Power, 'Import Substitution as an Industrialisation Strategy', *Philippine Economic Journal*, 5, 1966, 167–204; S. R. Lewis and S. E. Guisinger, 'Measuring Protection in a Developing Country: The Case of Pakistan', *Journal of Political Economy*, 76, Nov./Dec. 1968, 1107–1198; S. E. Guisinger, 'Negative Value Added and the Theory of Effective Protection', *Quarterly Journal of Economics*, 83, Aug. 1969, 415–433; A. H. H. Tan, 'Differential Tariffs, Negative Value-Added and the Theory of Effective Protection', *American Economic Review*, 60, March 1970, 107–116.

positive one and so bring forth domestic production. Thus in this example a 100 per cent tariff on the final good combined with a 10 per cent tariff on the input would yield a post-tariff effective price of $68. The domestic production that results is then correctly described as *negative value-added* when value-added is measured at free trade prices. The cost of the inputs is greater than the value of the final product. Even without taking any indirect or general equilibrium repercussions into account—a matter for later chapters—the act of replacing imports of the final good has an adverse effect on the balance of payments since the free trade value of the imports of the final good replaced by domestic production is less than the cost of the imported inputs. It is sometimes misunderstood to mean that, in some sense, under free trade there would actually be 'negative value-added'. But there would not be any production of the product concerned under free trade. It means only that the positive production (value-added) under protection has a negative value when measured at free trade prices.

In what circumstances can the free trade effective price be negative? How can it be that it costs more to import the components of a motor-car than the finished motor-car? Clearly, in the country which supplies the imports of motor-cars and perhaps the components the price of the car cannot be less than the price or cost of the required components to the car producers, for otherwise it would not pay to produce the cars. There are four possible explanations for a negative effective price under free trade in the home country. Firstly, transport costs (which can be regarded as including costs of packaging), expressed as a proportion of the f.o.b. export price in the supplying country, may be much greater for the components than for the finished cars. For example, the f.o.b. prices may be $2000 for a car and $1500 for the components. But transport and packaging costs add 10 per cent to the cost of the car, bringing the c.i.f. import price to $2200 and 50 per cent to the cost of the components, bringing their price to $2250. Secondly, production functions (input coefficients) may differ between countries, the home country being less efficient and wasting materials. In the efficient supplying country only one unit of the input may be required to make one unit of the final good. But in the inefficient home country two units of the input may be required. Assume now that there are no transport costs and that in both countries the price of a unit of the final product is $100 and of a unit of the input $60; hence the effective price is $40 in the supplying country. But with a less efficient production function, in the home country the cost of the necessary inputs is $120. Hence the effective price is then −$20. Thirdly, even with the same production functions and no transport costs, the effective price may be negative if the input price the users in the supplying country have to pay is lower than the export price of the input. This would be so if there were an export tax on the input (though the effects could be offset by an export tax on the final product), or if the input industry discriminated against foreign buyers for the same reason. Fourthly, in the supplying country there may be a monopolistic producer of both the final product and the input who may deliberately price exports of the input highly so as to discourage processing abroad. In practice one might expect the first two reasons to explain most cases. It should also be noted that figures implying negative value-added may simply result from inaccurate data or excessive aggregation. The results are much influenced by whether non-traded inputs are grouped with value-added or with traded inputs.[11] Use of foreign input-output coefficients as proxies for unobtainable domestic coefficients may also lead to inaccuracies. Further, foreign-owned companies may purchase their imported inputs at inflated prices from their parent companies or associated companies in order to shift the taxation burden abroad (if company tax rates are lower there) or to avoid domestic criticisms of high profits. Thus the use of statistics of declared import values will reveal input shares that are excessive and so may give an appearance of negative value-added.[12]

When the effective price is negative under free trade and is made positive by protection the effective protective rate, as calculated by the usual formula, behaves curiously. It is at first sight surprising that it turns out to be *negative* even though there is most certainly positive protection when a negative effective price is turned into a positive one. The

[11] See section II of Chapter 7.

[12] Input substitution (assumed away in this chapter) may also give rise to negative value-added. See section IV of Chapter 6.

explanation is quite simple. The effective rate relates the change in the effective price to the free trade effective price, the formula being $g_j = (p_v' - p_v)/p_v$. When the numerator of this expression is positive effective protection is positive: the effective price is raised by protection; in the case we considered earlier this numerator was negative because p_v' was negative. But now we have a situation where the denominator is negative while the numerator is positive. Hence positive effective protection leads to a negative g_j. One could avoid this paradox of getting an apparently negative effective rate when effective protection is really positive by defining the effective rate as the increase in the effective price divided by the post-tariff effective price, that is as u_j, where

$$u_j = \frac{p_v' - p_v}{p_v'}$$

This might be described as the proportion of domestic value-added which is subsidized by the protective structure; negative value-added at free trade prices will reveal itself in a figure greater than 100 per cent.[13] But this procedure would express the effective rate differently from the way in which nominal tariff rates are usually expressed, and hence has not been adopted here. Furthermore, it would not avoid the paradox that, when there is negative value-added, an increase in t_j or decrease in t_i would lead to a fall in the effective rate as calculated from the formula, even though both must raise p_v' and hence the rate of protection.

One must conclude that in all cases where there is negative value-added at free trade prices the actual figure that results when the usual effective protection formula is applied is meaningless. One can interpret the result as representing essentially an infinite rate of protection. But this raises the further question of how we can know when a negative rate yielded by the calculations of effective rates refers to genuinely negative protection, that is, to $t_j < a_{ij}t_i$, and when there is negative value-added. In the former case the rate must normally be between 0 and −100 per cent. In theory the rate could be less than −100 per cent (e.g. −150 per cent) but this would mean that the effective price under protection is negative, and

---

[13] This definition was used in Soligo and Stern, op. cit.

since there would be no production in such a case (unless an industry is temporarily running at a loss) one would not actually observe it from a study of existing industries in a country. One could of course set out to calculate rates of protection available for non-existent industries using foreign input-coefficients. Now consider the case of negative value-added. In that case the calculated effective rate would emerge as less than -100 per cent, for $g_j = (p_v' - p_v)/p_v$, which can be rewritten as $g_j = (p_v'/p_v - 1)$ and with p_v' positive and p_v negative it follows that $g_j < -1$. We have thus the convenient result that if the effective rate emerges as negative but not less than -100 per cent we must have truly negative effective protection while if it is less than -100 per cent it is a case of negative value-added. This is a sufficient rule for most purposes, but seems to rest rather too much on the -100 per cent border-line. Another approach is as follows. Consider formula (6) of section II. This, it will be recalled, is the formula generally used for calculations of effective rates, a_{ij}' being the post-tariff input share.

$$g_j = \left[\frac{1 - a_{ij}'}{\dfrac{1}{1+t_j} - \dfrac{a_{ij}'}{1+t_i}} \right] - 1 \qquad (6)$$

How does negative value-added reveal itself in this formula? A negative effective price in free trade means that a_{ij} is greater than unity, and from (5)

$$\frac{a_{ij}'}{1+t_i} = \frac{a_{ij}}{1+t_j} \qquad (12)$$

Hence a negative effective price under free trade means that

$$\frac{a_{ij}'}{1+t_i} > \frac{1}{1+t_j} \qquad (13)$$

This, it will be observed, means that the denominator in the bracketed expression in formula (6) is negative. This is how the peculiar case of negative value-added reveals itself. By contrast, if there is genuinely a negative rate of protection the denominator will be positive, and the bracketed expression as a whole will be positive and less than unity.

VII. *Some Implications of the Theory of Effective Protection*

When one takes into account the vertical relations between products or industries much that has seemed straightforward in a world of vertically integrated industries—the world of Chapter 2—turns out to be somewhat more complicated. But the new technique of the effective protective rate gives us a way of handling these complications. We stay still within the confines of the partial equilibrium approach, though laying the foundations for the later general equilibrium discussion.

Consider first the effects on imports and domestic production of imposing a tariff. In the simple model of Chapter 2 this would reduce the value of imports and raise the domestic output of the import-competing industry. Now suppose that this tariff is on an intermediate good. If the domestic supply elasticity is positive the tariff will certainly lead to lower imports and greater domestic production of this good. But the tariff will also reduce the effective protection for the using industry. Imports of the using industry's product will increase and domestic production will decline. A change in the nominal rate for an intermediate good will in fact alter at least two effective rates in opposite directions. On balance total protected production may rise or fall, with trade moving in the opposite direction. Turning the problem around and thinking of a tariff reduction, a country which offers in international negotiations to reduce tariffs on an intermediate good appears to be making a 'concession' that will reduce protection and increase trade. But in fact the extra imports and lower domestic production of the intermediate good must be set against the consequences of the higher effective rate for the using industry. This is clearest in the special case where the elasticity of supply of the intermediate good is zero so that the only consequences of the tariff reduction result from the rise in the effective rate for the user industry.

Consider a simple case where a tariff t_i is imposed on an input, with no tariff on the final good. The effective rate g_j for the final good will of course be negative. Output Y_i of input i will rise and output Y_j of the final good will fall, with imports moving in the opposite direction. Defining Y as the sum of output of i and the value-added by j, both valued at free trade prices, e_i and e_j as the elasticities of the two supply curves, e_j being the elasticity of supply of the value-added product with respect to the effective price, and h_i as the initial ratio of domestic output of i to total usage of i, we have:

$$dY = dY_i + dY_j(1-a_{ij}) \tag{14}$$

$$e_i = \frac{dY_i}{Y_i} \cdot \frac{1}{t_i} \tag{15}$$

$$e_j = \frac{dY_j}{Y_j} \frac{1}{g_j} \tag{16}$$

$$h_i = \frac{Y_i}{a_{ij}Y_j} \tag{17}$$

$$g_j = \frac{t_j - a_{ij}t_i}{1 - a_{ij}} \tag{4}$$

From (14), (15), (16), (17), (4), with $t_j = 0$

$$dY = t_i a_{ij} Y_j (e_i h_i - e_j) \tag{18}$$

Thus (18) shows that whether total protected output valued at free trade prices rises or falls as a result of imposing the tariff t_i, depends on the two supply elasticities and the ratio h_i. If $e_i h_i = e_j$ there will be no net change in protected output and in the combined imports of i and j. But the composition of production and imports will still change, the imposition of t_i shifting output towards and imports away from the intermediate good.[14]

Next consider the implications of our approach when we wish to compare one protective rate with another or when we wish deliberately to provide the same protective rates for two products. In the simple model of Chapter 2 the matter was straightforward. When the nominal tariffs for cloth and for cars were both 20 per cent then the rates of protection were the same, provided only both tariffs were fully utilized and the foreign supply prices were given. But now the nominal tariffs

---

[14] Our derivation assumes that the tariff and output changes are small. Alternatively one could assume the two supply curves to be straight lines, define the two elasticities at the free trade points, and so obtain

$$\Delta Y = t_i a_{ij} Y_j (e_i h_i - e_j)$$

may be equal and yet the effective rates may not be. Suppose
that there are no tariffs on inputs into cloth and cars. Then,
if the input ratios differ, equal effective rates will require
different nominal rates. For example, if the free trade input
ratio is 60 per cent for cloth and 20 per cent for cars, if tariffs
on inputs are ruled out and if it is desired to attain an equal
effective rate of 25 per cent, then the nominal tariff for cloth
must be 10 per cent and for cars 20 per cent. Equality of
nominal and effective rates would be possible only if the input
ratios were the same or if it were possible to impose an identical
nominal tariff on both inputs and both final goods.

We can also compare the rates of effective protection provided to different activities in a vertical chain. We know from
our formula (4) that if the nominal tariffs on yarn and cloth
are both 20 per cent the effective rate on cloth will also be
20 per cent. But what will be the effective rate on yarn?
If yarn is vertically integrated its nominal and effective rates
will be equal; otherwise we must look at the nominal rate on
raw cotton, the input into yarn. If the cotton nominal rate is
20 per cent then the yarn effective rate will also be 20 per cent.
In fact, if nominal rates are 20 per cent at every link in the
vertical chain, then all effective rates will be 20 per cent.
But it may be that the tariff on the raw material at the base is
zero, or less than 20 per cent, or that this raw material is an
exportable with no export subsidy or tax. If we then wished to
obtain a vertical uniformity of 20 per cent effective protection
for every activity above this an interesting result ensues. With
the raw cotton rate zero, in order to have a 20 per cent effective
rate for yarn, the nominal rate for yarn would have to be
between zero and 20 per cent, say 15 per cent, since the nominal
rate is a weighted average of the effective rate and the rate
on the input. To give the next activity above this an effective
rate of 20 per cent, the nominal rate for its products would
have to be between 15 per cent and 20 per cent, say 18 per cent.
Thus we find that the nominal rates need to increase steadily
with the degree of processing just to maintain effective rates
constant.[15] From (4.3), if t_0, t_1, t_2, t_3 . . . are the nominal tariff

[15] The point was originally made in C. L. Barber, 'Canadian Tariff Policy',
Canadian Journal of Economics and Political Science, 2, Nov. 1955, p. 524. It
is thoroughly discussed in H. G. Johnson, 'The Theory of Tariff Structure with

rates on raw cotton, yarn, grey cloth, printed cloth, etc., a_{01}, a_{12}, a_{23} . . . are the input shares into the next stage at free trade prices, each being less than one (share of raw cotton, yarn, grey cloth . . .), and g is the constant effective rate, then

$$t_0 = 0$$
$$t_1 = g(1-a_{01})$$
$$t_2 = g(1-a_{12})+t_1 a_{12} \qquad (19)$$
$$t_3 = g(1-a_{23})+t_2 a_{23}$$

It can be seen from (19) that t_2 is the weighted average of g and t_1 where t_1 is less than g, so that t_2 is greater than t_1 and similarly t_3 is greater than t_2. If, rather fancifully, one imagined an infinite vertical progression, then $t_\infty = g$. But since no activity is in fact the nth activity, all nominal rates will be less than the effective rate, except for the material at the base where both nominal and effective rate are zero. The general point is that with zero or low-duty imports of the basic material, to maintain constant effective rates above the basic stage, nominal rates must rise or 'escalate' as one moves from lower-order to higher-order products. But a difficulty is that one product may not be clearly of a higher order than another. The products may not be related in a simple linear chain. Thus not only product 2 but also product 1 might be an input in product 3. Or there may be feedback, so that, while product 2 is an input in product 3 this product is an input in product 2 or in product 1.[16] In these circumstances the simple argument given here breaks down.

Escalation is a common characteristic of the nominal tariff structures of most countries. It is common for tariffs on finished goods to be higher than tariffs on intermediate goods and raw materials. Three observations about this can be made.

Special Reference to World Trade and Development', in H. G. Johnson and P. B. Kenen, *Trade and Development* (Geneva, 1965), pp. 18–20, where the qualification mentioned below that the products may not be related in a simple linear chain is stressed.

[16] In other words, the input-output matrix may not be triangular. On this subject see H. B. Chenery and P. G. Clark, *Interindustry Economics* (John Wiley and Sons, New York, 1959), pp. 210–11. They present evidence which suggests a high degree of triangularity in the input-output matrices of a number of countries and suggest that 'this uniformity lends support to the idea of a natural hierarchy of sectors'.

The first is that, apart from the protection of the material at the base, escalation of nominal rates may not mean escalation of effective rates; on the other hand, just because a vertical chain displays escalation of nominal rates it does not mean that it is precisely that rate of escalation which maintains the effective rate the same at each stage (other than the first). With the input ratios differing as one moves up the chain, to achieve the same effective rate at each stage there would have to be an irregular rate of escalation. The second point is that escalation means always that an effective rate is higher than a nominal rate, so that a misleading impression tends to be conveyed of the rates of protection that are being provided. And thirdly, insofar as escalation means non-uniformity of effective rates—and at least the effective rate for the activity at the top is bound to be higher than the rate for the raw material at the base—the pattern of production and imports within the vertical chain will be affected, unless relevant supply elasticities are zero; if the effective rate for raw cotton is zero while for all other links in the chain it is 20 per cent, there will be no such shift in the pattern of output if the elasticity of supply of domestic cotton production is zero.

To conclude, consider one more complication introduced by vertical relationships. In section V of Chapter 2 it was pointed out that a tariff may be so high that it completely excludes imports. One must then distinguish the *utilized* from the *available* tariff. Given the domestic and foreign supply curves and the domestic demand curve, whether a part of the tariff is redundant depended in this analysis purely on the level of the available tariff. Once we allow for effective rates, this remains almost, but not quite, true. Suppose we have a given tariff on input i, and then imagine a gradual increase in the nominal tariff on j. The rise in the nominal tariff will reduce domestic consumption of j. Furthermore, it will raise the effective protective rate for j, and hence increase domestic production. When the nominal tariff is 12 per cent, say, imports of j may cease. This may be associated with a 20 per cent effective tariff on j. If the tariff on j increases further, bringing the available effective rate to, say, 25 per cent, the extra tariff will be redundant: the *available* effective tariff is then 25 per cent and the *utilized* one 20 per cent. This distinction presents the same problems as discussed earlier. But it is not true that in our example a 25 per cent effective tariff must always contain a 5 per cent redundant element. Suppose the input tariff t_i and the nominal tariff on the final good, t_j, were reduced simultaneously so as to maintain the effective tariff for j at 25 per cent. Domestic output will then remain unchanged but the reduction in t_j may raise domestic consumption and imports may start again. Thus tariff redundancy may end even though the effective rate has not changed. Hence, whether an effective tariff contains a redundant element depends not only on the level of the effective rate (which affects domestic supply) but also on the level of the nominal tariff (which affects domestic demand). If the input tariff can be varied then a given effective rate can be associated with different nominal rates.

VIII. *Complications: Non-Homogeneity, Inter-Firm Differences*

The theory of effective protection appears to be very neat. But this hinges on some rather crucial assumptions. The three crucial assumptions are probably those listed at the beginning of this chapter—fixed coefficients, small country assumption, and that 'trade remains'. But there are some others, which we discuss briefly here.

It has been assumed so far that imported yarn and domestically-produced yarn are quite homogeneous—identical in every respect. But there may be fixed differences between them. One possibility is that domestic yarn is of a lower quality than imported yarn. This may mean that the amount required to make a given unit of cloth is greater than when imported yarn is used. We could then define units so that the horizontal axis in Fig. 3.1 shows units of constant quality; a point on the axis might represent two pounds of imported yarn but three pounds of domestic yarn. Alternatively, while the input coefficients might be the same, the cloth produced with domestic yarn may be of lower quality and thus have a lower import price than the cloth produced with imported yarn. This could again be overcome by appropriate choice of units, so that units of the two types of cloth can be brought to the same price.

Another possibility is that domestic and imported yarn

are of the same quality, but that the use of one of them requires more complementary primary factors—that is, more value-added product—than the other. For example, there may be advantages in vertically integrated production, so that when yarn is produced within the same factory as the cloth, or at least within the same town or country, it requires less internal transport and packing costs than when it is obtained from abroad. There may thus be 'breaking-up costs' resulting from separating vertically related processes. Let us define a unit of value-added product as the input of primary factors required to make a unit of cloth when *imported* yarn is used. It may then be that only 75 per cent of a unit of value-added product is required to make the same amount of cloth when domestic yarn, or more specifically, yarn spun within the same weaving mill, is used. Thus there is a saving in value-added through vertical integration. This is best handled in our analysis by subtracting the value of this saving per unit of cloth from the supply curve of domestic yarn, hence obtaining a new supply curve below the old one. In Fig. 3.1, EE' is the supply curve of domestic yarn, telling us that the marginal cost of the yarn required for OK' units of cloth is $K'L$. This can be compared with the free trade price of imported yarn, $K'R$. Now suppose that RL is the saving in value-added cost per unit resulting from using domestic rather than imported yarn. This means that the adjusted supply curve of domestic yarn is the dotted line through R. To obtain the supply curve of cloth it is necessary to add as before on top of the adjusted supply curve the value-added supply curve *as it is with imported yarn*. In the absence of a tariff on yarn it will pay to produce OK' domestically, and import the rest. If there were very great advantages in vertical integration the adjusted yarn supply curve would be well to the right and there would be no imports of yarn at all. So yarn would be a non-traded input. It is only if the possibility of importing it, or at least of buying it from outside the factory, arises that the concept of effective protection is relevant. Vertically disintegrated production must be possible; in a sense the degree of vertical integration, at least within the country as distinct from within the factory, must be a decision variable for the distinction between inputs and final goods to be significant.

A further complication is that the input coefficients are likely to differ between firms. This means that for every given set of nominal prices the effective prices will differ between firms. One could still draw a supply curve of the industry's value-added product, showing quantities supplied at various effective prices, but it would be of little significance since there would no longer be a single effective price ruling throughout the industry. Even this would present no difficulties if the relationships between the effective prices facing the various firms stayed constant, but when the input coefficients differ one cannot assume this. Firm A may have a high a_{ij} and firm B a relatively low one. The imposition of tariffs on the final product and the input will then yield them different effective rates, unless t_j happened to be equal to t_i (see implication (ix) of equation (4)). If t_j is greater than t_i the effective rate for firm A will be greater than for firm B. If t_j is less than t_i the effective rate could be positive for one firm and negative for the other; one firm might expand output and the other contract it. Here then is a real difficulty, in fact, an aggregation problem.

One might pursue the matter further and ask why input coefficients should differ between firms. We are still assuming fixed coefficients in each firm, so that differences cannot be explained by differences in substitution possibilities. But there are two possible explanations. One is that the products are not strictly homogeneous. This can be handled by the methods discussed above. Another, very plausible, possibility is that some firms are more efficient than others. On first thought one is inclined to handle this by incorporating the excess costs of the inefficient firms in their supply curves. The efficient firms, that require less inputs per unit of output, would have lower costs and earn rents. But the excess costs of the inefficient firms will not be independent of prices of the inputs and hence tariffs on the inputs, so that if this method were used the inefficient firms' value-added supply curves would shift with every change in the input tariff. This would defeat the purpose of effective protection theory, in which changes in traded input prices are reflected in changes in the prices of the value-added products (the effective prices) and not in shifts in the supply curves of the value-added products. So this is not a satisfactory solution. The use of the concept of effective protection really requires one to assume that input coefficients are reasonably similar between the domestic firms that produce a particular product.

Finally, it is quite possible that all firms in the country producing a given product have the same input-output co-efficients, but some are more vertically integrated than others. Some firms weave cloth and buy their yarn from independent spinning firms while other firms are both weavers and spinners. Thus there does not appear to be a 'natural' input-output scheme.[17] But this does not present any real difficulty for our analysis. The effective rate refers to protection for a process, not a firm, and the fact that some firms are engaged in only one process and others in more than one is not relevant unless 'breaking-up' costs differ between firms.

[17] See W. P. Travis, 'The Effective Rate of Protection and the Question of Labor Protection in the United States', *Journal of Political Economy*, 76, May/June 1968, p. 445.

4

THE GENERAL EQUILIBRIUM
APPROACH AND THE THEORY OF
PROTECTIVE STRUCTURE

I. *The Orthodox Two-sector Analysis*

It is the aim of this chapter and the next to set out a new way of analysing the general equilibrium effects of trade taxes and subsidies. This will go well beyond the two-sector approach which is commonly used in the literature of trade theory. But the orthodox approach is our point of take-off and is also illuminating in its own right.

So we begin with expounding it briefly. For more rigorous and fuller expositions and more thorough specifications of its assumptions the reader is referred to the many books and articles which use this approach.[1] Readers familiar with pure trade theory are advised to pass directly on to section II.

In this approach one assumes that only two products are produced and consumed in the economy, the exportable X and the importable M. Each of these could be thought of as a bundle of goods. Production of each is vertically integrated. Some kind of mechanism, which we shall discuss in the next chapter but which for the moment can simply be termed *price flexibility*, ensures full employment of the given stock of factors of production and equality of the value of exports to the value of imports. From the factor stocks and the two production functions can be derived a production possibility curve, drawn as HH' in Fig. 4.1. It is concave to the origin, so that a diminishing marginal rate of transformation of one

---

[1] See, for example, J. E. Meade, *A Geometry of International Trade* (Allen and Unwin, London, 1952); M. C. Kemp, *The Pure Theory of International Trade* (Prentice-Hall, Englewood Cliffs, 1964); H. R. Heller, *International Trade: Theory and Empirical Evidence* (Prentice-Hall, Englewood Cliffs, 1968).

product into another is assumed. We need not concern ourselves with what lies behind this curve, noting only that a sufficient, though not necessary, condition for such a curve is that the production functions of the two industries are both linear homogeneous with continuous substitution between inputs and that the factor-intensities differ between them—that is, when the two industries face identical factor price ratios they employ different quantity ratios of the factors. Next we make the *small country assumption*, hence assuming that the country faces a given world price ratio (terms of trade) represented by the slope of SS'. The point of tangency to the production possibility curve of a line with such a slope determines production under free trade. In Fig. 4.1 the point of free trade production is P, so that there is some production of both goods.

Next we shall assume that the overall pattern of consumption depends only on relative prices and total real income and not on income distribution. This means that we are assuming the demand patterns at the margin of the owners of different factors of production to be identical. If they were not, then the change in income distribution induced by a movement along the production possibility curve would affect the pattern of consumption. In Fig. 4.1, OZ is the income-consumption line associated with the price ratio given by the slope of SS'. At that price ratio consumption has to be somewhere on OZ. Given production at P and the price ratio as shown by SS', income is OS in terms of M or OS' in terms of X, and given this income, consumption must be at C, where OZ intersects SS'. The diagram shows that in free trade production of X exceeds consumption of X by BP, the excess being exports, while consumption of M exceeds production of M by BC, the excess being imports. Exports are equal to imports at the given price ratio. The free trade *trade triangle* is shaded. This is where we start. Now, what are the effects of a tariff?

A tariff raises the domestic price of M relative to that of X. The new tariff-distorted domestic price ratio is indicated by the slope of GG'. It induces production to shift away from X towards M, the new production point being P'. Thus the movement from P to P' is the *production* or *protection effect* of the tariff. The tariff also raises to the same extent the relative domestic price of M facing consumers and so induces the consumption pattern to shift away from M towards X. The income-consumption line appropriate to the new domestic

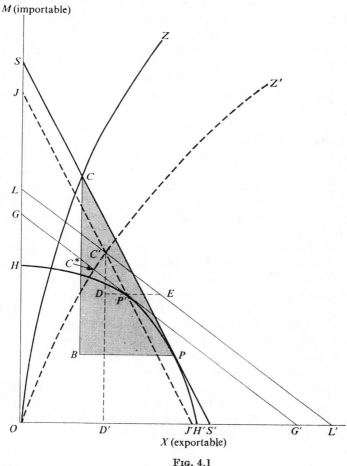

Fig. 4.1

price ratio is OZ'. The movement from one income-consumption line to another represents the *consumption effect*—the price-induced shift in the pattern of consumption.

The point of consumption has not yet been determined. Given the new domestic price ratio and the new point of

6

production, income now appears to be OG in terms of M or OG' in terms of X. So the consumption point would seem to be C^*. This would indeed be so if the revenue from the tariff were retained by the government and not spent. The government might spend the revenue, allocating it between X and M on the basis of its own marginal propensities. If these propensities differed from those of the community in general there would be various implications which have been explored in the literature.[2] We shall make the simple assumption here and elsewhere in the book that the revenue is returned to consumers in a non-distorting way and consumers then spend it like any other part of their total income. This is a common assumption in trade theory. Thus consumers will move up OZ' from C^*. The actual consumption point is C' and is derived as follows. With production determined at P', the trade possibilities are given by the world price ratio: the country can trade anywhere along $JP'J'$, which is parallel to SS'. But the new tariff-distorted domestic price ratio has determined that the consumption point must be on OZ'. It follows that it must be at the intersection of $JP'J'$ with OZ'. The new trade triangle resulting from the tariff is $DC'P'$. As drawn, the tariff is not prohibitive, so that some trade remains. If we compare the protection consumption point C' with the free trade point C we find that it differs from it in two respects. First, it is on a different income-consumption line, this being the consumption-substitution effect of the tariff. Secondly, it is at a lower level of income at world prices (OJ' instead of OS'), this in turn being the result of the production-substitution effect of the tariff.

What are income and tariff revenue in the protection situation? To sort this out, draw the line $LC'L'$ through C', with the slope of the tariff-distorted domestic price ratio. At this price ratio the incomes of producers from producing X and M add up to OG' in terms of X. But this is supplemented by an income of $G'L'$ which is the redistributed tariff revenue. We shall see in a moment where this comes from. At the resultant total income OL' consumers choose to consume the amounts

[2] A. P. Lerner, 'The Symmetry between Import and Export Taxes', *Economica*, 3, Aug. 1936, 306–13, reprinted in R. E. Caves and H. G. Johnson (eds.), *Readings in International Economics* (Richard D. Irwin, Homewood, 1968).

ORTHODOX TWO-SECTOR ANALYSIS

indicated by the point C'. Consumption of M is $D'C'$ of which $D'D$ is home-produced and DC' is imported. The cost of these imports to consumers at domestic tariff-distorted prices is DE in terms of exports. Of this cost, DP' actually pays for the exports needed to buy the imports at the world price ratio while $P'E$ is the tariff revenue. And it is this tariff revenue which is then redistributed, yielding the income supplement $G'L'$.

A great deal of information can be drawn out of this diagram. One could compare the tariff with a production subsidy or a consumption tax. One could show the *subsidy-equivalent* of the tariff (namely $J'G'$) and one could show what would happen if the government spent the tariff revenue itself. Furthermore, one could use the diagram to illustrate the effects of an export tax or an export subsidy and one could show that a specified export tax would have exactly the same effect as the tariff—a point to be further developed in the next chapter. In fact, most and perhaps all of the conclusions of Chapter 2 could be derived here, but in addition the general equilibrium approach brings out income effects which are lost in the partial equilibrium method.

Finally, one could represent in a diagram like Fig. 4.1 the case where world prices are not given, foreign elasticities being less than infinite. The tariff would then affect the terms of trade. This would involve some further complications and the use of the *offer curve*, a concept central to two-sector trade theory that will not be used in this book. There would again be a production and a consumption effect, with the relative price of M facing domestic producers and consumers again identical and above the foreign price. Normally the domestic relative price of importables, would, as before, rise, but this time the foreign price would fall.[3] For the full exploration of this case for the two-sector model the reader is referred to the literature.[4] We shall now return to our *small country assumption*, to be maintained right through this and the next chapter.

[3] The domestic relative price of importables *may* fall because of the *Metzler paradox*; see Appendix II.

[4] See Meade, op. cit.; Kemp, op. cit.; Heller, op. cit. Many have contributed to the development of the model. See R. E. Caves, *Trade and Economic Structure* (Harvard University Press, Cambridge, 1960) and references cited therein.

11. *Limitations of the Orthodox Analysis*

The analysis which has just been presented clearly is of value. If a country imposes a uniform ad valorem tariff on all its imports, and does not tax or subsidize exports, then broadly it suggests that resources will move from the export to the import-competing industries, provided all adjustments have taken place. At the same time consumption is likely to move in the opposite direction and, if foreign prices are given, income at world prices is likely to fall. Trade is likely to decline. This all seems rather obvious, but perhaps only the diagram makes it obvious. Nevertheless, it is a very limited analysis. Some effects are just assumed away, while others are obscured by being implicit rather than explicit. The author of this book is not one to undervalue simple diagrams or to denigrate the heuristic value of simple theories. Those who seek to explain everything usually explain nothing. So all that is claimed here is that by becoming a little more complicated we could in this case become much more realistic and useful.

The limitations of the method are really of two main types. Firstly, this orthodox approach deals explicitly with only two products. It can thus have only one tariff rate or one export tax rate in it. This is hardly overcome by describing each product as a bundle. Nor is it overcome by presenting the analysis mathematically rather then geometrically.[5] The second limitation is that it obscures the process of adjustment— how full employment and balance of payments equilibrium are maintained—by assuming that the adjustment has always successfully taken place. It thus makes no explicit reference to the exchange rate. Let us consider these two limitations in turn.

The first limitation can really be broken down into three elements. First of all, it is assumed that all production is vertically integrated, so that the two products are final goods. In a world where a large proportion of trade consists of intermediate goods this is patently unrealistic. It is clearly necessary to introduce vertical relationships between products and hence the effective protective rate. One could produce a rather odd

---

[5] Cf. Kemp, op. cit. This book is confined almost wholly to a two-product model, but the author uses algebraic methods because 'algebraic analyses point most clearly to their own generalizations' (p. 4).

though simple model with just one final good and one intermediate good in it, but to bring out the implications of vertical relationships a useful model would need to have at least two final goods in it, and then in addition one or more intermediate goods.[6] Secondly, the analysis limits the consumers' and the producers' choices horizontally to only two goods. Trade is a *barter* of one export for one import, so that pure trade theory is often described as 'barter theory'. Leaving aside the vertical complication for a moment, it allows only for one tariff. But this makes it quite irrelevant for most practical problems of protection. Sometimes a problem consists of looking at the effects of protection in just one industry, an industry that is not a major element in the economy. Then the partial equilibrium analysis of Chapter 2 provides the best technique of analysis, supplemented perhaps by allowance for a few specified general equilibrium effects. But at other times the problem consists of looking at the effects of protection in a number of industries, the inter-relationships between tariffs in different industries being crucial. To assume only one tariff, or that all tariffs are uniform, is to assume away often the most important problems. In reality there is not 'a' tariff or 'an' export tax but a *structure* of such tariffs, taxes and subsidies. The problem to be studied is one of *protective structure*, a term to be used here to include not only the structure of tariffs but also to allow for the other taxes and subsidies on trade and traded goods. We must have a model in which there are many importables and many exportables, with the possibility of many tariffs, export taxes and so on. Thirdly, the analysis does not refer to non-traded goods and services, that is to goods (and, above all, services) the prices of which are not determined in the world market. This is a profound limitation with important implications.[7] The line between traded and non-traded goods

---

[6] It is also possible to have a two-good general equilibrium model with input-output relationships where each good is both a final good and an input into the other. See J. Vanek, 'Variable Factor Proportions and Inter-Industry Flows in the Theory of International Trade', *Quarterly Journal of Economics*, 77, Feb. 1963, 129–42. Vanek's model anticipates in certain respects the model of section III of this chapter.

[7] But see R. Komiya, 'Non-traded Goods and the Pure Theory of International Trade', *International Economic Review*, 8, June 1967, 132–52; I. A. McDougall, 'Tariffs and Relative Prices', *Economic Record*, 42, June 1966,

is not always a clear one since world market conditions certainly *influence* the prices of non-traded goods, but there is little doubt that in most economies a large part of domestic production consists of goods that can more reasonably be described as non-traded than as traded goods. This category would normally include services, distribution, building, and often parts of the production of power. In addition, many goods which are potentially tradeable are, because of their weight or their peculiar appropriateness to local tastes, not in fact traded.

The second main limitation of the analysis is the assumption of full employment and balance of payments (strictly, balance of trade) equilibrium. The analysis does not bring out how this is achieved and what happens if the adjustment process does not work smoothly. It is indeed a striking limitation of international trade theory that the 'pure' or barter theory is so rigidly separated from the 'monetary' theory. In the pure theory internal and external balance are *assumed* while the monetary theory is concerned with the mechanisms that bring or fail to bring them about. The two are rarely linked up in the literature. Thus there is little emphasis on the effects on economic structure of various so-called monetary rigidities. More important, there is little attempt to show how the effects of a policy such as a tariff designed to influence, say, the structure of production depend on the adjustment process. If in response to the logic of the classical argument for free trade a country eliminated its tariffs, would resources really move from the import-competing into the export industries, or would they just stay unemployed? Would the rise in imports be balanced by a rise in exports, or would the balance of payments just stay in deficit until the tariff reduction were supplemented by some other explicit act of policy? It is obvious that one cannot look at tariff policy in isolation from exchange rate policy, but it is just this that the artificial separation of the pure from the monetary theory encourages. It follows that we must here introduce considerations of internal and external balance more explicitly and especially put in

---

219–43; I. A. McDougall, 'Non-Traded Commodities and the Pure Theory of International Trade', in I. A. McDougall and R. H. Snape (eds.), *Studies in International Economics* (North-Holland, Amsterdam, 1970).

the exchange rate as a variable. Nevertheless, we will not be concerned here in any detailed way with the concept and the problems of internal balance or with the techniques of monetary policy.

We thus have an agenda for the remainder of this chapter and for the next chapter, first to introduce vertical relationships and effective rates into the general equilibrium model (section III), secondly to extend horizontal relationships by having many traded goods (sections IV to VII), thirdly to introduce non-traded goods (section VIII) and fourthly to introduce the adjustment process and especially the exchange rate (in the next chapter).

III. *Effective Rates in the Simple General Equilibrium Model*[8]

We shall now combine the effective protective rate analysis of the previous chapter with the orthodox general equilibrium two-sector analysis. Almost all the simple assumptions of the orthodox model will be retained at this stage.

There are two final products, j_a and j_b, and two produced inputs, m_a being the input into j_a and m_b the input into j_b. Thus we have a four good model. There are again, as in Chapter 3, fixed input-output coefficients; these coefficients apply to the input of m_a into j_a and m_b into j_b. In addition there are the two *value-added products*, v_a and v_b, their units being so defined (as in Chapter 3) that one unit of v_a is required, together with the appropriate m_a, to make one unit of j_a, and one unit of v_b, with the appropriate m_b, is required to make one unit of j_b. Finally we have two primary factors, L and K, these being inputs into v_a and v_b. The stocks of the primary factors are fixed. There is no domestic production of the produced inputs, m_a and m_b; they are all imported.

It follows that consumption consists of j_a and j_b and production of v_a and v_b. The production functions of v_a and v_b are both constant returns to scale with continuous substitution between the two primary factor inputs. We are thus still at the simplest type of model with just two goods produced and consumed. But this time the goods that are consumed are

---

[8] This is a slightly amended version of my 'Effective Protective Rates in the General Equilibrium Model: A Geometric Note', *Oxford Economic Papers*, 21, July 1969, 135–41.

strictly not the same as the goods that are produced. The
pattern of consumption will now be affected by one price ratio,
namely the *nominal* price ratio, and the pattern of production
by another, namely the *effective* price ratio. One characteristic
of the model should be stressed now and will be highlighted
by the diagram to follow: there are fixed coefficients in the

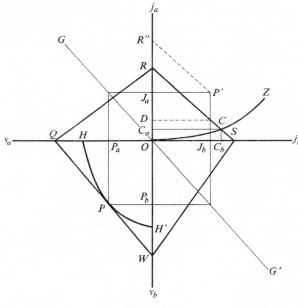

Fig. 4.2

production functions of j_a and j_b, but there is scope for substitution in the production functions of v_a and v_b. Factors can
move from v_a to v_b and production of v_b can be substituted
for production of v_a along a continuous production possibility
curve. But within the production functions of the two final
goods substitution is at this stage of the analysis not permitted.
The assumption of fixed coefficients in the final goods production
function will be maintained right through this chapter and the
next and reconsidered only in Chapter 6.

In Fig. 4.2 consider first the north-eastern quadrant.
Quantities of j_a are shown along the vertical axis and of j_b

along the horizontal. The quadrant shows consumption of these two goods. Suppose that national income measured in terms of j_a is OR and that the given price ratio between the two goods in the world market is indicated by the slope of RS. OZ is the income-consumption line associated with this price ratio. Consumption will then be at C, the intersection of OZ with RS. The slope of RS is a ratio between *nominal* prices and so we shall call it the *nominal* price ratio.

Next we come to the north-western quadrant. The vertical axis shows again quantities of j_a and the horizontal axis shows this time quantities of v_a. Now the price of v_a—the effective price, p_{va}—is determined as a residual by the price of j_a—the nominal price, p_{ja}—and the price of a unit of $m_a(p_{ma})$, defining units of m_a so that one unit of m_a is required for each unit of j_a. The price of m_a is of course also given in the world market. On the lines of the algebra of Chapter 3, if a_{mja} is defined as the share of m_a in the cost of j_a at free trade prices, then $p_{va}/p_{ja} = 1 - a_{mja}$. This price ratio—the ratio of the effective to the nominal price of j_a—is represented by the slope of RQ, the price of v_a being OR/OQ.

Similarly we can obtain the price of v_b—that is the effective price of j_b—from the nominal price of j_b and the price of m_b, defining units of m_b and v_b again so that a unit of m_b and a unit of v_b are required to produce a unit of j_b. If a_{mjb} is the free trade share of m_b in the cost of j_b then $p_{vb}/p_{jb} = 1 - a_{mjb}$. Turning to the south-eastern quadrant, the southern part of the vertical axis shows quantities of v_b, and the price of v_b is assumed to be OS/OW measured in terms of j_b or OR/OW measured in terms of j_a. Thus the slope of the line SW gives the ratio of the effective to the nominal price of j_b just as the slope of RQ gives such a price ratio for j_a.

Finally we link up the points Q and W to obtain the ratio between the prices of v_a and v_b, namely the *effective price ratio*. This will determine the pattern of production just as the *nominal price ratio* has determined the pattern of consumption. But before looking at production more closely, let us pause for a moment. We have a quadrilateral $QRSW$. This is not the only possible quadrilateral, but is the one that goes with an income of OR. The slope of RS gives the nominal price ratio, determined from outside by the world prices of j_a and j_b. The slope of RQ

gives the ratio of the nominal to the effective price of j_a, determined by (a) the nominal price of j_a, (b) the nominal price of m_a and (c) the choice of units of m_a and v_a, which depends in turn on the input-output coefficients in j_a. Similarly the slope of SW gives the ratio of the nominal to the effective price of j_b. Finally, the slope of QW is derived from these three price ratios, and is the effective price ratio. The latter can alter if any one of four prices (p_{ja}, p_{jb}, p_{ma}, p_{mb}) given from outside alters or if one or both of the two input coefficients change. One can experiment with changing shapes of the quadrilateral in response to exogenous changes in any of the prices or in the input coefficients.

The next step is to draw a production possibility curve for v_a and v_b, derived from the stocks of the primary factors L and K and the two production functions. Geometrically we might imagine an Edgeworth box with the stocks of L and K as the dimensions, points in the box representing possible primary factor allocations between v_a and v_b, optimal points being along the usual contract curve which traces out tangency points of the isoquants. To each point on the contract curve corresponds a point on the production possibility curve HH'. This curve is drawn as continuously concave to the origin, implying that there is substitution between the factors in each industry and that the factor-intensities between v_a and v_b differ.

Movements along HH' have effects on absolute and relative factor prices familiar from pure trade theory. The direction of effect depends on which product is intensive in which factor.[9] The changes in *factor* prices that result from the protective structure are thus derived from the changes in *effective* prices—which refer to activities—and from the relative factor-intensities. In this simple model, with two factors, labour and capital, with constant returns to scale and marginal productivity factor pricing, if it is desired to raise the real wage, the effective price of the labour-intensive product (the product with the higher labour-capital ratio) must be increased relatively to the

---

[9] W. Stolper and P. A. Samuelson, 'Protection and Real Wages', *Review of Economic Studies*, 9, Nov. 1941, 58–73, reprinted in H. S. Ellis and L. A. Metzler (eds.), *Readings in the Theory of International Trade* (Blakiston Co., Philadelphia, 1949).

effective price of the capital-intensive product. But it must be clearly understood that the proportional increase in the effective price of the former does *not* in any sense measure the change in the real wage. The change in relative factor prices will lead to appropriate factor substitutions in each industry. For example, if v_a is L-intensive relative to v_b a movement along the curve towards v_a will lead to a rise in the price of L relative to that of K, and to substitution of K for L in both activities v_a and v_b.

Assuming perfect competition and no externalities the production point is determined in the usual way by the tangency of the relevant price ratio—this time the effective price ratio—so that the point of production is P. It should be noted that the four given world prices and the two fixed input coefficients determine not just a single quadrilateral, but a map of such quadrilaterals, all with the same slopes. One of them will yield a tangency point with the production possibility curve, and so represent the level of income appropriate to free trade and full employment. It is this particular one which we have drawn as $QRSW$.

We now know production P and income OR, both determined by the production possibility curve and the effective price ratio, and consumption C, determined by this income, by the nominal price ratio and by the community preference map from which the income-consumption lines appropriate to various nominal price ratios are derived. It remains to show trade. Draw a 45° line GOG' through the north-western and south-eastern quadrants. By drawing a perpendicular and a horizontal from P to the axes we find that production of v_a is OP_a and of v_b is OP_b. Continuing these two lines to the 45° line and then drawing a horizontal to the j_a axis and a perpendicular to the j_b axis we obtain the outputs of j_a and j_b, namely OJ_a and OJ_b, that must be associated with the outputs of v_a and v_b given originally by the point P. This follows from our assumption that one unit of v_a is required to make one unit of j_a and one unit of v_b to make one unit of j_b. The point P' in the north-eastern quadrant is the production point, showing outputs of j_a and j_b, and corresponds to P in the south-western quadrant. Drawing a horizontal and a perpendicular to the axes from C we find that consumption of j_a is OC_a and of

j_b is OC_b. The differences between the production quantities and the consumption quantities yield exports of j_a of C_aJ_a and imports of j_b of J_bC_b. At the given price ratio between A and B exports of A exceed imports of B, because exports of C_aD pay for imports of J_bC_b, leaving exports of DJ_a. These are required to pay for imports of m_a and m_b. A little more geometry could show imports of m_a and m_b separately, each valued in terms of j_a, and it could be proven that these imports must sum to DJ_a. Furthermore the gross value of output OR'' (derived by drawing $R''P'$ parallel to RS) must exceed the net value of output (= income) of OR by the value of imports of the two produced inputs, i.e. $RR'' = DJ_a$.

All this is designed to show the relationship between the roles of the nominal and the effective price ratio, one helping to determine the pattern of consumption and the other the pattern of production. It also emphasizes that the simplifying assumption of fixed input-output coefficients in the production functions of j_a and j_b does not exclude substitution between primary factors in the production functions of v_a and v_b and so permits output patterns to change while maintaining full employment.

The next step is to introduce tariffs, import subsidies, export subsidies and export taxes. All revenues are assumed to be redistributed and subsidies financed in non-distorting ways. The essential point is simple. Nominal protective rates on j_a and j_b will change the nominal price ratio facing domestic consumers and hence the pattern of consumption. These two nominal rates (tariff or import subsidy for j_b and export subsidy or tax for j_a), together with any tariffs on m_a and m_b, will change the two effective prices facing domestic producers, the extent of these changes for given nominal protective rate changes depending on the input coefficients. The proportional changes in the effective prices are the effective protective rates, derived for each product exactly as in the partial equilibrium model described in Chapter 3. Production and consumption taxes and subsidies on the four traded goods concerned can also be taken into account. So we obtain the change in the effective price ratio facing producers and hence the change in the pattern of production. This will then also bring about a change in relative and absolute factor prices. It is important to stress that changes in price *ratios*, not absolute price changes, matter. If, for example, the rate of nominal tariff for j_b happened to be the same as the rate of export subsidy for j_a there would be no change in the pattern of consumption since the nominal protective rates would then be equal. Similarly the movement of resources will depend on *relative* effective rates. The effective rate for v_a may be positive but nevertheless resources will move out of v_a into v_b if the effective rate for v_b is higher.

We shall now represent a new tariff-distorted equilibrium.

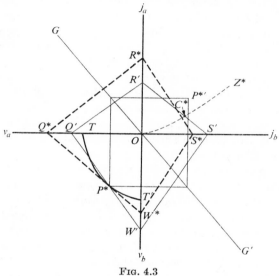

FIG. 4.3

It must satisfy requirements which are essentially the same as in the orthodox model of Fig. 4.1 apart from the distinction between the effective and the nominal prices. Firstly, the pattern of domestic production must be determined by the tariff-distorted domestic effective price ratio, and the pattern of domestic consumption by the tariff-distorted domestic nominal price ratio. Secondly, trade must satisfy the given set of undistorted world prices.

In Fig. 4.3 the new tariff-distorted quadrilateral is given by $Q^*R^*S^*W^*$. There is a map of such tariff-distorted quadrilaterals, $Q^*R^*S^*W^*$ being the one which yields a tangency point P^* with the production possibility curve. So output is given by that point and the corresponding point $P^{*\prime}$ in the north-eastern quadrant. Now through P^* we draw an undistorted (free trade) quadrilateral $Q'R'S'W'$. This quadrilateral $Q'R'S'W'$ belongs to the set of free trade quadrilaterals to which $QRSW$ in Fig. 4.2 also belongs, but $Q'R'S'W'$ is *within* $QRSW$. Comparing the slope of R^*S^* with that of $R'S'$, and the slope of Q^*W^* with that of $Q'W'$ we see that, as drawn, the nominal tariff on j_b must have been greater than the nominal export subsidy (if any) on j_a and the effective protective rate for j_b must have been greater than the effective rate for j_a. The nominal and/or effective rates for j_a could, of course, have been zero or negative; as pointed out above, in this model only changes in *relative* prices, not the *absolute* price changes, are relevant. The new consumption point has to satisfy two conditions: First, it must be on the free trade quadrilateral $Q'R'S'W'$—and hence must be on the line $R'S'$—so as to satisfy the requirement that exports equal imports at free trade prices. Secondly, it must be on the income-consumption line OZ^* appropriate to the tariff-distorted domestic nominal price ratio represented by the slope of R^*S^*. The new consumption point is thus at C^*, the intersection of OZ^* with $R'S'$. As drawn, production of j_b is greater than consumption of j_b so that j_b has turned from an import into an export; hence it must have obtained not just a tariff but also an export subsidy (unless an import subsidy was given for m_b). In addition, as in free trade, production of j_a is greater than consumption of j_a ($P^{*\prime}$ is above C^*), so that there are exports of j_a. Hence exports of j_a and j_b now pay for imports of m_a and m_b. This was of course only one possible, and not a necessary, result.

This analysis has answered a question which was left open in Chapter 3. What is the point of calculating effective rates, that is, of relating a product's tariff to its effective rather than its nominal free trade price? It was shown there that at the level of partial analysis one might just as well calculate the *adjusted nominal rate* which relates the nominal tariff per unit minus the input tariff to the product's free trade nominal price.[10] In the partial model resources move into the industry

---

[10] The adjusted nominal rate is $(p_v'-p_v)/p_j$ or $(t_j-a_{ij}t_i)$ compared with the effective rate, which is $(p_v'-p_v)/p_v$ or $(t_j-a_{ij}t_i)/(1-a_{ij})$. The symbols are defined as in Chapter 3.

concerned if its effective rate is positive, and move out if it is negative. And if the effective rate is positive the adjusted nominal rate would be also, while if one is negative the other is also. Thus a calculation of adjusted nominal rates would indeed give us the direction of the resource movement (assuming that the domestic supply elasticity is positive). But this is no longer so in the general equilibrium model. The resource movement depends now on *relative* effective rates. Even with a positive effective rate resources will move out of an activity if the effective rate of the other activity is higher. Thus the calculation of effective rates is now an essential prerequisite to determining the resource allocation effects of a tariff structure.

IV. *The Multi-Product Model and the Scale of Effective Rates*

We shall now generalize the preceding analysis and attempt to construct a much more ambitious and realistic model. There will now be many importables and many exportables. All goods are either one or the other and some imports or some exports of each good remain. Some of the goods are final goods only, some are inputs only and some are both inputs and final goods. Some inputs are inputs into other inputs while others are inputs into final goods. We define a *using industry* as an industry that uses produced inputs. An input can have many using industries and a using industry can have many inputs. The vertical relationships need not go one way, and a good could be both an input *into* product X and at the same time could itself either use product X as an input or use another input which in turn uses product X. Thus the possibilities are complex.

The model is fairly easily manageable at this stage because we maintain all the assumptions of the preceding discussion, apart from increasing the number of traded products. To repeat these assumptions, (1) there are no non-traded final goods, (2) there are no non-traded inputs, (3) coefficients between produced inputs and outputs are fixed, (4) foreign import supply and export demand elasticities are infinite (small country assumption), (5) price flexibility ensures full employment and balance of payments equilibrium, (6) tariff revenue is redistributed and subsidies are financed in non-distorting ways, (7) the consumption pattern is independent of income distribution, and (8) the protective structure does not completely end imports of any good of which there were imports under free trade or end exports of a good which was exported under free trade; hence no tariff is prohibitive and there is no reversal of trade. It is also convenient for simple exposition to continue to assume a fixed stock of factors of production. This assumption will be maintained throughout this book, except in sections V and VI of Chapter 7, but it would probably be possible to adapt the analysis to allow for a positive response of factor supplies to increases in their real rewards. We are concerned primarily with how resource flows respond to changes in relative prices of value-added products, and one element in this response could consist of the entry or exit of factors of production into the economy in response to price changes. But to avoid paradoxical effects it would be necessary to rule out backward-bending factor supply curves.

First, let us describe the free trade equilibrium. For each good there is a nominal price given by the world market. In addition, for each good there is a given set of input coefficients. Knowing thus its own nominal price and the nominal prices of its inputs, together with the input coefficients, we obtain then for each good its effective price. Given the basic conditions of consumption demand (the community preference set), the set of nominal prices for final goods will determine the pattern of consumption of final goods at any given level of income. Though our model is static we need not exclude demand for investment goods from our discussion, and final 'consumption-goods' can be taken here to include investment-goods; when we refer to the pattern of consumption this could be taken to refer to the pattern of expenditure. Complications connected with investment goods will be discussed in Chapter 7. Similarly, given the basic possibilities of production as determined by the production functions of the various value-added products and the supply of primary factors of production (that is, given the production possibility set) the set of effective prices will determine the pattern of production. The basic consumption and production conditions are the equivalents of the demand and supply curves in our partial models, and of the community preference (indifference) map and the production possibility curve in the two-sector general equilibrium model. Exports and imports of each good will be determined as residuals. Flexibility of factor prices will bring total exports into equality with total imports, and the total value of domestic production of all goods will be equal to the total value of domestic consumption.

Now consider a *protective structure*, to be interpreted as a structure of tariffs, import subsidies, export taxes, export subsidies, and consumption and production taxes and subsidies on importables and exportables. For each good separately one can calculate a nominal rate and an effective protective rate which take all these into account. The method was described in Chapter 3. If good Y is an input into product X, and vice versa, then the nominal tariff on Y will play a part in the calculation of the effective rate for X and the nominal tariff for X will influence the effective rate for Y. The method required is elaborate in the sense that there may be many taxes and subsidies to take into account, but it is in principle simple because each product, together with its direct inputs, can be looked at separately. As was pointed out in Chapter 3, to calculate the effective rate for product X it is not necessary to know the tariffs on indirect inputs into X. Having calculated the set of effective rates, the next step is to order all these effective rates on a continuous scale through zero. The order is likely to be quite different from a similar scale based on nominal rates. Note that along the scale exportables and importables will be mixed up. Only if exportables, say, obtain generally lower effective rates than importables will the former be at one end of the scale and the latter at another. It is quite possible that the nominal rates consist wholly of tariffs and export subsidies, and hence are all *positive* nominal rates, and yet the scale of effective rates may include many negative rates.[11] This may be so if nominal rates on inputs tend to be high in relation to nominal rates on final goods. But whether an effective rate is positive or negative does not really matter for the present: all that matters is the order on the scale. The scale summarizes the total protective rate structure. In addition there will be a scale of nominal rates. Oversimplifying a little, the scale of effective rates will determine the way in which the protective structure affects the pattern of production and the

[11] Truly negative rates are meant here, not negative value-added. We discuss the latter in section VI below.

7

scale of nominal rates the way in which it affects the pattern of consumption.

Now let us look at the production effects of the protective structure more closely. It must be said straight away that these effects can be complex. Almost anything is possible, and strictly speaking, nothing simple can be said. In my original article on this subject[12] an argument along the lines to be given immediately below was advanced. This still seems to me broadly sensible, so it is now repeated. But it will be qualified in sections VI and VII since there are some weaknesses in it.[13]

Assuming normal non-zero substitution elasticities in production (or, in more precise language, a well-behaved transformation function relating the various value-added products, which is differentiable and strictly concave to the origin), the scale of effective rates tells us the *direction* in which the protective structure causes resources to be pulled as between activities producing the various value-added products. Domestic production will *tend* to shift from low to high effective-protective rate activities and hence the demand for those primary factors in which the high effective-rate activities are intensive will rise relative to those in the low effective-rate activities. If four activities producing traded goods can be ordered along a scale, A, B, C, D in ascending order of effective rates, we can say that output of A must fall and of D must rise and that resources will be pulled from A to B and from A and B to C; but without more precise information about production substitution elasticities, we cannot say whether the outputs of B and C will rise or fall. But we can deduce that if the factors of production used by B and C are similar and are mobile between these two activities, while the factor-intensities of B and C differ greatly from those of A and D or there is little factor mobility between B and C on the one hand and A and D on the other, then whether resources move into or out of B

[12] W. M. Corden, 'The Structure of a Tariff System and the Effective Protective Rate', *Journal of Political Economy*, 74, June 1966, p. 224.

[13] It has been criticized by a number of authors, essentially on the grounds that it neglects the sorts of considerations introduced in sections VI and VII below. See, for example, A. H. H. Tan, 'Differential Tariffs, Negative Value-Added and the Theory of Effective Protection', *American Economic Review*, 60, March 1970, 107–16; and J. E. Anderson, 'General Equilibrium and the Effective Rate of Protection', *Journal of Political Economy*, 78, July/Aug. 1970.

depends mainly on whether its effective rate is higher or lower than that of C. Thus the effect of a tariff structure on an activity depends not just on the position in the scale of effective rates, but on the activity's position relative to those other activities which are significant substitutes on the production side. If there is an activity (value-added product) which employs factors quite specific to it and cannot use any other factors, its production substitution elasticity relative to other activities will be zero; hence, irrespective of how high or low its effective rate, resources will not move into or out of it.

All this concerns only the production effect of the protective structure. The approach has been rather intuitive and we shall look again at the production effects in sections VI and VII, introducing some complications. But let us accept this approach for the moment. It is particularly convenient that the production effect depends in this model only on the scale of effective rates and the production-substitution elasticities and not at all on consumption effects. So if one is concerned only with the production effects one can just ignore consumption substitution. In addition the pattern of consumption of final goods will be affected by the protective structure; consumption will shift from final goods with high nominal tariffs towards goods with low nominal tariffs. But the consumption effect depends not only on the scale of nominal tariffs, nominal export subsidies, etc., and on the consumption (expenditure-) substitution elasticities. It depends also on the income change which results from the production effects, and on income-elasticities of demand (which determine the shapes of the income-consumption lines). This is clear from the geometry of Figs. 4.1 and 4.2 and remains true in our multi-product world. But if one is prepared either to ignore income effects or to assume that income elasticities are all unity, then changes in the pattern of consumption will indeed depend only on nominal rates of protection of final goods and on consumption-substitution elasticities. In addition, consumption or usage of inputs depends of course on outputs of final goods and hence on the effective rates for the final goods (which depend in part on the nominal rates of the inputs) and on production-substitution elasticities.

This general approach can be used not only to compare

the effects of a protective structure with the effects of free trade but also to analyse the effects of changes in a protective structure. Consider one possible change, namely an increase in the nominal tariff on a good which is an input into other goods. First, this will lead to an increase in its effective rate; hence resources will be drawn into the domestic industry producing it and out of other industries. Outputs of those industries, particularly, which compete closely for factors with it will fall. Secondly, if this good is not just an input but is also a final good there will be a switch in the consumption pattern away from it. Thirdly, the effective rates for all using industries will decline, some more than others, depending on the input coefficients. This will lead to a shift in the output pattern away from these using industries, especially those where this particular input is a large element in cost. The nominal tariffs of the using industries might be raised appropriately so as to compensate for the higher input tariff and thus maintain the effective rates of the using industries constant. In that case the only shift in the output pattern affecting the using industries will result from the higher effective rates for the input industry. If the using industry's products are final goods the higher nominal rates will shift the consumption pattern away from these products while if the using industries themselves produce intermediate goods we would have to go on further and trace out the effects of either lower effective rates or higher nominal rates for their using industries. In any case, at some point the higher tariff for the input must either reduce an effective rate, or raise a nominal rate facing final purchasers.

In principle this approach to analysing the effects of a protective structure or of changes in it seems to be very simple. But to find out how a particular protective structure has affected resource allocation, and hence which activity has been expanded and which contracted, is not easy. First effective protective rates must be calculated; the complex nature of this task will already be evident. Formal rates, which may be specific, must be converted into nominal rates, and the various problems of defining the rate of protection discussed in section VI of Chapter 2 must be resolved. Next, nominal rates must be converted into effective rates; this raises further problems discussed in Chapter 3, but above all the problem of obtaining the relevant input-output data, and especially of relating data obtained from domestic or foreign producers to tariff classificaations.[14] Some further problems connected with the concept of effective protection will be discussed in Chapters 6 and 7. And finally some estimates or guesses of substitution elasticities must be made. Normally some compromise between a partial and a general equilibrium analysis will be appropriate. One may be able to partition off some activities which have high substitution elasticities relative to each other but low ones relative to the rest of the economy and treat them separately, just focusing on relative effective rates within the group. If no such grouping is plausible and there is no reason to believe that the production substitution elasticity is higher between one pair of activities than between another pair, then one may be justified in deducing the effects of a structure on a particular industry from its position in the total scale; the protective structure will have led to a movement of resources into industries high in the scale and out of industries low in the scale, though there will of course be some doubt about industries near the middle of the scale. The size of the value-added products of the industries will also be relevant: for given elasticities the greater the size of the industry the more weight it needs to be given.

v. *Multiple Exchange Rates*

The protective structure may result not from a system of tariffs, export subsidies, and so on, but rather from a multiple exchange rate system. Such systems were common in less developed countries, especially in Latin America, until a few years ago.[15] They differ from systems of tariffs, export subsidies, etc., in five ways: First, they are administered by the

[14] These are all difficulties which, with patience and a readiness to compromise a little, can be overcome. After all, effective rates have now been calculated for many countries. To see how these problems have been handled, see especially J. R. Melvin and B. W. Wilkinson, *Effective Protection in the Canadian Economy* (Economic Council of Canada, Ottawa, 1968); and B. Balassa (ed.), *The Structure of Protection in Developing Countries*, 1971.

[15] In 1956 twenty-six countries had multiple rates of some kind. See Margaret G. de Vries, 'Fund Members' Adherence to the Par Value Regime: Empirical Evidence', *IMF Staff Papers*, 13, Nov. 1966, 504–30. See also F. H. Schott, *The Evolution of Latin American Exchange Rate Policies Since World War II* (Princeton Essay in International Finance No. 32, Princeton University, Princeton, Jan. 1959); and S. Macario, 'Protection and Industrialization in Latin America', *Economic Bulletin for Latin America*, 9, March

monetary authorities, usually the central bank, and the profits go to the central bank, while import and export taxes are usually administered by a department of central government and the revenue goes to the Treasury. Secondly, multiple exchange rates are enforced through the availability of foreign exchange at the financial point of a transaction, while import and export taxes are enforced through customs control at the borders or ports. Thirdly, they are limited or affected by a different set of international obligations and institutions. Fourthly, in many countries exchange rate variations do not require parliamentary legislation or endorsement while import and export taxes go through the government budget and are subject to parliamentary control. And fifthly, a multiple rate system makes it possible to apply varying rates to capital movements and to invisibles as much as to visible trade, while with a tariff-export tax-subsidy system capital movements are usually (though they need not be) untaxed and unsubsidized.

These are significant distinctions, but from the point of view of the focus of the present book multiple exchange rate systems are essentially the same as protective structures. Let us analyse such systems now. One exchange rate may apply to exports and another, a lower one, to imports. Say the rate for exports is 8 pesos to the dollar and for imports 12 pesos. (The 12 peso rate represents a *lower* value of the peso than the 8 peso rate.) Thus an exporter who earns a dollar will obtain 8 pesos for it from the central bank, but when the bank sells this dollar to importers they have to pay 12 pesos, the bank making a profit of 4 pesos per dollar. This system is essentially the same as if there had been a unified exchange rate of 8 pesos to the dollar combined with a 50 per cent tariff or a unified rate of 12 pesos combined with a $33\frac{1}{3}$ per cent export tax. In these cases the Treasury would receive tariff or export tax revenue instead of the central bank receiving exchange profits. The result is also, for example, the same as that from a

---

1964, 61–101. Detailed descriptions of multiple rate systems are in W. M. Corden and J. A. C. Mackie, 'The Development of the Indonesian Exchange Rate System', *Malayan Economic Review*, 7, April 1962, 37–60, and in W. M. Corden, 'The Exchange Rate System and the Taxation of Trade', in T. H. Silcock (ed.), *Thailand: Social and Economic Studies in Development* (Australian National University Press, Canberra, 1967).

unified exchange rate of 10 pesos combined with a tariff and export tax of 20 per cent. In fact one could choose arbitrarily any exchange rate and express the system in terms of a combination of import tariff (or subsidy) and export tax (or subsidy). The method of analysing a complicated system of multiple exchange rate systems is thus as follows. First choose any arbitrary exchange rate and define it as the *base* rate. One might take the rate that is described in the country concerned as the 'official rate', though any other rate would do. Then all actual rates charged on imports and paid on exports can be converted into nominal rates, import subsidies, export taxes and export subsidies. The set of nominal rates is next converted into a set of effective rates using the procedure of Chapter 3 for each product. The scale of nominal and effective rates that results can then be interpreted as indicated in the present chapter.

This discussion has been quite general, but multiple exchange rate systems have come in many forms, most of them very complex and amalgams of various techniques or elements. Before going on, let us look at them in more detail. The simplest is a dual rate system where one rate applies to all imports and another to all exports. This is the equivalent of having a uniform ad valorem nominal import tariff (or alternatively a uniform export tax) with all the implications of such a structure; it need not mean uniform effective protection for importables or zero effective protection for exportables. Another type of dual rate system is one where each of the two rates applies both on the import and the export side. Thus the rate for agricultural imports and exports might be 10 pesos and for manufactured imports and exports 12 pesos to the dollar. This is the equivalent (for example) of having a unified exchange rate of 10 pesos to the dollar combined with a uniform nominal tariff of 20 per cent on all imports of manufactures and a uniform subsidy of 20 per cent on all exports of manufactures.

It has been more common to have a dual rate system where the high rate, say 10 pesos, applies to 'traditional' exports and to imports of 'essentials', which usually include raw materials, intermediate goods, capital-goods and government imports, while the low rate, say 12 pesos, applies to 'new' exports, to imports of finished consumer goods and to invisibles and

capital movements.[16] This has complicated implications which
can be readily worked out with our method; since buyers of
inputs pay a lower price for dollars than buyers of finished
manufactures, the effective rates of the latter will not be
uniform and will be higher in relation to effective protection
for traditional exports than will appear from the nominal
rates. In terms of nominal rates the system is a dual rate one,
but in terms of effective rates it is a multiple one.

A system may appear to have only two nominal rates but
in fact it may be a multiple rate system even in nominal
rate terms. This is so when there are 'mixed' rates. The two
basic rates may be 10 and 12 pesos, but exporters of product X
have to convert 80 per cent of their foreign exchange at the
higher rate (the rate at which *less* pesos are obtained per dollar),
exporters of product Y need only convert 50 per cent while Z
exporters can convert all their earnings at the lower rate.
Thus the true nominal exchange rates for the three are
respectively 10.4, 11 and 12 pesos.[17]

In many countries the two rates in a dual system have
been the 'official' and the 'free market' rate. The latter has
often been far below the former, and has fluctuated in the
market, so that the margin between them has not been fixed.
Hence the whole complex protective structure with its 'mixed'
rates and its non-uniform effective rates has been changing,
possibly day by day. It is interesting to note that such fluctua-
tions cannot actually alter the order in the scale of effective
rates, at least provided that there is no change in the rate
classification or 'mix' for any product. Treating the official
rate as the base rate and expressing the free trade rate as a
tariff equivalent t_f, a proportional rise in t_f will lead to the same
proportional rise in all the effective rates.[18] But this may

[16] In 1970 Uruguay had such a system. Two other countries with dual rates
in 1970 were Chile and Afghanistan. See *International Financial Statistics*
(International Monetary Fund, monthly) for descriptions of such systems. A
description of a changing dual rate system of the type mentioned is in J. H.
Power, 'The Structure of Protection in the Philippines', in B. Balassa (ed.),
The Structure of Protection in Developing Countries, 1971.

[17] 'Mixed rates' have been very common. See, for example, W. M. Corden,
in *Thailand: Social and Economic Studies in Development*, op. cit.

[18] For any one product, let t_j be its nominal tariff rate as required for the
effective protection formula, t_i similarly the nominal tariff rate on the input,
a_{ij} the input share at the official rate, t_f the tariff equivalent of the free rate,

represent a very significant change in the scale of effective rates. Products with zero rates (perhaps because their earnings are converted and their inputs bought at the official rate) will maintain their zero rates; hence products with positive effective rates will be increasingly protected in relation to them. More generally, products with high effective rates will gain in relation to products with low rates in terms of the relative price advantage the protective system gives them. The following example will make this clear. Initially product X has a 5 per cent effective rate and product Y a 10 per cent rate; choosing units so that their prices at the official rates are equal, the effective price of Y exceeds that of X by 4·8 per cent as a result of the two effective tariffs. A 100 per cent rise in t_f then raises the two effective rates to 10 per cent and 20 per cent respectively; so the price margin will have risen to 9·1 per cent. When the official rate is fixed and the free rate responds to market forces, in a period of internal inflation the free rate is likely to fall more and more below the official rate, so increasing the margin between them and giving a greater and greater advantage to those import-competing producers who are able to purchase their inputs at the official rate while their competing imports have to be paid for at the free rate. Over time the resource movement into favoured industries of this kind out of, say, traditional export industries which have to convert their earnings at the official rate, will then increase. This type of system is normally a stage in what has been called the 'pattern of reluctant exchange rate adjustments'.[19] A country starts with a unified rate combined with some physical import or exchange controls. Great excess demand for certain imports leads to a black market in foreign exchange and the development of a low black-market rate. Eventually this is legalized

---

z_j the ratio t_j/t_f and z_i the ratio t_i/t_f. If the product is sold at the official rate, $z_j = 0$, if at the free rate $z_j = 1$, and if at a mixed rate, z_j will be between 0 and 1; similarly z_i depends on the rate applying to the input. It follows that

$$g_j = t_f \left[\frac{z_j - a_{ij} z_i}{1 - a_{ij}} \right]$$

with z_j z_i and a_{ij} as constants, g_j will vary proportionately with t_f.

[19] J. Bhagwati, *The Theory and Practice of Commercial Policy: Departures from Unified Exchange Rates* (Special Papers in International Economics No. 8, Princeton University, Princeton, Jan. 1968), pp. 48–50. See Corden and Mackie, op. cit., for a detailed account of one such case (Indonesia).

and becomes the free-market rate. As internal inflation proceeds the official rate becomes more and more uneconomic for exporters and makes foreign exchange too cheap for imports; to reduce imports, encourage exports and protect domestic import-competing producers, more and more goods are transferred to the free rate. Eventually the official rate is given up, the free rate becomes the new unified rate, and perhaps, if inflation is brought to a halt, is turned into the new unified fixed rate.

VI. *The Multi-Product Model: Some Special Cases*

Consider now four special cases of interest.

Firstly, there may be no production of a particular product under free trade even though its effective price is positive. Given the basic supply conditions and the effective prices of other goods the minimum or *threshold* effective price required to induce any output may be higher than the actual free trade effective price. A low though positive effective rate may then be insufficient to get output started, given the effective prices of other goods. In this case the supply response to a change in the effective price would be zero over a range; effective protection would not affect resource allocation into this potential activity. But if the effective rate were sufficiently high to bring the effective price to the threshold, output would commence. The level of the threshold will depend on effective rates for other activities which compete for factors with this activity. Even if the effective price for this particular activity did not change (that is, if the effective rate were zero) output might start if other activities obtain negative effective protection, so lowering the threshold and shifting this industry's supply curve to the right.

Secondly, there may be goods where the effective price is negative under free trade and positive under protection (*negative-value-added* at free trade prices). This is really a special case of the one just discussed, since there will certainly be no production under free trade but production may start provided the effective price is raised above the threshold. The problem is how to order these cases in the scale of effective rates. As pointed out in Chapter 3, the algebraic result of a negative figure yielded by the usual effective protection formula is meaningless. There seems no logical basis for forming an order *within* the group of negative-value-added activities, but the whole group should in principle be placed at the top of the scale, since it really obtains an infinite rate of protection. Provided there is production under protection this type of activity would certainly lose resources if free trade were restored since output would cease completely.

Thirdly, it is possible that the imposition of a protective structure leads to the closing down of some industries which were producing under free trade. This may happen if an activity obtains negative effective protection while other effective rates are zero or positive; it is bound to result if its effective rate is so negative that the effective price under the protective structure actually becomes negative. More unexpectedly, an activity may cease even though its effective rate is positive. This could happen if the effective rates for other activities that compete for factors with it are higher. The central point is that the response of the production pattern to a protective structure— including the starting or stopping of various activities— depends not on the *absolute* effective protective rates but on *relative* rates.

Fourthly, there is the possibility of a *dominant non-protected* industry. At the bottom of the scale of effective rates there may be a single but very large industry, perhaps the principal export industry. It is then conceivable that the protective structure has moved resources into all the other industries, including even those quite low in the scale, though above the very large industry. Let us assume now that the large industry obtains zero protection and that the production substitution (transformation) elasticities between all the other industries are very low, so that, if any of them are to obtain extra resources, these would have to come out of the large industry. In that case a positive effective rate would indeed be a sufficient sign that resources have been drawn into an industry. It would not be necessary to look at the position in the scale to determine this. We would in fact be back to a situation which can be handled by partial equilibrium techniques. The higher the effective rate the more resources will have moved, irrespective of the effective rates for other industries, and of course for a given production substitution elasticity. This type of model could be developed further in a direction appropriate for some smaller less developed countries. One could assume that in free trade only one single large industry (representing the export industries or the agricultural sector) exists. For each potential import-competing industry there is a minimum or *threshold* effective price at which output would start, the resources coming out of the export industry. The effects on resource allocation of a protective structure depend then on the relation of each effective protective rate to the threshold protective rate needed to get output started. But once various import-competing industries do exist and the possibility of factors moving from one to the other arises, relative effective rates and hence the scale of effective rates become relevant.

VII. *Resource Allocation Effects in a Three-product Model*

The discussion in section IV of the resource allocation effects of a protective structure in a multi-product model was somewhat intuitive. It is clear from the previous section that there are many possibilities, especially when there are 'corner solutions', that is when there is no production or trade of some products. But here let us return to the simplest type of case with production and trade in every product. Can one say anything more precise about the effects of a protective structure on resource allocation by having a fully-specified model? Here we shall look at a model with three products, hoping to obtain some insight into the relevant considerations in a model with more products. We shall only be concerned with production effects and shall assume linear homogeneous production functions in each industry and competitive factor pricing. Thus we are operating within the framework of the orthodox pure trade theory model, differing from it only by adding an extra product. We retain the small country assumption. There are three vertically integrated products, manufactures, wool and butter. They could be thought of as value added products and the prices as effective prices, but this is not central to the argument. In this case nominal and effective prices are equal; the issues that arise do not depend on a vertically disintegrated system and the distinction between nominal and effective prices. Precision is only possible because the model is limited to three products; results that are certain in this model might be regarded as only *possible* in a multi-product model. Finally, with a three-product model we need at least three factors of production for a determinate result.

To begin with a very simple case (Model I), there is a single mobile primary factor of production, labour, and each product is produced with labour and a specific factor. This model is attractive not only because its unsurprising results confirm the author's intuition but also because more or less specific factors are probably common. Furthermore, one could allow for more than one mobile factor provided the mobile factors are always used in the same ratio in the three industries.

Suppose that manufactures are protected, so that the price of manufactures rise, while the prices of the other two products stay unchanged. The wage rate in manufacturing will rise and this will lead to a movement of labour out of wool and butter into manufacturing until the marginal product of labour has risen sufficiently in wool and butter production for the value of the marginal product to be equal in all uses. Finally the ratio of labour to the specific factor has risen in manufactures and fallen in wool and butter. The value of the marginal product of labour has risen in all three industries, but in manufactures a higher price for the product has more than offset a lower physical marginal product, while in wool and butter the marginal physical product is higher. One thing is clear. Given the mobility of labour, outputs of both wool and butter fall when manufacturing is protected and they are not. This type of model confirms the intuitive discussion of section IV. If the price of wool had also risen there would have been some pull of labour into wool out of butter, though, if the price of wool rose less than that of manufactures, there would still be a pull into manufacturing out of wool.

Now we come to the quite surprising, but by no means unrealistic Model II.[20] There are two sectors, the manufacturing sector, consisting of just one industry, and the agricultural sector, consisting of the wool and the butter industries. Each sector uses labour and a factor specific to the sector, capital

[20] The model was developed in connection with an Australian case in F. H. Gruen and W. M. Corden, 'A Tariff that Worsens the Terms of Trade', in I. A. McDougall and R. H. Snape (eds.), *Studies in International Economics* (North-Holland, Amsterdam, 1970).

in the case of manufactures and land in the case of agriculture. In the agricultural sector wool is land-intensive relative to butter (at every given wage-rent ratio the ratio of land to labour is higher in wool). Labour is mobile between all three industries while land is mobile between the two agricultural industries. It can now be shown that protection of manufacturing will *increase* the output of wool. The crucial ingredients in the analysis are the Stolper-Samuelson and the Rybczynski theorems.[21] Suppose in the first instance that labour is immobile between manufacturing and agriculture. When the domestic price of manufactures rises the wage-rate in that sector rises, since the value of the marginal product of labour rises. In agriculture the real wage rate and the real rent in terms of the two agricultural products are fixed by the wool-butter price ratio, which will remain unchanged. This follows from the Stolper-Samuelson theorem. Allowing for the higher price of manufactures (if they are protected by a tariff), the real wage and rent in agriculture have actually fallen. Now allow for labour mobility. Labour will move out of agriculture into manufacturing until labour has been substituted for capital in manufacturing sufficiently for the value of the marginal product of labour, and hence the real wage, to fall back to the given wage in agriculture. So manufacturing expands and agriculture contracts, as one would expect. But within agriculture the labour-land ratio has declined, and it follows from the Rybczynski theorem that, with the factor prices given in terms of the two agricultural products, this then calls for an absolute expansion of the land-intensive industry (wool) and contraction of the labour-intensive one (butter). In each of the two agricultural industries the labour-land ratio will remain unchanged because the wage-rent ratio remains unchanged, so that to accommodate a lower labour-land ratio for the two industries combined the land-intensive industry must expand and the labour-intensive industry contract.

We have thus the interesting result, neglected in the more intuitive approach of section IV, that protection of one industry

[21] Stolper and Samuelson, op. cit.; T. M. Rybczynski, 'Factor Endowment and Relative Commodity Prices', *Economica*, 22, Nov. 1955, 336–41, reprinted in R. E. Caves and H. G. Johnson (eds.), *Readings in International Economics* (Richard D. Irwin, Homewood, 1968).

may lead to increased output of another. Taking general equilibrium repercussions into account manufacturing and wool might be described as 'complementary' on the production side. In addition to the positive protection for manufactures and the zero protection for wool one might introduce a modest rate of protection (lower than that for manufactures) for butter. One could then get the result that the industry in the middle with the modest protective rate (butter) contracts, while the two industries at the extreme, one with a high protective rate and the other with a zero rate, expand.

One could use the same model to show the effects of protecting the two agricultural industries, with zero protection for manufacturing. If the rate of protection for wool is the same as that for butter the real wage and the real rent in terms of these two goods will stay unchanged, but in terms of manufactures will rise. In the manufacturing sector the real wage will fall owing to the higher price of agricultural products. So labour will move from manufacturing into agriculture. The effect is exactly the same as if there had been a negative protective rate for manufacturing with zero protection for agriculture. The rise in the labour-land ratio in agriculture will then (on the basis of the Rybczynski theorem) cause butter production to expand and wool production to contract. This result is rather interesting since it suggests that a uniform rate of protection in one sector of an economy will cause some industries in that sector to contract. If the rate of protection for butter exceeded that for wool the real wage would rise even in terms of the agricultural products, and these effects would be strengthened. Both the initial change in the wool-butter price ratio and the subsequent movement of labour into agriculture would lead to contraction of the wool industry. If, on the other hand, the rate of protection for wool sufficiently exceeded that for butter, then the real wage in agriculture might fall. It would be certain to fall in terms of the two agricultural products (since wool is land-intensive and the factor prices in terms of the agricultural products depend on the domestic agricultural product price ratio) and might do so in terms of all three products. So labour would then move out of agriculture. Both the initial change in the wool-butter price ratio and the subsequent movement of labour out of agriculture would lead to contraction of the butter industry. So, as in our earlier case, the high protection industry (wool) and the zero protection industry (manufacturing) would have expanded while the industry in the middle (butter) contracted.

It is hard to say how important this type of consideration is in practice. Our earlier example is meant to suggest its plausibility; in Australia it is at least arguable that protection of manufacturing has expanded land-intensive agriculture at the expense of labour-intensive agriculture, and possibly absolutely so. The general conclusion is that a protective structure may expand the outputs of some activities which do not themselves receive high effective protection but which benefit in this indirect sense from the high effective protection of certain other industries, and that it may contract industries which are high on the scale of effective rates. Thus one must interpret a scale of effective rates with some care, and bear in mind possible general equilibrium 'complementarities' on the production side.

Finally, there are various other conceivable reasons why a protective structure may have paradoxical resource allocation effects (though the practical importance of these cases may be doubted). They lead to the result that in a two-sector model, with the rate of effective protection for A higher than for B, output of A may contract and of B expand. One possibility is that there are backward-bending factor-supply curves, instead of fixed factor supplies; thus if A is labour-intensive and a higher wage reduces the labour supply (or the supply of effort) output of A could fall.[22] Another is that uniform factor prices do not rule throughout the economy, the wage in A, perhaps, being lower than in B, so that while A is labour-intensive in a physical sense it is not so in a value sense. Relative protection of A may then lower the wage and cause the physically labour-intensive industry A to contract.[23] These

[22] M. C. Kemp and R. W. Jones, 'Variable Labour Supply and the Theory of International Trade', *Journal of Political Economy*, 70, Feb. 1962, 30–6.

[23] M. C. Kemp and H. Herberg, 'Factor Market Distortions, the Shape of the Locus of Competitive Outputs, and the Relations between Product Prices and Equilibrium Outputs', in J. Bhagwati et al. (eds.), *Trade, Balance of Payments and Growth: Papers in Honor of Charles Kindleberger* (M.I.T. Press, Cambridge, 1970); and R. W. Jones, 'Distortions in Factor Markets and the General Equilibrium Model of Production', *Journal of Political Economy*, 78, 1971.

two paradoxes, like the new one introduced in this section, do not depend on the concept of effective protection, but are possible also in vertically integrated models. A third reason why the output of the activity with the higher effective rate could conceivably contract will be explained in Chapter 6 and hinges on the effective protection concept.

VIII. *Non-Traded Goods and Indirect Protection*

So far we have assumed that all goods in the model are actually imported or exported both under free trade and after the protective structure is imposed. Combining this with the small country assumption the nominal prices of all goods have thus been fixed by world prices, modified only by tariffs, subsidies and so on. Furthermore, given the input coefficients it has been possible to derive a set of free trade and protection effective prices. Now we introduce *non-traded* goods and services. These are goods (and, above all, services) where no significant part of domestic consumption is imported or of production is exported so that they do not have their prices set in world markets. They may be conceivably or physically *tradeable*, but because of transport costs or for other reasons are not actually traded. For the moment we shall be concerned only with goods that are non-traded under free trade, but later shall also allow for goods that are traded under free trade but become non-traded as a result of the protective structure.

The line between a traded and a non-traded good is often difficult to draw for the same reason that it is difficult to define a 'commodity'; the gaps in the chain of substitution are not always clear. One brand of car may be produced domestically only for the home market while another similar but not identical car is imported. One might regard the domestic car as a non-traded good, its price not being set completely by the price of the import. On the other hand, the import price certainly influences its price, and since the two cars are very close substitutes one could group them as one traded commodity. This problem of defining commodities is well-known and will not be resolved here; one can only stress the arbitrariness of any classification.

The introduction of non-traded goods presents a very

8

important problem for our analysis. It introduces a link that did not exist before between the consumption effects of imposing a protective structure and the production effects. It appears thus that one of the great simplifications of our analysis disappears. This problem can be explained in terms of the simplest three-good model, with two traded goods, X and M, and only one non-traded good N. We start in free trade with a price of N relative to the prices of X and M that makes demand for N equal to its supply. A tariff on M is then imposed. As in our earlier analysis this shifts the consumption pattern from M to X and the output pattern from X to M. But now there is an additional effect. *Given the price of N relative to X*, it also shifts desired expenditure from M to N and output from N to M. But this would create excess demand for N so that the price of N cannot in fact stay constant. Note that up to this point production and consumption effects have been distinct (aside from any income effects on consumption). Next the relative price of N must rise. The extent of the price rise required depends both on consumption and production effects. This will modify the production and consumption shifts between M and N and in addition will bring about shifts between N and X. The final effect of the tariff on the pattern of production depends now, among other things, on how much the price of N has to rise to restore equilibrium in the market for N. And the extent of this price rise depends both on consumption and production substitution elasticities. The point is that demands and supplies for individual traded goods do not have to be brought into equality since the excess demands and supplies are covered by imports and exports. But for the non-traded good equilibrium requires consumption to be equal to production, so that consumption effects cannot be separated from production effects. And if the non-traded good is linked to the traded goods through production and consumption substitution this means, regrettably, that for the whole system production and consumption effects cannot be separated. In describing the effects of a protective structure the solution appears to be to employ a two-stage analysis. First one can describe what would happen to production and consumption if the price of the non-traded good (or the average price of all non-traded goods) stayed constant, and then one can work out the implications of the required change in the relative price of the non-traded good. This two-stage approach will be used when we explicitly introduce the exchange rate in the next chapter.

Now let us allow for many non-traded goods. The complication that now arises is that a protective structure not only affects the output pattern within the exportables and importables sectors, but also causes the outputs of some non-traded goods to rise and of others to fall. It thus creates *indirect protection* and anti-protection. Is there any clear way of analysing this and can it be distinguished from the direct protective effects? To analyse this problem we must first classify the possible relationships between traded goods and non-traded goods. The relationships may be horizontal or vertical. The horizontal relationships may be on the consumption side—which means that a traded and a non-traded good are substitutes (or perhaps complements) in the pattern of expenditure; or they may be substitutes on the production side, so that a traded and a non-traded good compete for factors of production. (They could also be complements on the production side, but this possibility is ignored here.) In our model with one non-traded good above we allowed for such horizontal relationships. The vertical relationships may also take two forms: a non-traded good may be an input into a traded good, or a traded good may be an input into a non-traded good. For any particular non-traded good several of these relationships may coexist; thus it may have a traded good as a consumption substitute, another as a production substitute, it may be itself an input into a traded good and also may have traded inputs into it.

Consider first horizontal relationships and assume to begin with that they are wholly through production, the elasticities of substitution in consumption between traded and non-traded goods being zero. A protective structure is imposed. In the first instance, assuming constant prices of all non-traded goods and that excess demands or supplies of them are absorbed by stock movements, outputs of those non-traded goods that are production substitutes for traded goods which have obtained positive effective protection will fall while outputs of production substitutes for traded goods which have obtained negative effective protection will rise. Then price adjustments will follow which will further affect the production pattern and will also shift production and consumption as between different non-traded goods. When it is all over we can broadly say that outputs of those non-traded goods that compete for factors with those traded goods that are high in the scale of effective protection will fall while outputs of non-traded goods that compete for factors with those traded goods that are low in the scale of effective rates will rise. Now add consumption effects to this. This time it is the scale of nominal rates that counts. Non-traded goods that are consumption substitutes for traded goods high in the scale of nominal rates will tend to increase in output: consumption will be diverted from traded goods to them, and this will lead to extra domestic production of them. To sum up, whether the output of a non-traded good rises or falls as a result of a protective structure depends (assuming only horizontal relationships) on which traded goods it is a close substitute for both in production and in consumption, and where these traded goods come in the scale of effective and nominal rates.

The line between direct and indirect protection is as difficult to draw as the line between traded and non-traded goods. To return to our earlier example, if the imported car is considered a separate commodity from the domestically produced car, then we would say that the tariff on imported cars causes the demand for domestic cars to increase, so that their prices rise, which in turn brings forth more production. As they are not perfect substitutes for the imported cars the price rise will be proportionately less than the nominal tariff rate; there has then been indirect protection. Alternatively, we might regard the import and the domestic product as part of one commodity group, and then would simply treat the rise in domestic output as a direct consequence of the tariff.

Next we come to vertical relationships between traded and non-traded goods. A non-traded good may be an input into a traded good, or vice versa. When non-traded goods are inputs into traded goods a problem is presented for the concept of the effective protective rate even in a partial equilibrium context, and even more so in the general equilibrium framework. It is such a critical problem that it will be confined to a separate discussion in Chapter 7; meanwhile we continue to assume that all produced inputs into traded goods are themselves traded. Next consider the case where traded goods are inputs into non-traded ones. This is a very common relationship. Indeed one might even say that almost all traded goods are inputs into non-traded goods rather than being final goods. For the service of internal transport and distribution is a non-traded value-added product, and almost all traded goods will have some significant element of that service added on top of them before being sold to final consumers. Though embodying possibly a large content of traded goods, the final product as delivered across the counter must be described as a non-traded good. The most convenient way of approaching this is to think of the non-traded and the traded element as being jointly demanded, hence being complementary on the demand side. Consider an example: newsprint is a traded input into the (more or less) non-traded product, newspapers. A nominal tariff on newsprint raises the price of newspapers, reduces the demand for them, and so reduces the demand for the value-added product (printing and journalism). Output of the value-added product will decline. A protective structure will tend to give indirect anti-protection to those non-traded value-added products that are complementary with (that is, use as inputs) traded inputs that obtain relatively high nominal protection.

One can now summarize the possible effects of a protective structure on the outputs of non-traded goods. First, those non-traded products which compete for factors with traded goods high in the scale of effective protection will tend to contract in output. Secondly, those non-traded products which are close consumption substitutes for traded goods high in the scale of nominal protection will expand in output, obtaining indirect protection. Thirdly, those non-traded products which are complementary in consumption with traded goods high in the scale of nominal protection will contract in output; the latter embraces the vertical relationship just discussed. All these effects of course operate in reverse when the competing or complementary traded good is low in the scale of effective or nominal rates. There could also be general equilibrium 'complementary' effects on the production side, as explained in section VII, so that a high effective rate causes the output of a 'complementary' non-traded product to expand. A fourth effect, resulting from the other vertical relationship—non-traded inputs into traded goods—will be introduced in Chapter 7.

5

THE GENERAL EQUILIBRIUM
APPROACH AND THE
EXCHANGE RATE ADJUSTMENT

So far no mention has been made of the exchange rate and nothing precise has been said about the way in which full employment (internal balance) and balance of payments equilibrium (external balance) are maintained in our various models.

A simple approach might be the following. Fiscal and monetary policies are used to vary domestic expenditure—that is the sum of consumption and investment spending—so as to maintain internal balance, while the exchange rate is varied so as to maintain external balance. Starting in internal and external balance, what then are the effects of imposing a protective structure? If this structure consists mainly of positive nominal and effective protective rates, rather than negative rates, it is likely in the first instance to create an external surplus. This then requires an appreciation of the exchange rate to restore external balance. The final protection equilibrium situation will thus have an exchange rate different from the free trade one. Looking back from the protection situation, if the protective structure were removed and free trade restored, there would have to be a devaluation of the exchange rate so as to avoid the external deficit which would otherwise result. All this time domestic expenditure in real and money terms would need to be varied to maintain internal balance. When the protective structure is imposed and before the subsequent exchange rate appreciation, real expenditure would have to be reduced to make possible the external surplus, while, when the exchange rate is appreciated real expenditure would be raised again, though, if there have been losses from trade distortion, it would not be raised up to the real expenditure level of the free trade situation.

This is a familiar, but very general way of putting the matter. It can be made more precise by focusing explicitly on equilibrium in the markets for traded and non-traded goods and hence on the relationship between the prices of traded and non-traded goods. Throughout this chapter we shall continue to make the small country assumption. This means that an exchange rate alteration affects the domestic prices of all traded goods equally. Hence if we had a model with only traded goods it would bring about no changes in price relationships between products and hence would not induce resources to move between them. This indicates the crucial role of non-traded goods in this context. Once non-traded goods are introduced an exchange rate alteration affects relative goods prices, namely the price relationship between traded and non-traded goods.[1]

I. *Non-traded Goods and the Net Protective Rate*

Suppose we have two traded goods, X (the exportable) and M (the importable), and one non-traded good, N. We start in internal and external balance with a given exchange rate and given money income and money prices of the three goods. Now a tariff is imposed. For the moment hold the exchange rate constant. The domestic money price of M will rise by the extent of the tariff while the money price of X stays constant. As we have seen, this will lead to a production shift from X to M and a consumption shift in the opposite direction. But what will be the movements relative to N? This hinges on what happens to the price of N. Let us assume that the money price of N is rigidly fixed. This is a key assumption. In the context of the analysis to follow it may appear not unreasonable. It really means that we are using N as the numeraire. Then resources will move out of N into M and consumption will switch, or attempt to switch, from M towards N. The price of M will have risen in relation *both* to the price of X and the price of N. It appears in fact that the tariff has protected M not

---

[1] The role of non-traded goods in general equilibrium analysis of exchange rate adjustment has tended to be ignored, for example in all except Chapter XVIII of J. E. Meade, *The Balance of Payments* (Oxford University Press, London, 1951). A notable exception is I. F. Pearce, 'The Problem of the Balance of Payments', *International Economic Review*, 2, Jan. 1961, 1–28. See also I. F. Pearce, *International Trade* (Macmillan, London, 1970), 78–83.

only in relation to X but also in relation to N. There will be no production or consumption movements between X and N because their relative prices have not changed.

This is not an equilibrium situation. If total expenditure is equal to income derived from production, there will be excess demand for N (internal imbalance), this excess being equal to the balance of payments surplus (external imbalance). The excess demand, or internal imbalance, could be eliminated by a sufficient reduction of expenditure through fiscal or monetary policy. This would bring demand for N down to production of it, but would also reduce domestic demands for M and X, so increasing the external imbalance. As pointed out in the previous chapter, in this case the restoration of full equilibrium requires a rise in the relative price of N. This could be brought about in two ways: by a rise in the money price of N or by an appreciation of the exchange rate. Since we are holding the money price of N constant we must choose the second way. The appreciation lowers the domestic prices of M and X equally, but does not change the domestic price of N. So it causes consumption to flow from N towards M and X and production to move from M and X towards N. This will eliminate the balance of payments surplus and at the same time, if expenditure is brought back into equality with income, will involve equilibrium in the market for N.

Now let us introduce the concept of the *net protective rate*. Suppose that the free trade price of a unit of M had been £125. A tariff of 40 per cent then raised the domestic price to £175. The proportional increase in the domestic price of M over that of X and over that of N before the exchange rate alters is thus 40 per cent. Then the necessary appreciation lowers the domestic prices of all traded goods by 20 per cent (so that the appreciation in the value of the domestic currency is 25 per cent), the price of M excluding tariff falling to £100 and the price including tariff to £140. Since the appreciation will also have reduced the price of X by 20 per cent it remains true that the price of M has risen relative to that of X by 40 per cent. The tariff rate correctly measures the protective margin relative to X. But relative to N, the money price of which is constant, the price turns out to have risen only from £125 to £140, or 12 per cent. We shall call the proportional rise in the price of M relative to that of N as a result of the tariff after the exchange rate adjustment has been taken into account the *net protective rate*. Provided this *net* rate is positive there will finally have been some resource flow from N into M. If the elasticity of substitution in both consumption and production between X and M and X and N had been zero, then the appreciation would have had to reverse completely the original flow of resources between M and N induced by the tariff, and so would have had to be sufficient to yield a net rate of zero. Since one is usually interested in analysing a situation where countries already have tariffs it may be more convenient to start the story in the protection situation with a price excluding tariff of £100 and a price including tariff of £140. If the tariff were removed there would have to be a devaluation to retain internal and external balance. This would raise the domestic price of M excluding the tariff to £125. The devaluation is thus equivalent to a 25 per cent tariff, at least in its effect on the money price of M and so on its relationship with the given money price of N. We shall say that 25 per cent is the *devaluation rate*. It is the same as the proportional appreciation of the domestic currency if we had started from free trade. The net protective rate t_n (the proportional increase from £125 to £140) can be expressed in terms of the ordinary protective rate t (40 per cent here) and the devaluation rate q, namely $t_n = \dfrac{t-q}{1+q}$.

It was pointed out in the previous chapter that when there are non-traded goods it may be convenient to analyse the effects of a tariff or protective structure in two stages, first assuming the price of N constant and then allowing it to vary so as to maintain equilibrium. This is the approach used here. First one can analyse the effect of the tariff when the money price of N and the exchange rate are unchanged. Next the relative price of N is altered through the appropriate exchange rate alteration. The net protective rate expresses the net result of the two processes on the price relationship between N and traded goods.

So far we have assumed that the money price of N stays constant, so that any change in the price relationship between N and X, and N and M (after tariff), must be brought about by an exchange rate alteration. Is this a reasonable assumption? We could simply assume that monetary policy is so directed as always to keep the money price of N constant. This is perfectly possible and if N formed the dominant sector of the economy quite plausible. But if the policy is rather to keep money income constant, then the money price of N need not stay constant. There are various possibilities here, but essentially, whether its price rises or falls depends then on its relative substitutability in production and consumption with M and X. It may be that N is not particularly intensive in one factor of production rather than another so that its price is affected only by the change in the *average* factor price, not by changes in the ratios of individual factor prices brought about by the tariff. In that case its price will not change if money income (and hence the average money factor price) does not change. Alternatively, the money wage may be fixed and N may be highly labour-intensive, consisting mainly of services. Its money price will then change very little if at all. Thus the assumption of a constant money price of N is quite plausible and will be maintained below. But it is not inevitable. The money wage and the money price of N may have been somewhat flexible, so that the price of N may have been raised by the excess demand which initially resulted from the tariff before appreciation or expenditure reduction. Similarly, the excess supply of N resulting from removal of a tariff might lead to some fall in its price and so reduce the extent of the devaluation required. In that case, the net rate, as calculated from the tariff rate and the devaluation rate, would overstate the rise in the price of M relative to N that has resulted from the tariff combined with the appropriate exchange rate adjustment. But, to repeat, we shall continue to use N as the numeraire and hold its money price constant. If its price were indeed flexible we could redefine the devaluation rate as the proportional fall in the money price of N that would be required, with a fixed exchange rate, to maintain internal and external balance if the protective structure were removed.

II. *Partial Equilibrium Analysis of the Exchange Rate Adjustment*

One would like to give some precision to the idea of the exchange rate adjustment associated with a tariff change. It is quite simple to express the devaluation rate required when a tariff is removed in terms of the usual elasticities of demand and supply. These elasticities are partial equilibrium concepts and so one has to revert to an essentially partial model. This is not to say that there is not a precise solution available in terms of a general equilibrium model, but it would not be a simple one. Let us just try for a simple solution, making the simplifying—but not always grossly unrealistic—assumptions that (1) the cross-elasticities between X and M both in production and consumption are zero, so that we can draw demand and supply curves for X and M independent of each other, and (2) consumption and production of N are so large relative to consumption and production of traded goods that income effects of tariffs, exchange rate alterations, and so on, can be ignored. In addition, (3) it is assumed, as before, that monetary and fiscal policy hold constant the price of N, and (4) that world prices are given.

We could now draw domestic demand and supply curves for X and M reflecting the substitution possibilities of X and M relative to N. From these curves can be derived the export supply curve SS' of Fig. 5.1a and the import demand curve DD' of Fig. 5.1b. Units are so chosen that the foreign currency price of a unit of X is the same as the foreign currency price of a unit of M. Given the exchange rate of the protection situation the price of both is OP. The tariff is PT/OP and the import quantity with the tariff is OK. If the tariff were removed and the exchange rate remained unaltered, imports would rise to OL. Assuming that with the tariff there was balance of payments equilibrium, removal of the tariff would lead to a deficit. So the exchange rate must be devalued at the same time. The necessary devaluation raises the domestic price of X and the duty-free price of M to OP', so that the devaluation rate is PP'/OP. The rise in exports is BC. The rise in imports relative to the original tariff situation is KH. For balance of payments equilibrium to be maintained, BC must equal KH and the devaluation rate has been so chosen as to attain this. The increases in export and import values resulting from tariff reduction combined with the appropriate devaluation, valued at the free trade exchange rate, are shaded, the two shaded areas being equal.

Now we wish to express the devaluation rate PP'/OP in

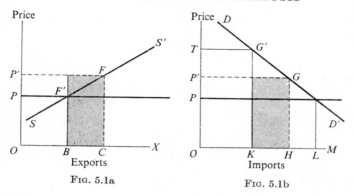

FIG. 5.1a

FIG. 5.1b

terms of the tariff rate PT/OP and the elasticities of the two domestic curves. We shall assume that over the relevant ranges the SS' and the DD' 'curves' are both straight lines. Their elasticities will then differ at different points. It is convenient to choose the points F and G which are the equilibrium points in the free trade-with-devaluation situation since these yield the simpler formula.
Let

Export value in free trade situation (at free trade exchange rate)	$= X$
Import value in free trade situation (at free trade exchange rate)	$= M$
Rise in export value (at free trade exchange rate) resulting from devaluation (shaded area in diagram)	$= dX$
Rise in import value excluding tariff (at free trade exchange rate) resulting from removal of tariff and devaluation combined (shaded area in diagram)	$= dM$
Tariff rate	$= t$
Devaluation rate	$= q$
Elasticity of export supply in free trade situation	$= e_x$
Elasticity of import demand in free trade situation	$= e_m$

Then

$$e_x = \frac{dX}{X}\left(\frac{1}{q}+1\right) \tag{1}$$

$$e_m = \frac{dM}{M}\left(\frac{1+q}{t-q}\right) \tag{2}$$

If the balance of payments is to stay in equilibrium

$$dX = dM \tag{3}$$

From (1), (2), (3)

$$e_x X\left(\frac{q}{1+q}\right) = e_m M\left(\frac{t-q}{1+q}\right) \tag{4}$$

From (4)

$$q = \frac{t}{1+\dfrac{e_x X}{e_m M}} \tag{5}$$

This then is the formula for the devaluation rate. The net protective rate is $(t-q)/(1+q)$. Note that when $e_x = 0$, then $q = t$, and the greater the ratio of the elasticity of export supply (e_x) to the elasticity of import demand (e_m) the lower the devaluation required. If $X = M$ and $e_x = e_m$ the formula reduces to $q = t/2$. Assuming $X = M$, if e_x is greater than e_m the devaluation rate is less than half the tariff rate, and if less than e_m, greater than half the tariff rate.

One could allow for import supply and export demand elasticities that are less than infinite, though this would yield a much more complicated formula.[2] Since one usually thinks in terms of moving from protection to free trade it might also seem more sensible to use the elasticities at the protection points F' and G' (Figs. 5.1a and 5.1b) and the export and import values in the protection situation. Defining these respectively as e_x', e_m', X' and M', the equation would then be more complicated, namely

$$q = \frac{t}{1+(1+t)\left(\dfrac{e_x' X'}{e_m' M'}\right)} \tag{6}$$

The more important development, very relevant to our subsequent analysis, is to allow for more than one import, and hence more than one tariff, and for a subsidy or tax on the export.

[2] See G. Basevi, 'The Restrictive Effect of the U.S. Tariff and its Welfare Value', *American Economic Review*, 58, Sept. 1968, 840–852.

Let

s = export subsidy rate (subsidy as proportion of
price excluding subsidy)

then

$$e_x = \frac{dX}{X}\left(\frac{1+q}{q-s}\right) \tag{1.1}$$

dX is the rise in export value resulting from removal of the subsidy combined with devaluation. Since exports could fall as a result of these two changes, dX could be negative.

Let there be two imports, with tariff rates t_1 and t_2, elasticities at the free trade points e_{m1} and e_{m2}, and free trade imports M_1 and M_2
then

$$e_{m_1} = \frac{dM_1}{M_1}\left(\frac{1+q}{t_1-q}\right) \tag{2.1}$$

$$e_{m_2} = \frac{dM_2}{M_2}\left(\frac{1+q}{t_2-q}\right) \tag{2.2}$$

If the balance of payments is to stay in equilibrium

$$dX = dM_1+dM_2 \tag{3.1}$$

From (1.1), (2.1), (2.2), (3.1)

$$q = \frac{se_xX+t_1e_{m_1}M_1+t_2e_{m_2}M_2}{e_xX+e_{m_1}M_1+e_{m_2}M_2} \tag{5.1}$$

Hence the devaluation rate is simply the weighted average of the various protective rates, the weights being the relevant elasticities at the free trade points and the free trade values of imports and exports.

One could also introduce the distinction between nominal and effective rates. If consumption elasticities were zero the devaluation rate would simply be a weighted average of the effective rates, the weights being either the relevant domestic value-added supply elasticities and the initial outputs in value-added terms, or alternatively the import demand elasticities in value-added terms and the initial trade values (also in value-added terms).[3] With consumption effects as well, both nominal and effective rates would enter the formula.[4]

III. *Balance of Payments Effects and Exchange Rate Adjustment in the Multi-Product Model*

The preceding analysis of the exchange rate adjustment with non-traded goods must now be combined with the multi-product analysis of the previous chapter. The basic idea is very simple. Each traded product has its nominal and its effective protective rate, the net result of tariffs, export subsidies and the rest. We shall assume the average money price of non-traded goods constant (treating them initially as if there were only a single non-traded good) and that internal balance is maintained continuously by appropriate fiscal and monetary policy. Then each of the protective rates will have a balance of payments effect. The combined result of all the effects may be to improve or worsen the balance of payments. There would then have to be an exchange rate adjustment to restore equilibrium.

Consider first nominal rates and consumption effects. In all cases where nominal rates are positive some expenditure will switch from the traded goods concerned to non-traded goods, unless the elasticities of substitution in consumption (expenditure) are zero. This will lead to a balance of payments improvement. On the other hand, where nominal rates are negative, perhaps as a result of export taxes, consumption will move towards traded goods and the balance of payments will tend to worsen. In addition, if the nominal rates differ between different traded goods consumption will shift within the traded goods sector. But this will not affect the balance of payments, though it may affect the volume of trade.[5] Next consider effective rates and production effects. We shall assume, for

---

[3] W. M. Corden, 'The Effective Protective Rate, the Uniform Tariff Equivalent and the Average Tariff', *Economic Record*, 42, June 1966, 200–16.

[4] H. G. Johnson, 'The Theory of Effective Protection and Preferences', *Economica*, 36, May 1969, 129–30.

[5] A given amount of expenditure may be switched from one importable to another. Given domestic production of the importables (which depends on the effective rates) this will lower imports of one by the same amount it raises those of another. If the switch is from an importable to an exportable, import and export value will fall by the same amount. We are of course assuming given world prices of imports and exports here.

exposition, that the elasticities of substitution in production between traded goods and the non-traded sector are all positive. Positive effective rates will draw resources from the non-traded sector into production of the traded goods concerned, and will improve the balance of payments; negative effective rates will have the opposite result. In addition, if the effective rates differ, resources will move as between different industries producing traded goods; this may worsen the balance of payments.[6]

Taking all these effects together, the balance of payments may at this stage improve or worsen. If the nominal rates and the effective rates are mainly positive it is likely to improve. But negative rates, nominal or effective, create a tendency in the opposite direction. It may be that the protective structure consists wholly of positive nominal rates. Nevertheless, the balance of payments need not improve because this structure may have produced negative effective rates.[7] The positive nominal rates would make for a balance of payments improvement and the negative effective rates for a deterioration. The net result, conceivably, may be for the balance of payments to stay in equilibrium.

This analysis has an interesting application. It can be shown that a uniform ad valorem tariff on all imports could worsen the balance of payments. Let us assume that there are no export subsidies or taxes and that the tariff rate is 20 per cent. Some of the importables are inputs in other importables, some are inputs in exportables and some exportables are inputs in importables. Those importables which have only other importables as inputs will then get 20 per cent effective protection; those importables which have some exportables as inputs will get effective protection greater than 20 per cent; and exportables that have importables as inputs will get negative effective protection. There will now be three effects on the balance

---

[6] With given total expenditure (fixed by the need to provide sufficient demand for non-traded goods) and with given resources in the traded goods sector, the question is whether total output of traded goods, valued at constant (world) prices rises or falls. It will fall as a result of the protective structure if free trade had yielded the static efficiency optimum; in this case the balance of payments will have worsened owing to this effect.

[7] H. G. Johnson, 'A Model of Protection and the Exchange Rate', *Review of Economic Studies*, 33, April 1966, 159–63.

9

of payments. First, the positive nominal rates for all import-ables will improve the balance of payments through the shift in the expenditure pattern towards the non-traded sector. Secondly, the positive effective rates for all importables, whether they obtain 20 per cent effective protection or more, will improve the balance of payments through the shift of resources from the non-traded sector into the sector producing import-competing goods. Thirdly, the negative effective protection for exportables will worsen the balance of payments. If the input share of importables in exportables is high and the elasticity of substitution in production between exportables and non-traded goods is high the latter effect may be very large; so it could outweigh the other two effects with the net result that the balance of payments worsens.

How does *negative value-added* (negative free trade effective price and positive protection effective price) fit into our story? Just like negative protection it worsens the balance of payments. But just like normal positive effective protection it leads to a movement of resources from the non-traded sector into the traded-goods sector. In Chapter 3 we regarded it as a form of positive effective protection because of this latter effect; but it is true that from the point of view of the balance of payments it should be grouped with negative effective protection. The point is that normally effective protection, whether positive or negative, leads to a switch of resources as between the traded and the non-traded sectors which has an associated balance of payments effect: either resources move out of the non-traded sector to improve the balance of payments or move into it and worsen the balance of payments. But in this case there is not just a reallocation of resources but essentially a destruction of them.

Before proceeding to the next step, namely the equilibrium exchange rate adjustment, it must be pointed out that in the intermediate position which we have reached here total money expenditure will have to be varied so as to maintain equilibrium in the market for non-traded goods—that is, internal balance. And this variation in expenditure will have effects on the balance of payments that will reinforce the effects attained by the consumption and production switches just described. For example, suppose that positive nominal and effective rates have improved the balance of payments by increasing desired consumption of non-traded goods and reducing production of them. Hence there has been *switching* of consumption away from traded goods and of factors of production towards them. This means that there would be excess demand for non-traded goods. So we must go on to allow for a reduction in expenditure, sufficient to bring the demand for non-traded goods down to the reduced supply of them. But this expenditure reduction will also lead to reduced purchases of importables and exportables, and so will improve the balance of payments further. The only complication arises here in the *negative value-added* case just described. In the first instance, as we saw, this worsened the balance of payments, while also leading to reduced production of non-traded goods. The latter effect will have required an expenditure reduction to bring consumption of non-traded goods down to their lower production, and this expenditure reduction in turn will tend to improve the balance of payments. Hence when this internal balance adjustment is taken into account the balance of payments may improve as a result of negative value-added. This does not alter the fact that there has, in a sense, been a destruction of real resources.

The next step is to allow for the exchange rate adjustment. We shall assume, without referring further to it, that expenditure is appropriately readjusted so as to maintain internal balance. Let us suppose that the protective structure has caused the balance of payments to go into surplus. The necessary exchange rate appreciation will cause the domestic prices of all importables and exportables to fall by an equal percentage. In relation to non-traded goods, the money prices of which are constant, it is the equivalent of a uniform *ad valorem* import subsidy and export tax, the rates of subsidy and tax being the same and applying both to final goods and to inputs. We know from Chapter 3 that if the tariffs on the inputs into a final good are at the same rate as the final good's own nominal tariff, then its effective rate will also be equal to its nominal rate. Thus, when all nominal rates are at one rate, all effective rates will also be at this rate. It follows that the exchange rate appreciation provides a uniform rate of nominal *and effective* protection for all traded goods in relation to non-traded goods. It does not of course affect the scale of nominal and effective rates within the traded goods sector and so does not bring about any shifts in the expenditure and output pattern within that sector. These shifts result only from the imposition or removal of a protective structure, not from the exchange rate adjustment that may go with it. This exchange rate adjustment must clearly be regarded as an integral part of the effect of a protective structure.[8] If the appreciation were, for example, 25 per cent, all traded goods with an effective rate of less than 25 per cent will, in a sense, have been taxed in relation to non-traded goods, and only effective rates over 25 per cent mean protection in relation to them. If we subtract 25 per cent (equal to the devaluation rate) from all effective protective rates as previously calculated and take 80 per cent. of the result (so that a 40 per cent effective rate turns into a 12 per cent rate) we obtain the scale of *net* effective protective rates. Only when the net rate is positive is an activity protected relative to non-traded goods.

It is probably more realistic to look at this process starting in the protection situation, asking what would happen if free trade were restored. If the effective and nominal rates are mainly positive, there would have to be a devaluation. Suppose the devaluation rate required is 25 per cent. This would then 're-protect' industries to some extent in relation to non-traded goods. Only those activities obtaining effective rates above 25 per cent—that is, obtaining positive *net* effective protection —will then have been protected in relation to the free trade-with-devaluation situation. Activities with effective rates below 25 per cent, and hence with negative net effective protection, would actually gain resources from the non-traded goods sector if free trade were restored and associated with the appropriate exchange rate adjustment. The analysis can also be generalized for the case where there are many non-traded goods. One must then hold constant not the price of each separate non-traded good but rather some kind of average price-level of them. As a result of the protective structure the prices of some non-traded goods will go up—these being indirectly protected—

<hr />

[8] Estimates of the equilibrium exchange rate adjustment (the 'overvaluation' resulting from the protective structure) have been made in Basevi, op. cit. and in the various studies in B. Balassa, (ed.), *The Structure of Protection in Developing Countries*, 1971.

while the prices of others—indirectly anti-protected—will go down.

IV. *The Symmetry of Various Protective Structures*

An important proposition in the theory of international trade, owed to Lerner, is that there is a symmetry between import taxes and export taxes.[9] When this proposition is extended to the theory of tariff structure it can be shown to have very interesting implications.

Lerner's proposition was developed in the context of the orthodox two-sector model. Given only two goods, X and M, the consumption pattern and resource allocation depend on a single domestic price ratio, that between the price of X and the price of M. If a tariff of 25 per cent were imposed the domestic price of M would rise relative to that of X by 25 per cent, resulting in a shift in production and consumption, how much depending on the relevant elasticities. Alternatively there might have been no tariff and hence no change in the domestic price of M, but exactly the same change in the price ratio could have been attained by reducing the domestic price of X sufficiently. Say the price of X and M were initially £100. Then an export tax of 20 per cent would reduce the domestic price of X to £80. The price of M will thus be 25 per cent above that of X compared with the free trade situation. The effect on the price ratio is thus identical with that of a 25 per cent tariff. If one had expressed the export tax in relation to the post-tax price received by exporters, then a 25 per cent export tax would have the same effect as a 25 per cent tariff. This is Lerner's 'symmetry' proposition. Consumption and production would shift and the volume of trade would be reduced to the same extent. It could also be shown that the revenue from the export tax would be the same as the revenue from the tariff. Lerner provided a proof of all this in terms of the orthodox two-sector geometry.

In one important respect the export tax is by no means symmetrical with the tariff, a respect which the usual pure

[9] A. P. Lerner, 'The Symmetry between Import and Export Taxes', *Economica*, 3, Aug. 1936, 306–13, reprinted in R. E. Caves and H. G. Johnson (eds.), *Readings in International Economics* (Richard D. Irwin, Homewood, 1968). See also J. E. Meade, *Trade and Welfare*, 1955, pp. 165–66.

or 'barter' theory approach obscures. A tariff in the first instance improves the balance of payments while an export tax worsens it (with given world prices and constant money income). To restore the original balance of payments situation the tariff must be associated with an exchange rate appreciation and the export tax with a depreciation. Given the necessary assumptions, the proposition is thus really that an export tax *combined with the appropriate depreciation* is symmetrical with a tariff *combined with the appropriate appreciation*. If average factor prices are flexible upwards but not downwards the tariff would not need to be accompanied by an appreciation, though the export tax would still require a depreciation. All this is also true in a model with non-traded goods where their average money price is constant. Even if we stayed within the two-traded goods model the Lerner proposition could be extended. It is not just a 20 per cent export tax that has the same effect as a 25 per cent tariff, assuming the appropriate exchange rate or money factor price adjustment. The identical change in the price ratio could be brought about by a 10 per cent export tax (which reduces the domestic price to £90) combined with a $12\frac{1}{2}$ per cent tariff (which raises the domestic price of imports to 25 per cent above £90), or by a 20 per cent export *subsidy* combined with a 50 per cent tariff. There is an infinite number of possible protective structures which can attain a particular change in the price ratio, though each would (with given money income or money price of N) involve a different exchange rate. Furthermore, the proposition can be simply extended to a model with three traded goods.[10] We may have one exportable, X, and two importables, M_1 and M_2. A 25 per cent tariff on M_1, with no tariff on M_2 and no export tax or subsidy, will shift consumption from M_1 to M_2 and to X and will draw resources into M_1 from M_2 and X, leading to a fall in total trade and a shift in the pattern of imports. The identical result could be obtained by an import subsidy of 20 per cent on M_2 combined with an export tax of 20 per cent on X (calculating them in relation to their prices excluding subsidy or tax), or by a $12\frac{1}{2}$ per cent tariff on M_1 combined with a

[10] R. I. McKinnon, 'Intermediate Products and Differential Tariffs: A Generalization of Lerner's Symmetry Theorem', *Quarterly Journal of Economics*, 80, Nov. 1966, 584–615.

10 per cent import subsidy on M_2 and a 10 per cent export tax on X. This makes the general point that it is possible to protect an industry relative to other industries either by protecting it or by taxing (negatively protecting) other industries.

This then leads to a most illuminating generalization of the symmetry proposition to the theory of protective structure. We refer to Fig. 5.2 and for our illustration shall assume that

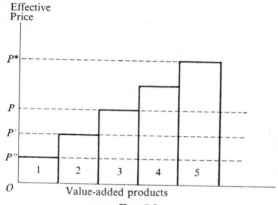

FIG. 5.2

there are five traded goods, though it will become evident that the story could be told for any number. Some goods may be importables and some exportables and the effective rates may be the complicated results of various combinations of import, export, consumption and production taxes and subsidies on the final goods themselves and their inputs (which must, in this model, be the same goods). We choose units of the five goods so that their foreign effective prices are all identical. In addition there is a non-traded good with a fixed money price. In Fig. 5.2, if there were free trade, with the exchange rate appropriate to free trade, the domestic effective price of each good would be OP. Suppose a protective structure is imposed yielding a negative rate for product 1, zero rate for product 2 and positive rates for products 3, 4, and 5. At the same time the exchange rate must be appreciated to maintain external balance. At the new rate the effective price, excluding tariffs, subsidies, etc., is OP' for each good, while the actual domestic prices allowing for the protective structure are as shown in Fig. 5.2, namely OP'' for good 1, OP' for good 2, and so on. Good 3 has the positive effective rate $P'P/OP'$ but its domestic price is the same as it would be under free trade. Hence its *net* effective rate is zero. The ordinary effective rates are measured in relation to OP' while the net rates are measured relative to OP. The devaluation rate is $P'P/OP'$. Now, imagine all effective rates to be raised such that product 1 obtains a zero effective rate and the domestic effective price relationships are maintained as before. So the exchange rate will have to be appreciated further, bringing the effective price excluding tariffs, etc., down to OP''. For example, the effective rate for product 3 will have risen from $P'P/OP'$ to $P''P/OP''$. Yet nothing has really changed. The domestic money prices of all goods are the same as before, the relativities between effective prices are the same so that there will be no resource shift within the traded sector and all the *net* rates remain unchanged, so that there will be no resource movements into and out of the non-traded sector. Hence the two protective structures, each with its appropriate exchange rate, are completely symmetrical. In fact there is an unlimited number of structures all yielding the same scale of net effective rates and so all having the same resource allocation effects. The point is made vividly if we suppose that all products obtain negative rates; there will then have to be a depreciation sufficient to bring the effective price of every product excluding tariffs, etc., to above OP^*. The scale of net rates, and hence the resource allocation effects, can remain unchanged. A scale of low effective rates associated with a depreciated currency can yield the same scale of net rates as a scale of high effective rates associated with an appreciated currency.

Exactly the same analysis could be applied to the scale of nominal rates. Figure 5.2 could be reinterpreted as referring to nominal, not effective, prices, and we would then be concerned with the effects of the protective structure on the pattern of consumption, not production.

v. *Four Concepts of Protection*

There emerge from this analysis four distinct concepts of when an industry producing a traded product is really protected.

First, there is the old-fashioned approach that an industry is protected if its nominal tariff or rate of subsidy is positive. But it is the message of our analysis that, while the nominal rate is relevant to the consumption effect, in itself it can tell us nothing about the production effect.

Second, there is the more sophisticated approach which emerges from the new theory of effective protection at a partial equilibrium level that an industry is protected if its effective protective rate is positive. It is true that it will be protected relative to all those traded goods that have zero effective protection. It is also true that, if the prices of non-traded goods are given and the exchange rate does not alter, any industry with a positive effective rate will tend to attract resources into it from non-traded goods and is thus protected relative to non-traded goods. But it clearly may not be protected relative to non-traded goods once exchange rate adjustment is permitted. Furthermore, it will not be protected—indeed it will be anti-protected—relative to traded goods obtaining higher effective rates.

Third, one might take into account the relationship with non-traded goods and consider an industry to be protected only when its *net effective rate* is positive. The concept of the net rate is useful, but it must be remembered that one net rate on its own tells us nothing about the place of a traded good in the scale of effective rates and thus nothing about whether the activity producing it is protected relative to other producers of traded goods.

Fourth, one might argue that an activity is only truly protected if the net result of the protective structure combined with the appropriate exchange rate adjustment (or adjustment in the money prices of non-traded goods) is to raise the *amount* of value-added (valued at free trade prices) in that activity. This is the concept of *total protection*. It is a quantitative, and not a price, concept. For this concept one needs to look at the complete general equilibrium repercussions of a protective structure. It is perhaps a theoretically satisfying concept as it does not rest on any limiting assumptions, but it is really not of much practical value. For this concept it is not sufficient to measure or guess at rates of protection or even to estimate exchange rate adjustments; rather, all substitution relationships must be taken into account. The direction of change in quantity of value-added depends not only on protection relative to non-traded goods but also on protection relative to other traded goods. It is not only the sign and size of the net rate but also the position in the scale of effective rates that counts. Even if we find that a particular activity has a positive net protective rate and its production-substitution elasticity with the non-traded sector is positive so that there is a movement of resources into that activity from the non-traded sector, it does not follow that output of that activity must increase. For there may be substitution against it because some other traded goods activity has obtained a higher effective rate. For example, in Fig. 5.2, industry 4, which has not only a positive effective rate but also a positive net effective rate, may nevertheless be anti-protected because industry 5 is even higher in the scale of effective protection and the two industries are close competitors for factors. Thus resources may have moved into industry 4 from the non-traded sector and from industries 1, 2 and 3, but these movements may be outweighed by the movement of resources from it to industry 5. To sum up, whether an industry is protected in our fourth sense (that is, is *totally* protected) depends not only on substitution relative to non-traded goods (the direction of which is indicated by the sign of the *net* rate) but also on substitution relative to other traded goods (which is influenced by its position in the scale of effective rates). Total protection refers to the final and complete effects of a protective structure. The rate of total protection would be the proportional increase in the quantity of domestic output at free trade prices resulting from the structure. It is a much more ambitious concept than the concept of the rate of effective protection. The latter is simply a proportional price change—the change in the effective price—which is one ingredient in a process of working out what the final answer must be. The rate of total protection, on the other hand, does not help towards the final answer but rather comes out of it.

In addition to *direct protection* of traded goods, however defined, there is *indirect protection*: the effects of a protective structure on prices and outputs of non-traded goods. Here also one might choose between defining protection in price or in output terms. Our approach in section VIII of the previous chapter has been in terms of output, and hence in terms of *total* indirect protection. A non-traded good is indirectly protected when its output is increased as a result of the protective structure, taking into account the exchange rate adjustment.

VI. *Foreign Protective Structures and Combined Protection*

It is the general approach in this book to regard foreign countries' trade taxes and other policies as constraints which help to determine the given foreign demand and supply curves facing the country. But it is also possible to use our techniques to analyse the effects of foreign tariffs, etc., on the pattern of consumption and output in our own country. Let 'our' country be Canada and the 'foreign' country the United States. Consistent with the assumptions in this and the preceding chapters, assume that the U.S. demand curves for Canadian exports and the U.S. supply curves to Canada of U.S. exports are all infinitely elastic. Now the tariffs and other taxes and subsidies imposed by the United States provide protection or anti-protection for the industries of Canada, and their effect on the allocation of resources in Canada can be analysed in the same manner as the effects of Canada's own tariffs and other taxes. For example, a U.S. tariff on furniture lowers the demand curve facing Canadian exporters and has the same effect on the allocation of resources in Canada as a Canadian export tax on furniture. The concern here is only with effects on the pattern of expenditure and on resource allocation. The fiscal and real income effects obviously depend on which country taxes and subsidizes.

A scale of effective rates can then be constructed which represents the protection or anti-protection imposed by the U.S. tax-subsidy structure on Canadian industry. The effects of this structure can be analysed alone, holding constant Canada's own structure; the effects of the Canadian structure could be analysed alone, this being the approach expounded in this book so far; or the combined effects of the two structures could be analysed, constructing a scale of *combined effective rates.*[11] In any particular case, the two components of a combined effective rate (say a Canadian export subsidy combined with a U.S. import tariff) could cancel each other.

The exchange-rate adjustment must again be taken into account. Even in the simple case when both the Canadian and the U.S. tax-subsidy structures consist mainly of tariffs on finished goods, the required exchange rate adjustment could go either way and would, in any case, be less than when the effects of one of the structures alone is considered. Thus if the Canadian protective structure alone were removed it might be necessary for Canada to devalue. If the U.S. structure alone were removed it might be necessary for Canada to appreciate. When both are removed at the same time the two effects will, at least to some extent, offset each other, and on balance indeed no exchange rate adjustment at all may be needed. But in theory at least other results are also possible. The Canadian structure might contain so many negative effective rates that a removal of the structure would require an appreciation. The simultaneous removal of the U.S. structure would then require an even greater appreciation.

---

[11] This approach is particularly relevant for policy discussion in Canada where the main issue is not unilateral tariff reduction but rather reciprocity with the United States, and especially the possibility of North American free trade. See R. J. and P. Wonnacott, *Free Trade Between the United States and Canada: The Potential Economic Effects* (Harvard University Press, Cambridge, 1967).

6

THE SUBSTITUTION PROBLEM IN THE THEORY OF EFFECTIVE PROTECTION

WE now remove the assumption that there are fixed input-output coefficients between any product and its produced inputs. As explained in Chapter 4, this assumption has still permitted substitution between primary factors in the various value-added production functions. The substitution effects with which we are concerned refer to the production function in any one industry, and must be distinguished from the production substitution effects of earlier chapters in the form of movements along transformation curves.[1] We continue to make the small country assumption, and to assume that the imposition of a protective structure does not end trade in any good that was traded under free trade, and that there are no non-traded inputs into traded goods.

The analysis is meant to provide answers to two questions. The first is how substitution (a) between different produced inputs and (b) between these produced inputs and the value-added product affect actual effective protection provided by a protective structure. The general answer is that substitution increases effective rates, and the higher the relevant elasticity of substitution the higher the effective rate yielded by a given set of nominal rates and initial input-output coefficients. The second question is what errors in measurement result from the two types of substitution. In particular, if the input-output coefficients of the protection situation are used for

[1] The substitution problem was first discussed in a partial equilibrium context in W. M. Corden, 'The Structure of a Tariff System and the Effective Protective Rate', *Journal of Political Economy*, 74, June 1966, 233–35. The present chapter substantially revises the relevant part of this article as well as extending it to general equilibrium. Many of the papers listed in the bibliography at the end of this book deal with substitution and effective protection.

measurements, will substitution cause the measured rates to exceed or fall short of the actual effective rates? The general answer is that measured rates based on data obtained under protection will tend to exceed actual rates, so that substitution leads measurements to *overstate* effective rates.

I. *Substitution Between Traded Inputs*

We begin by considering a final product j which is an importable and is produced by three inputs, namely its value-added product v and two importable inputs, m_1 and m_2. The production function is linear homogeneous. No substitution is possible between the value-added product and the two produced inputs, so that the v/j ratio is fixed. We want to allow for substitution between m_1 and m_2. Varying combinations of m_1 and m_2 can produce a unit of j in combination with the required unit of v. A tariff on the final good, j, will have no substitution effect so that we can hold it constant for the purpose of the present discussion, and it will be convenient to assume it to be zero. Furthermore, there will be substitution between m_1 and m_2 only if their tariffs differ, for only then will their relative prices change. We shall assume here that the tariff on m_1 is greater. The imposition of positive tariffs on the inputs will yield negative effective protection for j when the tariff t_j on the final good is zero, while if the latter were sufficiently high effective protection would be positive, though lower than it would have been if there had been no tariffs on the inputs. For the fixed coefficient case, as was shown in Chapter 3, the effective rate depends on t_j, on the weighted average of the two input tariffs, and on the free trade share of the two inputs combined in the cost of j.

Now we are assuming that the price of m_1 goes up by more than that of m_2. Hence producers of j will substitute m_2 for m_1. This has two implications. First, it means that they are able to modify the impact on them of the higher input prices by shifting towards that input where the price has not gone up so much. Thus it is intuitively obvious that their costs will rise less as a result of the higher tariffs than if they had not been able to substitute. It follows that the average cost of the inputs required per unit of j will not rise so much, and hence the effective price of j will not fall so much. So the effective rate will not be as negative as it would be with fixed coefficients. Algebraically, the effective rate will be raised by substitution. Next, let us consider the effect of substitution on the measurement of effective rates. Substitution will increase the share in cost (at free trade prices) of the input the domestic price of which has risen relatively less as a result of the tariffs. If then the data of the protection situation are used for calculating the average input tariff they will give a higher weight to the low-tariff input relatively to the high-tariff input than if the data of the free trade situation had been used. This is a point familiar from the theory of tariff averaging. In an extreme case there might be complete substitution towards the low-tariff input, so that the use of the data of the protection situation would yield an average tariff equal to the lower of the two tariffs. All this suggests, again intuitively, that using the data of the protection situation to calculate the average input tariff will lead to an understatement of this average. Hence it will lead to an overstatement of the effective rate, since the higher the average input tariff the lower the effective rate.

Let us now give some geometric precision to these intuitive ideas. The geometry is familiar from expositions of the index number problem. For simplicity we shall assume that the tariff on m_2 is zero; hence we are considering the effects of substitution when one of the input prices rises and the other stays constant, the substitution being then towards the input with the constant price, in this case m_2.

In Fig. 6.1 quantities of m_1 are shown along the vertical axis and quantities of m_2 along the horizontal axis. The isoquant ii' shows the various combinations of m_1 and m_2 that can produce (with a given quantity of v) one unit of the final product j. The free trade price ratio between m_1 and m_2 is given by the slope of AB. One unit of j will then be produced with OH of m_1 and OG of m_2, the free trade equilibrium point X on the isoquant ii' being given by the tangency of the price line with the isoquant. We shall use m_2 as the numeraire here since its price will not change. In terms of m_2 the cost of the produced inputs required for one unit of j at free trade prices is OB.

Now a tariff at the rate of BD/OB is imposed on m_1. Hence a new internal price ratio is given by the slope of AD. Suppose for a moment that the coefficients were fixed. The equilibrium point would then stay at X, the same quantities of m_1 and m_2 as before being used to produce a unit of j. With the new price ratio and the same input quantities per unit of j the cost of the inputs per unit of j will thus rise to OE, where XE is parallel to AD. Thus the imposition of a tariff at the rate BD/OB on m_1, with no tariff on m_2, has led to a proportional rise in the input

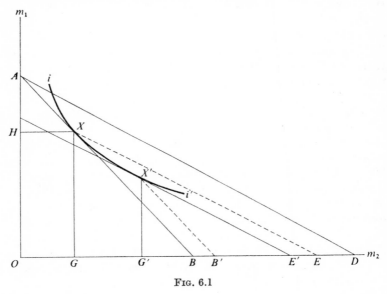

FIG. 6.1

cost of BE/OB, this being the average input tariff rate. It is simply a weighted average of the tariff BD/OB on m_1 and the zero tariff on m_2, the weights being the shares in cost of each input in total input cost at free trade prices, namely GB/OB for m_1 and OG/OB for m_2.[2]

Next, substitution can be introduced. This causes the equilibrium point to move to X' where the new tariff-distorted price line is tangential to the isoquant ii'. Drawing $X'E'$ parallel to XE and AD we find then that the input cost has risen only to OE', and not, as in the fixed coefficients case, to OE. Thus the increase in the cost of the inputs required for

---

[2] By similar triangles $BE/GB = BD/OB$
    hence $BE/OB = (BD/OB)(GB/OB).$

one unit of j is only BE'/OB. Substitution has enabled a saving of $E'E$ in input cost. This illustrates the point made above that substitution modifies the rise in input cost (and hence the fall in the effective price of j) resulting from tariffs on inputs.

The correct calculation of the average input tariff would yield the result BE'/OB. If the protection coefficients had been used the two tariffs would be weighted by what their shares in cost would be at free trade prices but with protection coefficients, namely $G'B'/OB'$ for m_1 and OG'/OB' for m_2 (the line $X'B'$ being parallel to AB). This would yield the result $B'E'/OB'$,[3] and would be an understatement of the correct average input tariff BE'/OB. On the other hand, if the free trade coefficients had been used as weights in the calculation the result would have been BE/OB and with substitution this would then represent an overstatement. It follows that use of the protection coefficients would lead to understatement of the average input tariff and hence overstatement of the effective rate while use of free trade coefficients would have exactly the opposite effect. We have, in fact, an index number problem.

II. *Substitution Between Primary Factors and Traded Inputs: The Model*

We now look at another type of substitution, namely that between the primary factors—or the *value-added product*—and the traded inputs. We shall consider an industry producing an importable product j which is produced by two inputs, i and v, where i is a produced importable input and v is the value-added product. There is a twice differentiable linear homogeneous production function with positive marginal products and a diminishing marginal rate of substitution. The assumption of positive marginal products excludes the case of zero elasticity of substitution (fixed coefficients). The assumption of linear homogeneity implies constant returns to scale. The prices of factors are assumed to be equal to their marginal products. We can regard the traded input as representing a bundle of inputs, but then relative prices within the bundle must not change; this means not only that relative world

---

[3] By similar triangles $\quad B'E'/G'B' = BD/OB$
$\qquad$ hence $\qquad\quad B'E'/OB' = (BD/OB)(G'B'/OB')$.

prices of the inputs must stay constant but that any tariffs on the inputs must be uniform. As before, the value-added product can be thought of as representing the contribution of the primary factors to the production of j; this v is in turn produced by the primary factors. But there is some difficulty about the concept of the 'value-added product' now. One cannot just say that one unit of v represents the contribution of the primary factors required to produce one unit of j since we shall allow the ratio v/j to change. What then is the meaning of a 'unit' of value-added product? This problem will be evaded for the moment and dealt with in section VI. It will be sufficient

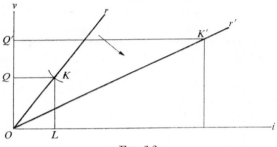

Fig. 6.2

for the moment to think of v as a factor of production which has 'natural' units that can be produced in turn by varying combinations of primary factors.

Let us now describe the free trade equilibrium for the product j. In Fig. 6.2, input i is shown along the horizontal axis and input v along the vertical axis, the quadrant containing a map of j isoquants. Along any given ray through the origin the marginal physical products of i and of v are constant. As the ray flattens, i.e. as i/v rises, the marginal physical product of v rises and of i falls. In Fig. 6.3 the marginal physical product of i (μ_i) is shown along the horizontal and the marginal physical product of v (μ_v) along the vertical axis; the quadrant contains a curve, FF', which shows the inverse relationship between the two marginal physical products. A flattening of the ray through the origin in Fig. 6.2—i.e. a rise in the factor ratio i/v—leads to a corresponding movement up the FF' curve, that is to a rise in μ_v and a fall in μ_i. It can be simply shown that the slope of FF' at any point $(\mathrm{d}\mu_v/\mathrm{d}\mu_i)$ is equal to the negative of the factor ratio associated with that point. This result will turn out to be important later.

By Euler's theorem

$$j = \mu_v v + \mu_i i \tag{1}$$

From the production function

$$\mathrm{d}j = \mu_v \, \mathrm{d}v + \mu_i \, \mathrm{d}i \tag{2}$$

From (1)

$$\mathrm{d}j = v\mathrm{d}\mu_v + \mu_v \, \mathrm{d}v + i\mathrm{d}\mu_i + \mu_i \, \mathrm{d}i \tag{1.1}$$

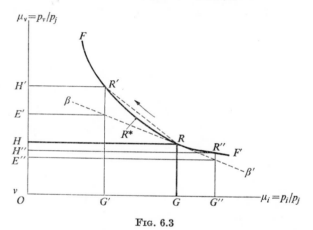

Fig. 6.3

From (2) and (1.1)

$$\frac{\mathrm{d}\mu_v}{\mathrm{d}\mu_i} = -\frac{i}{v} \tag{3}$$

Next prices must be introduced into the model. The prices of j, i and v are p_j, p_i and p_v (respectively the nominal price, the input price and the effective price). Given competitive pricing, prices of the inputs are equal to the values of their marginal products.

Hence

$$\mu_i = p_i/p_j \tag{4}$$

$$\mu_v = p_v/p_j \tag{5}$$

Before tariffs are imposed the prices p_j and p_i are given by the world market. Thus in the free trade situation p_i/p_j is determined, and hence μ_i is determined. In Fig. 6.3 we obtain thus a point G on the horizontal axis. This yields in turn an equilibrium point R on FF' and hence the marginal physical product of v, μ_v, namely OH. Furthermore, with the point R is associated a ray through the origin (and hence a factor ratio i/v) in Fig. 6.2. Clearly if either p_j or p_i changed, unless they changed in the same proportion, the ratio of the marginal physical products and of the inputs would change. The final step is to show how the effective price, p_v, is derived. It is represented in Fig. 6.4 along the vertical axis, the horizontal axis showing quantities of v used by industry j.

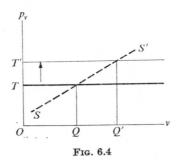

FIG. 6.4

Now p_v can be obtained from Fig. 6.3 and the free trade values of p_j and p_i. For the ratio p_i/p_j gives us μ_i which in turn yields, via the curve FF', μ_v, which is equal to p_v/p_j. But since p_j is given, p_v follows. The resultant value for p_v is then inserted in Fig. 6.4. It is assumed to be OT. Nothing has so far been said, or need be said, about the quantities of v used by industry j.

Now let us introduce tariffs. The tariff t_j raises p_j ($t_j = \Delta p_j/p_j$) and the tariff t_i raises p_i ($t_i = \Delta p_i/p_i$). The question is how these tariffs affect p_v. As before, we define the effective rate g_j as the proportional increase in the effective price, so that $g_j = \Delta p_v/p_v$. Suppose that t_j is greater than t_i. This means that p_i/p_j falls and hence μ_i falls. And this means that there is substitution from v to i. The fall in μ_i must be associated with a rise in μ_v. But a rise in μ_v must mean that $\Delta p_v/p_v$ is greater than $\Delta p_j/p_j$.

It follows that in this case $g_j > t_j > t_i$. The direction of movement is represented by arrows. In Fig. 6.3 equilibrium moves from R to R' and in Fig. 6.2 from the ray Or to the ray Or'. The story could also be told for the case where t_j is less than t_i. This time μ_i would rise and μ_v would fall so that the movement would be to the right along FF' in Fig. 6.3. Since μ_v would fall, g_j would be less than t_j and therefore $g_j < t_j < t_i$. It would now be possible for g_j to be negative. These results are the same in kind as emerge from the fixed coefficient formula for the effective rate. The effective rate exceeds the nominal rate when the latter is greater than the tariff on the input, and it is less than the nominal rate when the latter is less than the input tariff. Assuming that the effective rate is positive, the effective price p_v will rise, such an increase being indicated by the movement from OT to OT' in Fig. 6.4.

What is the formula for the effective rate g_j when there is substitution? We shall consider the case where the movement in Fig. 6.3 has been from R to R'.
Define

$$\Delta\mu_v/\Delta\mu_i = -\alpha \qquad (6)$$

Thus α is the slope of the line RR' defined as a positive number. It is the average rate of substitution between μ_v and μ_i over the relevant range.
From (4)

$$\Delta\mu_i = \left(\frac{\Delta p_i}{p_i} - \frac{\Delta p_j}{p_j}\right)\frac{p_i}{p_j + \Delta p_j} \qquad (4.1)$$

From (5), similarly

$$\Delta\mu_v = \left(\frac{\Delta p_v}{p_v} - \frac{\Delta p_j}{p_j}\right)\frac{p_v}{p_j + \Delta p_j} \qquad (5.1)$$

From (4.1) and (5.1)

$$\frac{\Delta\mu_v}{\Delta\mu_i} = \frac{\left(\dfrac{\Delta p_v}{p_v} - \dfrac{\Delta p_j}{p_j}\right)\dfrac{p_v}{p_i}}{\left(\dfrac{\Delta p_i}{p_i} - \dfrac{\Delta p_j}{p_j}\right)} \qquad (7)$$

From (6) and (7) and remembering that $\Delta p_v / p_v = g_j$; $\Delta p_j / p_j = t_j$; $\Delta p_i / p_i = t_i$

$$\alpha = -\left(\frac{g_j - t_j}{t_i - t_j}\right)\frac{p_v}{p_i} \tag{8}$$

From (8)

$$g_j = t_j + \alpha \frac{p_i}{p_v}(t_j - t_i) \tag{8.1}$$

Somewhere between R and R' on FF' is a point R^* where the tangent to FF' has the same slope as the straight line RR'. Let the factor ratio associated with this point be i^*/v^*. It follows from (3) and (6) that

$$\alpha = \frac{i^*}{v^*} \tag{9}$$

Now define the share of materials in total cost at free trade prices, given this factor ratio, as a_{ij}^*:

$$a_{ij}^* = \frac{p_i \dfrac{i^*}{v^*}}{p_i \dfrac{i^*}{v^*} + p_v} \tag{10}$$

From (9) and (10)

$$a_{ij}^* = \frac{p_i \alpha}{p_i \alpha + p_v} \tag{11}$$

From (8.1) and (11)

$$g_j = \frac{t_j - a_{ij}^* t_i}{1 - a_{ij}^*} \tag{12}$$

This is essentially the familiar formula for the effective rate. It differs only from the usual fixed coefficient formula in that a_{ij} has been replaced by a_{ij}^*. Both are input shares at free trade prices; but a_{ij}^* is derived from the input coefficient associated with R^*, which is *between* the free trade situation R and the protection situation R', while a_{ij} is derived from an input coefficient which is identical for the free trade and the protection situations.

The analysis which has been presented here is best thought of as an ingredient in a general equilibrium story. It yields the increase in the effective price of one product as a result of the protective structure. To know how resources will move requires this exercise to be carried out for all products so that one can obtain the *scale of effective rates*. These general equilibrium implications we shall develop further below. But let us for the moment see how it fits into the partial equilibrium analysis; this will give us, at least, some insight into the nature of the effects at work. It becomes then possible to close off the model. Draw a supply curve SS' for the value-added product in Fig. 6.4. Hence free trade output of this product is OQ. This output is inserted in Fig. 6.2, and is related to the ray Or appropriate to free trade, so obtaining the point K. The isoquant through K shows free trade output of j. If the tariff structure has raised the effective price to OT' (Fig. 6.4) output of the value-added product rises to OQ'. Inserting this in Fig. 6.2 and relating it to the ray Or' appropriate to the protection situation the point K' is obtained. It shows output of j and input i under protection.

One can get a little confused about this model and emerge with some pseudo-paradoxes. Note that in this case the physical ratio of value-added to gross output, that is the ratio v/j, has declined (since it must fall when i/v rises) but nevertheless the effective price has increased (the effective rate is positive), and this increase has induced the absolute amount of v to increase. It is also possible for the physical ratio of value-added to gross output to rise and the effective price to fall (the effective rate being negative), hence causing the absolute amount of v to decline. One apparent paradox emerges when one looks at what might happen to gross output. The effective rate might be positive, and yet gross output j could decline. The increase in the effective price will have increased v, but a rise in v/j may have been sufficient to lower j. A necessary but not sufficient condition for this result is that t_i is greater than t_j but not so much greater that it makes the effective rate negative. In the special case where t_i exceeds t_j just sufficiently to make the effective rate zero, v will stay constant and v/j will rise, so that gross output, j, must fall. (Of course, in general equilibrium, with tariffs on other products, a zero effective rate does not necessarily mean a constant v.) The effective rate indicates the change in the price of the value-added product, and in this case correctly predicts output changes in the latter. The concept is concerned with resource movements into the relevant *activity*, not with gross output.

The other apparent paradox arises when the effective rate is defined inappropriately. When there is substitution it is inappropriate to define it as the 'percentage increase in value-added per unit in an economic activity which is made possible by the tariff structure. . . .'[4] Let us call 'value-added per unit' in this sense $\bar{v}$ so that

$$\bar{v} = \frac{vp_v}{j}$$

If one defined the effective rate in this inappropriate way it would be $\Delta\bar{v}/\bar{v}$. When there are fixed coefficients, so that v/j is constant, $\Delta\bar{v}/\bar{v}$ will be equal to $\Delta p_v/p_v$, which is the effective rate as defined in this book. Hence the definition creates no problems for the fixed coefficient case for which it was originally developed. They will also be equal if $t_j = t_i$ for then there is no substitution. But with substitution, v/j may rise or fall and hence $\Delta\bar{v}/\bar{v}$ may be greater or less than $\Delta p_v/p_v$. In the example illustrated in the diagrams here, where $t_j > t_i$ (movement from R to R' in Fig. 6.3), v/j falls and $\Delta\bar{v}/\bar{v}$ is less than $\Delta p_v/p_v$. A number of writers have used the inappropriate definition for the substitution case and explored its implications.[5] They have found that when the production function is Cobb-Douglas, so that vp_v/jp_j stays constant whatever the tariff rates, we must always have $\Delta p_j/p_j = \Delta\bar{v}/\bar{v}$. Thus, with a Cobb-Douglas production function, the inappropriately defined effective rate is always equal to the nominal rate (since $t_j = \Delta p_j/p_j$) irrespective of the values of t_j and t_i or the input share—a paradox indeed . . . and yet of no importance since the definition of the effective rate used (when applied to the substitution case) is of no significance.

---

[4] Corden, op. cit., p. 222. The definition in this article referred to the fixed coefficient case, for which it is quite adequate.

[5] See W. P. Travis, 'The Effective Rate of Protection and the Question of Labor Protection in the United States', *Journal of Political Economy*, 76, May/June 1968, 443–61; and J. Anderson and S. Naya, 'Substitution and Two Concepts of Effective Rate of Protection', *American Economic Review*, 59, Sept. 1969, 607–12; and several other papers listed in the bibliography.

III. *Substitution Between Primary Factors and Traded Inputs:
The Questions Answered*

We now come to our two questions. The first question is how substitution between the value-added product and the traded input affects the size of the effective rate provided by a given protective structure. We must thus compare a situation where there is no substitution with one where there is. The analysis can also be used to show the effects on the effective rate of varying the elasticity of substitution.

Suppose we start in free trade with a particular set of prices and an input coefficient i/j and factor ratio i/v. In Fig. 6.3 the starting point is R. The slope of the tangent at R, $\beta\beta'$, is given by the factor ratio. If the ratio were fixed then the relationship between p_v/p_j and p_i/p_j would be a straight line one, given by $\beta\beta'$. On the other hand, when the elasticity of substitution is positive the relationship is given by a curve such as FF'. The greater the convexity of FF' from below the higher the elasticity of substitution, the line $\beta\beta'$ being the limiting case of zero elasticity of substitution.[6] Bearing in mind equation (3) above, the curvature tells us that if μ_i falls below G the factor ratio i/v will rise above its free trade level while if μ_i rises above G the factor ratio will fall below its free trade level.

Now consider the effects of tariffs. If $t_j > t_i$, then p_i/p_j will fall to a point such as OG' in Fig. 6.3. If there were fixed coefficients, p_v/p_j would then rise to OE'. But with substitution it rises to OH'. For a given rise in p_j, as determined by t_j, the increase in p_v (the effective rate, g_j) is thus greater with substitution than without. And it is clear that the more convex from below the FF' curve—that is, the greater the

---

[6] The elasticity of substitution of the production function is the reciprocal of the 'elasticity of substitution' on the curve FF' at its corresponding point. Thus, when the production function elasticity of substitution is zero the curve FF' is a straight line and its 'elasticity of substitution' is infinite.

Note that we are comparing various FF' curves with different curvatures, but all tangential to $\beta\beta'$ at R, and hence all yielding the same marginal products for the two inputs at one particular input ratio. In terms of an isoquant map, the slopes of the isoquants are identical at one input ratio, but vary at all other input ratios. It can be shown that this must mean that the production functions differ not just in respect of their elasticities of substitution; we cannot be holding everything constant and just varying the elasticity of substitution. In terms of the CES function the 'distribution parameters' must differ.

elasticity of substitution—the higher g_j would be. Exactly
the same result ensues when $t_j < t_i$. This time the movement
is to the right, to OG''. With fixed coefficients, p_v/p_j would
fall to OE'' while with substitution it actually falls to OH''.
A fall in the ratio p_v/p_j does not necessarily mean that the
effective rate is negative. All it means is that $g_j < t_j$. Substitution causes the ratio to fall less and so, for a given t_j, leads to a
higher effective rate g_j than with fixed coefficients. Thus it is
true that substitution causes the effective rate to be higher
relative to what it would be if there were fixed coefficients both
when $t_j > t_i$ and when $t_j < t_i$. Of course, when $t_j = t_i$ there is
no substitution so that it is irrelevant whether the production
function allows the possibility of substitution. When $t_j < t_i$,
it is also possible that the effective price falls; in that case
substitution will cause the effective price to fall less.

The simple economic explanation of our result is the same as
applied to the effects of substitution between traded inputs
in section I above which was also shown to increase the effective
rate. Substitution increases the choices open to the j industry.
The factor ratio of the free trade situation is still open to it,
but in addition, in adjusting to the new tariff situation it can
choose from other ratios. It can therefore increase its gain from
a tariff t_j on its own product or reduce its losses from an input
tariff t_i. These gains are measured by the effective rate; following
maximization principles it can obtain a higher effective rate
with substitution than without. If its effective price p_v falls,
perhaps because t_i is positive while t_j is zero, it can modify
the fall in the effective price and algebraically its effective
rate will be higher.

Our second question is what error in measurement results
from substitution between the value-added product and the
traded input. Again we refer to Fig. 6.3, beginning, as usual,
with the case where $t_j > t_i$, so that the movement is from
R to R'. We saw in the previous section that the correct
calculation of the effective rate requires use of the factor
ratio at the point R^* where FF' has the same slope as RR'.
With substitution this point must be somewhere between R
and R'. But if the data of the protection situation are used
for making calculations the factor ratio appropriate to the
point R' will be used. Now this ratio i/v will be higher than the

ratio at R^*. So if the ratio i/v is used to approximate to the latter ratio, there will be an overstatement. As a result the input share at free trade prices, a_{ij}^*, which is an ingredient in the effective rate formula, will be overstated. Referring to equation (12), if a_{ij}^* is overstated and $t_j > t_i$, then g_j will be overstated. Thus the use of the protection situation input coefficient or factor ratio leads to an overstatement of the effective rate. Next suppose that $t_j < t_i$ so that the movement is to the right in Fig. 6.3, from R to R''. The correct effective rate calculation would require a factor ratio which is given by the slope of the tangent to a point on FF' somewhere between R and R'', the tangent having the same slope as the line RR''. But the factor ratio i/v of the protection situation R'' will be lower than this, so that the input share a_{ij}^* will be understated. Referring to the effective rate formula (equation (12)), if a_{ij}^* is understated and $t_j < t_i$, then g_j will again be overstated. Thus the use of the data of the protection situation will lead to an overstatement of the effective rate irrespective of whether the substitution is towards i or v. A similar analysis will lead to the conclusion that the use of the free trade factor ratio, as given by the slope of $\beta\beta'$, will always lead to an understatement of the effective rate.[7]

This result fits in with our earlier result in section I that substitution between traded inputs leads to an overstatement of the effective rate if the data of the protection situation are used and an understatement if the data of the free trade situation are used. But it is still a little puzzling. Can it be related to the answer to our first question, that substitution raises effective rates? Let us look again at Fig. 6.3 and consider the movement from R to R' $(t_j > t_i)$. The correct factor ratio is given by the slope of RR'. This differs from the free trade

---

[7] This conclusion differs from that in Corden, op. cit., pp. 233–35. It was there argued that 'the effective rate should be the percentage rise in the return to the primary factor which would result if there were no substitution between inputs and, hence, if there were no change in the input coefficient' (p. 234). Given that definition, the use of the free trade coefficient leads to a correct calculation while the use of protection data leads to an overstatement. But in this book the effective rate is defined as the *actual* proportional increase in the return to the value-added product, taking substitution effects into account. J. C. Leith, in 'Substitution and Supply Elasticities in Calculating the Effective Protective Rate', *Quarterly Journal of Economics*, 82, Nov. 1968, 588–601, has used the same definition as in this book and arrived at the same answer.

ratio, given by the slope of $\beta\beta'$. The latter has shown us what would have been the result if the ratio had not changed. It was shown that a movement from the slope of $\beta\beta'$ to that of RR' would raise the effective rate. Now it follows that if a calculation is made on the basis of the tangent to R', which diverges in the same direction, *but more so*, from the slope of $\beta\beta'$, the effective rate thus calculated will be calculated even higher. The same argument applies when the movement is to R''. It follows also that if, for any reason, the free trade factor ratio were used to make the calculation the effective rate would be understated, the result being identical to what would have been the actual effective rate if there had been fixed cofficients.

We can thus sum up the answers to our two questions as follows. Substitution between the traded input and the value-added product always raises the effective rate but if the data of the protection situation are used then the increase in the effective rate owing to substitution will be overstated. Furthermore, the greater the elasticity of substitution over the relevant range, the greater the overstatement. This complication does not arise when $t_j = t_i$ for then, though substitution may be technically possible, there will not actually be any substitution. If the effective rate is negative the conclusion must be interpreted as meaning that substitution causes the effective price to fall less than it would with fixed coefficients, but that the use of the data of the protection situation will lead to an understatement of its fall, and indeed may yield a measured rate that is positive.

iv. *Negative Value-Added and Substitution*

How does the possibility of substitution affect the interpretation of the *negative value-added* phenomenon discussed in earlier chapters? It remains true that value-added at world prices can be negative in the protection situation. But it is no longer true that there would then necessarily be a negative effective price under free trade. If $t_j > t_i$ protection will have raised the factor ratio i/v, so that a restoration of free trade would lower the ratio, and with the lower free trade ratio the cost of the inputs may no longer exceed the value of the final product. Hence the high input coefficient under protection and so the high share of input costs may be the result of the substitution induced by the tariff structure.[8] It should be added that if we assume a production function with continuous substitution between v and i where the marginal products are always positive, there cannot be a negative effective price in any situation; a fall in p_v will always be modified sufficiently to avoid p_v becoming negative.

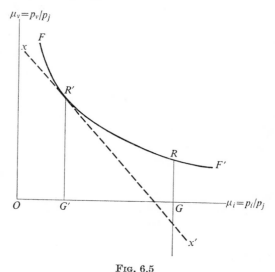

FIG. 6.5

These arguments can again be represented geometrically. We refer to Fig. 6.5, which is a version of the earlier Fig. 6.3, showing again the curve FF'. The free trade ratio p_i/p_j is given by OG and the free trade equilibrium is at the point R. We then suppose that a tariff t_j is imposed; for simplicity we can assume that $t_i = 0$ (though this is not essential to the argument). So p_i/p_j falls to OG' and the protection equilibrium

---

[8] The connection between substitution and negative value-added was first noted in G. Basevi, 'The United States Tariff Structure: Estimates of Effective Rates of Protection of United States Industries and Industrial Labor', *Review of Economics and Statistics*, 48, May 1966, p. 150, though not spelt out. For other discussions see S. E. Guisinger, 'Negative Value Added and the Theory of Effective Protection', *Quarterly Journal of Economics*, 83, Aug. 1969, 415–33; and A. H. H. Tan, 'Differential Tariffs, Negative Value-Added and the Theory of Effective Protection', *American Economic Review*, 60, March 1970, 107–16.

is at R'. Next draw the tangent to R', namely xx'. Let it inter-
sect the vertical through R below G, as drawn. Now suppose
that we start in the protection situation and our data include
the protection factor ratio represented by the slope xx'.
Assuming this factor ratio to be constant we could then work
back to the free trade situation by allowing t_j to be reduced to
zero, so bringing us back to OG. This would lead to the result
that p_v/p_j must be negative under free trade, as indicated by
the intersection of xx' with the vertical through R. It is the
result to which a calculation based on the protection factor
ratio would lead. But in fact the ratio would change in the
movement to free trade and p_v/p_j would be positive, namely
GR. And it is also clear that if FF' never touches the horizontal
axis—that is, the marginal product of v is always positive—
p_v must always be positive, whatever the ratio p_i/p_j.

v. *Substitution and General Equilibrium*

To present a coherent general equilibrium story we must
at this stage maintain the concept of the value-added product
and continue to think of value-added as having natural units.
The assumption behind this approach will be made clear in the
next section. Each traded product has its value-added product
and each value-added product has its price, the change in this
price brought about by the protective structure being its
effective protective rate. We have seen that for each product this
effective rate depends on the nominal tariff, on the tariffs on the
relevant inputs, and on the production function. In the fixed
coefficient case the production function could be summed up
by a single input-output coefficient (and hence a single factor
ratio) while in the substitution case there is a schedule of these
coefficients. This is the essential difference between the fixed
coefficient and the substitution case. Thus, when there is substitution the effective rate embodies certain reactions of the
industry to the protective structure. Changes in input coefficients are induced by the structure, and knowledge of these
changes is required to determine effective rates. We can thus
in principle obtain a scale of effective rates as in the fixed
coefficient case, this scale helping to determine the flow of
primary factors between the various industries. If we think of
a model with only two value-added products, the substitution

effect in each industry will influence the effective rate for each product, and primary factors will flow into the product with the higher effective rate. All this seems very simple, so that the introduction of substitution effects does not undermine the basic structure of the general equilibrium model as developed for the fixed coefficient case, even though it complicates the determination of the effective rate.

Nevertheless there is a serious difficulty. As has been stressed, the substitution effect creates a measurement error. If the data of the protection situation are used effective rates will be overstated. This would not create a problem if the proportionate extent of the error were the same for every product. But the errors may differ in size so that the order of industries in the measured scale of effective rates may not be the same as the order in the scale of correct effective rates. In the two-product model the measured effective rate for A may be less than that for B but the substitution elasticity in A may be very low and in B very high, so that the true effective rate of A may be higher than the true rate of B. It follows that the protective structure will actually have drawn resources from B into A and not the other way, as seemed to be suggested by the measured effective rates. More generally, we can conceive of one scale of measured effective rates and another of correct effective rates, the latter being generally below the former and possibly displaying industries in a different order.

Further research involving calculations with various plausible substitution elasticities and protective structures is needed to determine how important this consideration is.[9] Provisionally

___

[9] See J. C. Leith, 'Substitution and Supply Elasticities in Calculating the Effective Protective Rate', *Quarterly Journal of Economics*, 82, Nov. 1968, 588–601; B. Balassa, S. Guisinger, and D. Schydlowsky, 'The Effective Rates of Protection and the Question of Labor Protection in the United States: A Comment', *Journal of Political Economy*, 78, Sept./Oct. 1970; H. G. Grubel and P. J. Lloyd, 'Factor Substitution and Effective Tariff Rates', *forthcoming*. The latter have made some calculations using CES production functions which suggest that, for plausible substitution elasticities, substitution effects may not make a great deal of difference. But what is plausible? This hinges, among other things, on how narrowly or widely a 'product' is defined. An empirical test of the hypothesis that protection, by raising the prices of finished products more than those of their raw material inputs, causes significant substitution of raw materials for other factors of production, is in W. P. Travis, *The Theory of Trade and Protection* (Harvard University Press, Cambridge, 1964), Ch. VI, and the hypothesis seems to find some support. But Travis' evidence has been

one can suggest that the analysis of the effects of a protective structure be carried out with the use of measured effective rates but that some downward adjustments might be made in those cases where substitution effects are believed to be very important. Substitution may be important either because the elasticity of substitution is high or because the incentive to substitute is high owing to a large dispersion of the relevant tariffs.

VI. *Biased Substitution Effects and the 'Value-added Product' Concept*

Is the concept of the 'value-added product' useful or valid? Assume that we have a three-factor production function, product j being produced by one produced input i and by two primary factors, L and K. The value-added product is supposed to sum up the contribution of the two primary factors. Thus we say that j is produced by i and v, and v in turn is produced by L and K. But what is the unit of v? This indeed presents no problem when there are fixed coefficients between j and i. The unit of v is then the unit of the final product, v being simply the output of j less the input i. A higher price of j, owing to a tariff t_j, increases the amount available for the primary factor content in j, that is for v. No problem is presented by the fact that v itself can be produced in varying proportions of L to K. All those combinations of L and K which are just sufficient to produce one unit of j, when associated with the fixed amount of i, represent one unit of v.

The problem becomes more complicated when the ratio i/j is not fixed. What then is a unit of v, bearing in mind that it has no 'natural units'? The v/j ratio would change if relative prices changed, so we cannot define a unit of v in terms of units of j. It would appear that a unit of j can be produced with

---

re-examined in Balassa, Guisinger and Schydlowsky, op. cit., and they conclude that substitution does not appear to be important. The various studies in B. Balassa (ed.), *The Structure of Protection in Developing Countries*, 1971, do not suggest that the orders in the scales of effective rates of the countries concerned are greatly affected by whether 'standardized' (possibly an approximation to 'free trade') input-output coefficients or domestic (protection situation) coefficients are used.

differing amounts of v, an increase in the v/j ratio being associated with a decrease in the i/j ratio. The solution so far has been to assume that v has natural units, so that it can in principle be measured. But this was clearly an evasion. It has been argued that

'the root fallacy in the concept of effective protection is that it seeks to show how the price of value-added is affected by the tariff, when in fact there is no such thing as the price of value-added, for value-added has no natural unit. The economy generates prices only of goods and of primary factors.'[10]

So we must now look for a way of justifying the use of the 'value-added product' concept even when there is substitution. We shall now make the following crucial assumption. The ratio between the primary factors in industry j, that is, the L/K ratio, will change only if the price ratio between L and K alters, and the ratio between the produced input i and the final good j, that is the input coefficient i/j, will alter only if the price ratio between these two, the p_i/p_j ratio, alters. Hence the production function has the special form $J[V(K, L), i]$ where K and L are the amounts of the two primary factors, i is the amount of the produced input, and J and V are linear homogeneous functions of their respective arguments. Thus, suppose that the price ratio between L and K is in fact given from outside. Now a protective structure is imposed so that $t_j > t_i$. In our earlier analysis we would have said that this would lead to substitution of i for v since p_v will rise more than p_i. Now we can say that it will lead to substitution of i for both L and K to the same extent, so that the L/K quantity ratio will not change provided the L/K price ratio does not change. We can define v in this case as a bundle of L and K containing the two factors in fixed proportions.

But this is not the whole story. Effective protection for j increases the demand of the industry for the two primary factors. Similarly effective protection for other industries

---

[10] W. P. Travis, 'The Effective Rate of Protection and the Question of Labor Protection in the United States', *Journal of Political Economy*, 76, May/June 1968, p. 448. The problem is not new. See P. A. David, 'Measuring Real Net Output: A Proposed Index', *Review of Economics and Statistics*, 48, Nov. 1966, 419–25, for a general discussion of the problem of measuring *net* output (value-added) in real terms.

affects the demands for L and K. All this can initially be thought of as happening at a constant L/K price ratio. But the net result will be for the demand for one factor to expand relatively to that for another. Thus, in a two-product model, suppose that the effective rate for A is higher than that for B and that A is labour-intensive, in the sense that the L/K ratio is higher in A than in B. It will then be necessary for the price of L to rise relative to the price of K so as to maintain equilibrium in the factor markets. As the L/K price ratio changes there will be substitution in industry j between the two factors. How then can we talk about a bundle of primary factors in fixed proportions? We can handle this by holding constant now the prices of j and i, while allowing the L/K price ratio to change. We must remember that by assumption the i/j coefficient will not be affected by the change in the L/K price ratio. Hence we can say that a unit of v is all those combinations of L and K that can produce a unit of j, together with the appropriate amount of i, given the ratio i/j established by the p_i/p_j price ratio. All this seems a little complicated, but there is not really any logical difficulty provided we grant the assumption that the L/K quantity ratio depends only on the L/K price ratio and the i/j coefficient depends only on the p_i/p_j price ratio. It means that the elasticity of substitution of i for L is the same as the elasticity of substitution of i for K. The substitution effects are *unbiased*. The fictional concept of the value-added product, with the two-stage production function, is a convenient way of presenting our argument so as to yield the same result as would follow from making this assumption.[11]

If we remove this assumption complications result.[12] If the produced input is a much closer substitute for one primary factor than for another, and if the price of the produced input alters—that is, there is a tariff or import subsidy on it— then the technique of the value-added product, if crudely

[11] R. W. Jones, in 'Effective Protection and Substitution', *Journal of International Economics*, 1, 1971, shows in detail that the value-added concept has meaning even with substitution, and (if properly applied) even when substitution effects are biased.

[12] The subsequent discussion owes a great deal to the article by Jones, op. cit. The reader is referred to this important article for a much more thorough and rigorous analysis, only the main conclusions being indicated here.

applied, could give a misleading result. Consider an economy with two industries, A and B, each of which uses an imported input. B is the export industry. Suppose that A obtains positive effective protection, whether calculated at free trade or at protection coefficients, while effective protection for industry B is zero. In the unbiased case we would expect some quantities of both primary factors to move from B to A, though it is indeed possible that gross output of A falls for reasons explained earlier. But with respect to resource allocation effects there could be no paradox. Now allow for biased substitution effects, supposing that A's imported input is a much closer substitute for L than for K. We can now display the possibility of a paradoxical result.[13] Conceivably resources (or, at least one of the primary factors) could move from A to B. To narrow the problem down, assume that nominal protection for B and the tariff on its input are both zero. But the tariff on A's input is positive and its nominal tariff is sufficiently high for its effective rate to be positive. Also assume that A is labour-intensive, the L/K ratio in A being greater than that in B. Now there are two forces at work affecting the resource movement. The first might be called the *normal* effect. For reasons that follow from all our earlier analysis resources will tend to move from the industry with the zero effective rate to the one with the positive rate. The greater the nominal tariff on A and the lower the tariff on its input the stronger this normal effect. But now there is a second effect, the *bias effect*. This may pull in the same direction as the normal effect or may pull in the opposite direction. In our example it can be shown to pull in the opposite direction. The price of A's imported input has gone up because of the positive input tariff. Mainly labour will be substituted for this input since labour is a closer substitute for it than is capital. At a given ratio of the primary factor prices A will raise its L/K ratio. But this makes labour scarce relative to capital in the

<hr>

[13] The possibility of a paradoxical result was first indicated in V. K. Ramaswami and T. N. Srinivasan, 'Tariff Structure and Resource Allocation in the Presence of Factor Substitution', in J. Bhagwati, et al. (eds.), *Trade, Balance of Payments and Growth: Papers in Honor of Charles Kindleberger* (M.I.T. Press, Cambridge, 1970). The exploration of biased substitution effects in this chapter, and by Jones, was inspired by an attempt to explain their results.

economy as a whole. To accommodate this relative labour scarcity the size of the labour-intensive industry must contract and of the capital-intensive industry must expand. The effect is not unlike that of a labour-using bias in technical progress. Since A happens to be the labour-intensive industry in our example the *bias effect* thus creates a tendency for A to lose resources. Bearing in mind that the *normal effect* sets up the opposite tendency, on balance resources may move in either direction. Given that there is a positive tariff on A's input, the sign of the *bias effect* depends on whether the input is a closer substitute for K or for L and whether A is labour-intensive or capital-intensive. The bias effect works in the opposite direction from the normal effect if the input is a relatively closer substitute for that primary factor of production in which A is intensive. If there were an import subsidy, the bias effect would work in the opposite direction from the normal effect if the input were a relatively closer substitute for that primary factor in which B is intensive. All this assumes that A obtains positive effective protection, so that the normal effect causes resources to move into A. There are of course numerous possible combinations of cases one might consider, but let us here continue to assume that A's effective protection and the tariff on its input are positive, while for B these are zero. Then one can say that (a) the higher A's nominal tariff the higher its effective rate and hence the greater the strength of the normal effect, and (b) the higher the tariff on A's input, (i) the less the strength of the normal effect because a high input tariff means a low effective rate, and (ii) the greater the strength of the bias effect, which may of course pull either way depending on the substitution bias in relation to relative factor-intensities.

The general conclusion is that even in a two-sector model the direction of resource pulls may depend not just on relative effective rates, but also on biases in substitution effects and on relative factor-intensities. One can no longer look at each product, with its tariff and production function, separately and build up a scale of adjusted effective rates which can form the basis for a general equilibrium analysis. The complication is that the direction of resource movement depends also on relative factor-intensities. One question is whether biased substitution effects are important in practice. To obtain paradoxical results for given relative factor-intensities the biases must be of particular form and sufficiently large.[14] Furthermore, input tariffs must be sufficiently high or changes in them significant. This consideration is important in a world of escalated tariff structures where input tariffs tend to be low relative to nominal tariffs on final goods or using industries. For practical work it may be reasonable to assume that substitution effects are not significantly biased, but in special cases, where input tariffs are high, substitution effects are believed to be large and biased, and relative factor intensities significantly different, some modifications to our simple analysis could be introduced.

[14] Ramaswami and Srinivasan, op. cit., give several examples of biased substitution effects and believe them to be important. See Jones, op. cit., for a precise statement of necessary conditions for the paradox.

7

NON-TRADED INPUTS AND OTHER
COMPLICATIONS

In Chapters 3, 4 and 5 the three assumptions of fixed input-output coefficients, absence of non-traded produced inputs and given prices of traded goods in world markets greatly simplified the analysis. We have seen in the previous chapter that abandoning the first of these assumptions has led to some difficulties. We shall here remove the other two assumptions, while restoring the first (except in section III).

I. *Backward Linkage and Input Effective Rates*

The assumption that there are no non-traded produced inputs (such as services, or electricity) into traded goods has meant, together with the assumption of infinite elasticities of foreign import supply and export demand, that the prices of all produced inputs have been given from outside the system, altered only by tariffs and other trade taxes or subsidies. It has meant that the increase in the domestic price of a final good brought about by a tariff has gone wholly to raise the price of its value-added product, and not at all the prices of its produced inputs. Hence by expressing the whole of this increase as a proportion of the initial price of the value-added product we have obtained the proportional change in the price of the latter—that is, the effective protective rate.

Now we must introduce non-traded inputs. The main point is simply that the prices of non-traded goods, just like the prices of the primary factors, are determined within the system while—given the small country assumption—the prices of traded goods are given as parameters, changed only by taxes and subsidies on trade. Thus there is a sharp distinction between non-traded and traded produced inputs, a distinction which rests essentially on different assumptions about their elasticities of supply to the using industries. The distinction is much sharper between them than between non-traded inputs and primary factors. The distinction will be somewhat blurred later, but for the moment let us maintain it by assuming that any industry can obtain any amount of a traded input without raising the price against itself, but to obtain extra quantities of a non-traded input it must always pay a higher price.

Suppose then that a tariff is imposed on cloth or, if it is an exportable, that it is given an export subsidy. This increases the demand for yarn and other produced inputs which are important in the weaving industry. Yarn may be mainly produced domestically, but provided there are some imports or exports of it the world price will set the domestic price and so its price will not rise as a result of the extra demand from domestic weavers. Hence its domestic production will not change. Rather imports will rise or exports will fall. By contrast, another input, say power or a service of some kind, may not be traded at all, and extra demand from weavers will raise its price and so lead to extra output. Thus the tariff on cloth *indirectly protects* those industries producing non-traded inputs for the cloth industry. The consequences of the tariff or export subsidy on the final good filter back down that part of the input-output structure where there are non-traded goods. There is *backward linkage* within the country. This useful concept, first introduced by Hirschman[1] in another context, means that the expansion of industry X, perhaps because of a tariff, leads to expansion of domestic industry Y which produces an input into X. The demand for the product of industry Y is a derived demand. And if industry Z produces a non-traded input for industry Y then there will be further backward linkage towards Z, and indirectly industry Z will also have been protected. The main point here is that, given our present assumptions, the domestic backward linkage is only towards non-traded inputs, not traded inputs. In the latter case, if the input is an importable, there is linkage, but it goes outside the country.

If we think in general equilibrium terms we can say that protection of an industry not only raises the relative prices

[1] A. Hirschman, *The Strategy of Economic Development* (Yale University Press, New Haven, 1958), Ch. 6.

of those primary factors in which the industry is intensive, but through backward linkage also raises the relative prices of those non-traded inputs in which the industry is intensive. Non-traded goods are now indirectly protected or anti-protected in four ways by a protective structure, the first three having been described in Chapter 4, section VIII, and the fourth being the new backward linkage effect: positive effective protection of traded goods leads to additional demand for non-traded inputs; those non-traded inputs intensive in the protected industries will rise in price relative to the general price-level in the non-traded sector. The combination of all four effects will give rise to an appropriate exchange rate adjustment which will have further effects on the non-traded sector. In Chapter 5 it was suggested that if the net effective rate is positive an activity producing a traded good is protected relative to the non-traded sector as a whole, assuming that the average price-level of non-traded goods stays constant. Now it must be stressed that it will not be protected relative to all non-traded goods. Notably it will not necessarily be protected relative to those non-traded industries into which resources are likely to have moved because they produce inputs for highly protected traded industries.

Non-traded inputs create difficulties for the concept of the effective protective rate and reduce its usefulness. Let us first look at the matter in simple partial equilibrium terms, bearing in mind that this discussion will subsequently be qualified for general equilibrium effects. We have a final product j, produced by three inputs, namely the value-added product v, a traded input i and a non-traded input h. There is a supply curve facing the industry for each of these inputs, the supply elasticity being infinite for i and positive but less than infinite for v and h. Define units so that one unit of each input is required for a unit of j. The initial free trade prices are p_j, p_v, p_i and p_h and the initial shares of each of the inputs in the cost of j are respectively a_{vj}, a_{ij}, a_{hj} (which sum to unity). The elasticities of supply of v and h facing the industry are respectively s_v and s_h. A tariff t_j is then imposed, with no tariff on i. As a result the price of j rises by dp_j, this being divided up between a rise in the price of v and a rise in the price of h $(dp_v + dp_h = dp_j)$.

Now, what is the effective protective rate? Protection is being given both to v and to h, both of which move upwards along their supply curves, so we cannot just treat the non-traded input h as if it were traded, and then proceed to use our old formula. This would yield t_j/a_{vj}; it would imply incorrectly that the whole of the price rise has gone to the value-added product, and so would yield a higher figure than any of the preferable measures to be suggested here. The obvious approach appears to be to calculate an effective rate for each of the two protected inputs, v and h. This would simply measure the proportionate price rises of these two inputs. Denoting these *input effective rates* as g_v and g_h and the proportionate rise in output resulting from the tariff t_j as $\mathrm{d}q/q$, we would then get the following results:
If

$$t_j = \mathrm{d}p_j/p_j \qquad (1)$$

$$\mathrm{d}p_j = \mathrm{d}p_v + \mathrm{d}p_h \qquad (2)$$

$$s_v = \frac{\mathrm{d}q}{q}\frac{p_v}{\mathrm{d}p_v} \qquad (3)$$

$$s_h = \frac{\mathrm{d}q}{q}\frac{p_h}{\mathrm{d}p_h} \qquad (4)$$

$$g_v = \mathrm{d}p_v/p_v \qquad (5)$$

$$g_h = \mathrm{d}p_h/p_h \qquad (6)$$

$$a_{vj} = p_v/p_j \qquad (7)$$

$$a_{hj} = p_h/p_j \qquad (8)$$

Then, from (1) to (8), with a little manipulation:

$$g_v = \frac{t_j}{a_{vj} + a_{hj}\dfrac{s_v}{s_h}} \qquad (9)$$

and

$$g_h = \frac{t_j}{a_{hj} + a_{vj}\dfrac{s_h}{s_v}} \qquad (10)$$

So (9) and (10) tell us that the two *input effective rates* depend not only on the nominal tariff on the final good, t_j, and on the appropriate input shares, but also on the ratio between the two supply elasticities. The greater the supply elasticity for an input, given the supply elasticity of the other input, the lower its effective rate. If the two supply elasticities were equal, then the two effective rates would be equal. If not, then the input with the relatively lower supply elasticity would have the relatively higher effective rate.[2] A tariff on the traded input i can be introduced easily without affecting these conclusions, except that for t_j we must then write $(t_j - a_{ij}t_i)$, since (9) and (10) then become:

$$g_v = \frac{t_j - a_{ij}t_i}{a_{vj} + a_{hj}\dfrac{s_v}{s_h}} \tag{9.1}$$

$$g_h = \frac{t_j - a_{ij}t_i}{a_{hj} + a_{vj}\dfrac{s_h}{s_v}} \tag{10.1}$$

There are two difficulties about this approach. The first is that there will now be many effective rates for any final product, one for each non-traded input and at least one for the value-added product. Indeed, if one were consistent one would extend this method to the various primary factors, so forgoing the concept of the 'value-added product' and calculating or at least conceiving of a separate effective rate for each factor. Any simplicity in our new approach to the theory of tariffs will then be lost. The second difficulty is that each input effective rate depends not only on the elasticity of supply of the input concerned—and even that is an additional and not easily calculable variable which did not enter into the effective

---

[2] This partial equilibrium approach is used in B. Massell, 'The Resource-Allocative Effects of a Tariff and the Effective Protection of Individual Inputs', *Economic Record*, 44, Sept. 1968, 369–76. Massell uses the model to show how the proportionate rise in output, dq/q in our notation, (which is equal, given fixed coefficients, to the proportionate increase in factor inputs) depends on the final good tariff, the input supply elasticities and the input shares. Thus, one could derive from (1) to (8)

$$\frac{dq}{q} = \frac{t_j}{\dfrac{a_{vj}}{s_h} + \dfrac{a_h}{s_j}} \tag{9.2}$$

He uses the term *input effective rate*, but in his terms the input effective rate for v would be dp_j/p_v and for h dp_j/p_h. It has then, of course, a different meaning from that in this chapter. See also J. C. Leith, 'Substitution and Supply Elasticities in Calculating the Effective Protective Rate', *Quarterly Journal of Economics*, 82, Nov. 1968, pp. 590–91.

rate concept developed in the previous chapters—but it depends also on the supply elasticities of all the other non-traded inputs, including the value-added product. The effective rate ceases to be a conveniently simple measure which provides some indication of the resource allocation effects of a tariff structure. It requires now so much information that if this were indeed obtainable one might as well go on and calculate directly the resource allocation effects themselves.

Once we move to the general equilibrium system, the concept of input effective rates breaks down completely. The supply curve of an input facing any particular industry is then no longer given but depends on the tariffs elsewhere in the system. It would be meaningless to construct a scale of effective rates, for example, each calculation assuming that there are no other tariffs. If one wanted to know the effects of the whole tariff structure on the prices of the various non-traded inputs and value-added products, and on the prices of the primary factors, one would have to solve the whole system. The effective rates then emerge from the solution rather than helping one to assess the nature of the solution without having to solve it completely.[3]

II. *Non-Traded Inputs and the Measurement of Effective Protection*

The input effective rate is not a useful technique for a general equilibrium model. A preferable approach is to lump together all the inputs which are protected by a tariff and treat them as one. This is a logical extension of the method which has already been used with the concept of the 'value-added product', which lumps together all the primary inputs. This approach was suggested in the author's 1966 article and may be

---

[3] The general equilibrium solution would yield the proportional increases in all primary factor prices resulting from the protective structure, (some money price or average of prices, such as that of all non-traded goods, or all factors—i.e. money income—would have to be held constant). One might describe these as the *rates of factorial protection*. These are really general equilibrium rates of input effective rates; they do not seem to be measurable given the normal amount of data available and in the absence of the opportunity to experiment with the removal of the protective structure. On this subject, see W. P. Travis, 'The Effective Rate of Protection and the Question of Labor Protection in the United States', *Journal of Political Economy*, 76, May/June 1968, p. 450.

called the *Corden method*.[4] The argument is that the effects of a tariff on non-traded inputs are basically the same as the effects on the primary inputs so there is good reason for treating them in the same way. Protection for an activity producing a traded product represents not only protection for those primary factors intensive in that activity but also protection for those industries producing non-traded inputs in which that activity is intensive and thus, indirectly, protection for the primary factors intensive in these non-traded input industries. There is, thus, a complete identity between primary factors and non-traded input industries.

In our example this approach means combining v and h, and defining the effective rate g_j as $\mathrm{d}p_j/(p_v+p_h) = t_j/(a_{vj}+a_{hj}) = t_j/(1-a_{ij})$.

If $s_v = s_h$ then $g_v = g_j = g_h$
If $s_v > s_h$ then $g_v > g_j > g_h$
If $s_v < s_h$ then $g_v < g_j < g_h$

The essence of the distinction between traded and non-traded inputs stems from the two assumptions that foreign trade elasticities are infinite and that non-traded inputs are not in infinitely elastic supply. The tariff protects not only primary factors but also those non-traded inputs (and hence their factors) which are intensive in the using industries. But, unless one solves the whole system, the effects on the primary factors and the non-traded inputs cannot be separated out. Unless there are two inputs only and one is in infinitely elastic supply so that its price does not rise when the price of the output rises, it is impossible, short of such a total solution, to distinguish the effective protective rate for different inputs. For each product one can talk only about a single effective rate for all those inputs combined which are not in infinitely elastic supply to the industry.

If there are traded inputs in those non-traded goods which are themselves inputs in traded goods industries, this matter becomes more complicated. Only that part of the value of the non-traded input which is value-added by primary factors directly and indirectly (that is, via non-traded inputs into

---

[4] W. M. Corden, 'The Structure of a Tariff System and the Effective Protective Rate', *Journal of Political Economy*, 74, June 1966, pp. 226–228.

these non-traded inputs, and so on) should be treated like a primary factor and so grouped with value-added in the protected industry. In other words, ideally one should go down the input-output structure until one reaches a traded input. The share of traded inputs (a_{ij} in our formula so far) must be calculated as including the traded input content in non-traded inputs. This may be described as the *indirect traded input* content. For example, if 20 per cent of the cost of the final product is made up of direct traded inputs and 30 per cent of non-traded inputs, and if 50 per cent of the cost of these non-traded inputs consists in turn of traded inputs while the rest is value-added product, then the total traded input share for the final product is 35 per cent. To obtain the value-added share for our formula all direct contributions by primary factors should in principle be summed with all indirect contributions by primary factors through non-traded inputs. In the summation process traded inputs (even though they may actually be produced domestically) should be treated as leakages. Furthermore, tariffs on the indirect traded inputs must be taken into account. They have the same effect on effective protection of the final product as tariffs on direct traded inputs. In our example, a tariff of 33⅓ per cent on the indirect traded input (assuming no other tariffs) would give negative effective protection of 7·7 per cent for the final good.[5]

Failure to take *indirect traded inputs* into account when making calculations of effective rates by the Corden method may lead to measurement error. If there were no tariffs or export subsidies on the indirect traded inputs concerned it would lead to understatement. Suppose that there is a tariff t_j on the final good and no tariff on the direct traded input. The increase in the price dp_j would then be wrongly expressed as a proportion of $(p_v + p_h)$ where p_v refers to the value-added

---

[5] If t_j = nominal tariff, t_i = tariff on direct traded input, t_w = tariff on indirect traded input, a_{ij} = share of the traded input in cost of final good at free trade prices, a_{hj} = share of non-traded input, and w = share of the indirect traded input cost in the non-traded input, then

$$g_j = \frac{t_j - (a_{ij}t_i + wa_{hj}t_w)}{1 - (a_{ij} + wa_{hj})}$$

In the example, $t_j = t_i = 0$; $t_w = 33\frac{1}{3}$ per cent; $a_{ij} = 20$ per cent; $a_{hj} = 30$ per cent; $w = 50$ per cent. Hence g_j = approx. −7·7 per cent.

product of the industry concerned and p_h to the whole of the non-traded input. The correct calculation requires it to be related to p_v plus the truly non-traded element in p_h. Thus the wrong calculation will lead to a larger denominator and hence an understatement. But tariffs or export subsidies on the indirect traded inputs are cost-increasing and reduce effective rates, so that failure to take them into account leads to a larger numerator and hence overstatement of effective rates. On balance, neglect of indirect traded inputs when using the Corden method may lead to understatement or over-statement of effective rates.

One wonders whether there is not a way of rescuing the effective rate as a concept that refers to value-added in one industry only rather than incorporating the effects on the non-traded sector.[6] One alternative approach, already rejected, is that of input effective rates. Another is the *Balassa method*.[7] It is assumed that non-traded inputs are in infinitely elastic supply so that they can be treated just like traded inputs. But is this a reasonable assumption? There may be excess capacity in an input industry, implying a departure from our full employment assumptions. Alternatively, increasing returns to scale in the input industry may offset its rising factor costs as it expands; the input industry is then protected by a tariff for the using industry, though its price does not rise as a result of the tariff; it could then be treated like a traded input since the whole of the price increase goes to other inputs. But the difficulty in the general equilibrium model in treating some non-traded inputs in the same way as traded inputs is that a devaluation, while raising the domestic prices of all traded goods in an equal

---

[6] See Massell, op. cit., for a criticism of the Corden method and especially the weight it places on the 'finite-infinite dichotomy'. 'On a theoretical level, it is mathematically unsatisfactory to base a qualitative distinction on what is in fact only a limiting case. Moreover, there is the analogous empirical problem of how to distinguish between an elasticity that is finite-but-very large and an elasticity that is infinite.' (p. 370.)

[7] The method was used originally in B. Balassa, 'Tariff Protection in Industrial Countries: An Evaluation', *Journal of Political Economy*, 73, Dec. 1965, 573–94, and is also used in J. R. Melvin and B. W. Wilkinson, *Effective Protection in the Canadian Economy* (Economic Council of Canada, Ottawa, 1968) and in various other calculations (for example, in Australia). In the studies in B. Balassa (ed.), *The Structure of Protection in Developing Countries*, 1971, and in J. Bhagwati and P. Desai, *India: Planning for Industrialisation*, 1970, alternative figures using the Balassa and the Corden method are given.

proportion does not raise the prices of non-traded inputs. The scale of net effective rates will then differ from the scale of effective rates. For this reason alone it is probably desirable, if we are thinking in general equilibrium terms, always to group non-traded inputs with primary factors rather than with traded inputs.

If we take a very partial view, rather than being concerned with the whole tariff structure, then certainly some non-traded inputs may be in infinitely elastic supply to an industry, as indeed may be some primary factors, and they could then be grouped with the traded inputs. Furthermore, the difficulty of separating traded from non-traded inputs may compel use of the Balassa method.[8] Measured effective rates will then be higher than those resulting from the Corden method. Consider a simple example where there is a tariff t_j on the final good, no tariff on the traded input and no indirect traded inputs. The tariff raises the price by dp_j, the increase going partly to the industry's own value-added element and partly to the non-traded input. With the Corden method the effective rate is $dp_j/(p_v+p_h)$ while with the Balassa method it is dp_j/p_v. The latter must exceed the former as long as there is any non-traded content. In practice non-traded inputs can be quite important and the two methods can lead to substantially different results.[9] Insofar as there are indirect traded inputs on which there are no tariffs or export subsidies the overstatement resulting from the Balassa method will be reduced. On the other hand, the method neglects tariffs on the indirect traded inputs, since it treats non-traded inputs as if they were traded inputs without tariffs. Such tariffs lead it into overstating effective rates even more. One can conclude that the Balassa method must lead to an overstatement of effective rates for two reasons, first because it does not put any of the non-traded input content into the

[8] In practice the main difficulty is concerned with indirect traded inputs; it is not too difficult to identify the main direct non-traded inputs. See Balassa (ed.), op. cit.

[9] See I. Little, T. Scitovsky and M. Scott, *Industry and Trade in Some Developing Countries*, 1970, p. 430, for a table comparing effective tariff averages for seven countries using the two methods. See also S. R. Lewis and S. E. Guisinger, 'Measuring Protection in a Developing Country: The Case of Pakistan', *Journal of Political Economy*, 76, Nov./Dec. 1968, 1170–98; and Balassa (ed.), op. cit. Use of the Balassa method generally (especially in the case of Pakistan) has led to much higher figures than use of the Corden method.

denominator for the effective rate calculation when at least part of this content should be put in, and secondly because it neglects the negative effect on the numerator of tariffs or export subsidies on indirect traded inputs.

Another possibility is the *Scott method*.[10] Let us assume that there is only one non-traded good in the economy and that it is an input into various traded goods. We know that the imposition of a protective structure may require the relative price of this sole non-traded good to change. This change can take place either by holding the exchange rate constant and allowing the money price of the non-traded good to alter or by holding the money price of the non-traded good constant and allowing the exchange rate to alter (or some combination of these two). It will be convenient here to assume the mechanism to be the first one and that, as one might expect, the imposition of the protective structure required the money price of the non-traded good to rise, say by 10 per cent. (This is the same as the *devaluation rate* of Chapter 5). It is as if there has been a 10 per cent tariff on the non-traded input. Hence we should make our calculations in the protection situation as if the ruling price of the non-traded good incorporated a 10 per cent tariff, since, if the protective structure were removed, the price of the non-traded good would have to fall by 9·1 per cent.[11]

This approach is simple since it allows all non-traded inputs to be treated like traded inputs which have had their prices raised by a uniform tariff and export subsidy equal to the devaluation rate. Its usefulness hinges on the reasonableness

[10] Little, Scitovsky, Scott, op. cit., pp. 430–2, where it is called the 'ideal' method.

[11] It would be more awkward, though in line with the method of Chapter 5, to assume exchange rate adjustment and a constant money price of the non-traded good. One would first calculate effective rates as if the non-traded good were like a traded good with zero tariff, so getting a scale of effective rates. Then one would allow for the devaluation adjustment, which would raise the prices of all final goods and traded inputs, but leave the price of the non-traded good unaffected. For each product a *net* effective rate would result. Since the price of the non-traded good is constant this net rate will not be derived in a simple way from the ordinary effective rate and the devaluation adjustment as in Chapter 5. The order in the scale will alter: those goods with a relatively large non-traded content will have lower places in the scale of net rates than in the original scale. But the scale of net rates indicates the resource allocation effects.

of its central assumption. It is not strictly necessary to have a single non-traded good in the economy. There may be many different non-traded inputs, but their relative prices must not change as a result of a protective structure. Hence the input intensities—the ratios to each other at which different non-traded inputs are employed at given relative prices—must be the same for all traded goods. A change in the pattern of output of traded goods must not alter the pattern of prices within the non-traded sector so that one can conduct the analysis as if there were a single price. This approach really neglects the *indirect protection* effects of a protective structure but may be justified if there is no particular reason to expect a protective structure to alter the price relationships between non-traded goods.

III. *Substitution Between Non-traded and Traded Inputs*

What is the effect of substitution between non-traded and traded inputs? This question brings together the complications of Chapter 6 and the present chapter. It is an important question because the following situation is rather common. We may have an input which is domestically produced and is of a kind peculiarly suited to the domestic market. Hence there are no exports of it. Furthermore foreigners are not able to produce an identical product, so that there are no imports. But there are imports of a somewhat similar product which is a close substitute for it. Thus we have a non-traded input and a traded input, perhaps both belonging to the same product category but just somewhat differentiated from each other. How does this particular substitution influence effective protective rates?

At a simple level the answer is also simple and requires no further formal proof. It has been argued that non-traded inputs are essentially like primary factors, and for the purpose of effective rates should be lumped together with the value-added product. In a model where final good j is produced by three inputs, namely the value-added product v, the non-traded input h and the traded input i, the effective rate then refers to protection for v and h combined. It follows that if there is substitution either between v and i or between h and i the analysis of Chapter 6 applies completely: substitution raises effective rates and if protection data are used will lead to an overstatement. The closer substitutes h and i are the higher the effective rate.

It may be useful to move beyond this approach to consider the effects on v and h separately in terms of *input effective rates*, one for v and one for h, bearing in mind of course the partial equilibrium nature of this analysis. Suppose t_j is imposed, so that p_j rises while there is no tariff on i. Demand for v, h and i then increases. Given fixed coefficients, the prices of v and h rise, the proportional increases depending on the initial shares and the supply elasticities, as outlined in section I above. If there is substitution between i and h the input coefficient for h will fall and for i will rise. This means that the input effective rate for h will fall *relative to* the input effective rate for v. The rate for them together must, on the basis of our earlier argument, rise. Now it was also shown earlier that this effective rate for the two together must be between the two input rates. It follows that substitution clearly raises the input rate for v but apparently may raise or lower the rate for h. It would need an elaborate analysis to define precisely the conditions in which dp_h/p_h would rise or fall owing to substitution. But consider the case where the elasticity of substitution between h and i is very high. Then clearly, as the demand for h and i rises owing to the tariff t_j and as consequently h moves up its supply curve so that its price rises, there will be heavy substitution of i for h, hence greatly modifying the price rise of h. In the extreme case where h is a perfect substitute for i the input rate for h will be zero. Since the price of i is given the price of h cannot increase. So increasing substitutability, at least beyond a certain point, reduces the protection for h while at the same time increasing the protection for v.

iv. *Conversion of Non-traded into Traded Inputs*

Tariffs (or other trade taxes or subsidies) may convert non-traded inputs into traded inputs or vice versa. As already discussed in Chapter 4 with respect to final goods, the line between traded and non-traded goods is by no means as clear-cut as our simpler approaches suggest and as would be desirable for a simple theory of protective structure.

The effects can usefully be expounded here in partial equilibrium terms, using Fig. 7.1 (which is essentially the same as Fig. 3.1). Quantities of cloth and yarn are shown along the horizontal axis, the units being so chosen that one unit of yarn is required to make one unit of cloth. The free trade price of

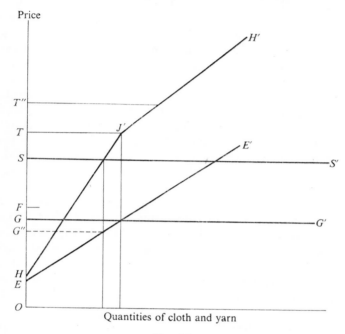

Fig. 7.1

cloth is OS and of yarn OG, the supply curve of domestic yarn producers is EE', and the cloth supply curve (which incorporates the cost of yarn) is $HJ'H'$. Note that in free trade, as drawn, there are no imports of yarn; it is non-traded. The f.o.b. export price of yarn is assumed to be below OE, so that the possibility of exporting yarn is ruled out. If the tariff on cloth were no greater than ST, the input would remain non-traded. As the tariff on cloth is raised from zero towards ST the price of yarn rises. Thus there is backward linkage and the preceding analysis concerning non-traded inputs applies. But when the tariff on cloth is raised beyond ST, say to ST'', and provided there is no tariff on yarn, imports of yarn commence; the price of yarn ceases to rise further so that there is no further backward linkage. The increase in the tariff on the final good has converted the non-traded input into a traded input.

Now there is a problem. How should the effective rate be calculated? Should yarn be treated as traded or non-traded? Clearly if one thinks of the total effect of the tariff, thus comparing the protection situation with the free trade situation, we have a typical case of a non-traded input. The increase in the price of the final good by ST'' has gone partly to the value-added product and partly, by $G''G$, to the input. So, strictly, one can use only the nominal rate ST''/OS. It seems then that for our analysis it is relevant not only whether a good is traded or non-traded in the protection situation, but also whether it would be traded or non-traded in the alternative free trade situation. If in either situation it is non-traded it should be treated as a non-traded good. But this is a somewhat defeatist solution. If one is concerned with fairly small changes in the degree of protection or with relative degrees of protection one might be justified still in calculating orthodox effective rates (in this case ST''/GS) and drawing, if hesitantly, some conclusions about the effects of tariffs on resource allocation from them. Alternatively one might break down the tariff ST'' into its two elements, ST and TT''. The first element would be expressed in nominal rate terms and the second in effective rate form.

Next consider the effect of imposing a tariff on the input. This will raise the threshold where the input is converted from a non-traded into a traded input. In the diagram, if the yarn tariff is GF, the cloth tariff would have to be above $ST+GF$ for yarn to be converted into a traded good and so for backward linkage to cease. In other words, the input tariff extends the scope for the backward linkage effect of the final good tariff. If yarn were traded in the free trade situation (as represented in Fig. 3.1) a tariff on it might convert it into a non-traded good. A tariff on cloth would then have backward linkage effects and should be expressed in nominal not effective rate terms. But if the cloth tariff were raised high enough yarn might again turn into a traded good. In considering the protection for the value-added product in all these cases the tariff on the input must simply be taken as given. If it has converted the input into a non-traded good then the final good tariff, or at least a part of it, may need to be expressed in nominal rate terms, while otherwise the usual effective rate calculation can be made.

Suppose that it is desired to protect an input—that is, to expand domestic output of it relative to free trade. Our analysis now suggests that any one of three different policies may be appropriate, depending on circumstances.

(1) In free trade there may be imports of this input. This is the case that has been assumed in previous chapters. A tariff on the final good would then not affect output of the input. Its output could only be expanded by a tariff on the input itself. But there is a limit here. A tariff on it will both increase its supply and reduce the demand for it through imposing on the final good negative effective protection. Hence if the tariff on the input is high enough imports of it will cease. At this limiting point a further increase in the input tariff, unaccompanied by a tariff on the final good, would have no effect on its output.

(2) In free trade the input may be non-traded. This is the case considered in the present chapter. The situation is then exactly the reverse: the output of the input can only be expanded by a tariff (or export subsidy) for the using industry, the output expansion of the input resulting from the backward linkage effect. A tariff on the input itself would be redundant. But here also there is a limit. If the tariff on the final product is high enough, and its output and hence the demand for the input expand far enough, the domestic price of the input will rise to the free trade price and beyond that any further demand for the input will be satisfied from imports. The limit is in fact the same as in the previous case. The input is on the margin between being traded and non-traded.

(3) Finally, the input may be at such a point of transition. Any increase in its own tariff unaccompanied by an increase in the tariff on the using industry would be redundant; any increase in the tariff on the using industry unaccompanied by an increase in the tariff for the input itself would lead to extra imports. To increase output of the input both tariffs must be increased simultaneously. The rise in the final good tariff will increase the demand for the input and the rise in the input

tariff will increase the supply of it. Thus at this point, where the input is non-traded but on the verge of being traded, protection of it depends on its own tariff *and* on the tariff on the final good. We know that the effective protection of the final good is influenced by the tariff on the input; it follows thus that there is a two-way relationship, protection of each of the two goods depending on both tariffs.

v. *Labour in Infinitely Elastic Supply*

So far we have assumed the stocks of the primary factors in the country concerned to be given. But, in this section and the next only, we assume that either labour or capital is in infinitely elastic supply. This has interesting implications for the effective protection concept.

The distinction has been made between traded inputs assumed to be in infinitely elastic supply, and non-traded inputs plus the primary factors where extra quantities are likely to come forth only at higher cost. The argument has been that a tariff on a final good raises the returns per unit only to the non-traded inputs and primary factors and therefore should be related only to the sum of their shares in total cost. This principle could also be applied to any primary factors which are in infinitely elastic supply. Suppose that there are no non-traded inputs but only traded inputs and three factors of production: labour, capital, and land. If labour were in infinitely elastic supply, it could be grouped with the traded inputs; and the effective rate would be calculated in relation to the combined shares of capital and land, being then the effective protective rate for the value-added products defined in terms of these two factors only. Alternatively, capital might be in infinitely elastic supply, in which case capital cost would be treated as just another traded input, and the value-added product would refer to labour and land combined. To extend our previous method in this way, and if the complications of substitution effects are to be avoided, fixed physical input coefficients must be assumed for all those factors in infinitely elastic supply which are to be grouped with the traded inputs.

The case where labour, or some types of labour, are in infinitely elastic supply may be relevant for some less developed countries. While the cause is likely to be a given income or wage level in the subsistence hinterland, or perhaps in a neighbouring country which supplies immigrants, the given money wage facing the protected industry need not be at the same level as that in the hinterland, the margin between them being the equivalent of the difference between the f.o.b. and the c.i.f. price of an import. Now, when the services of labour are treated as just another input, what is the equivalent of a tariff on the input? All such 'tariffs' will of course reduce the effective protection for the employing industries. One such 'tariff' is a payroll tax on the use of labour, and another is any tax which raises costs of transport of immigrants or costs of transfer from the hinterland (and hence the rate of return labour needs to recoup its once-for-all costs of movement).

If it is the real wage rather than the money wage which is fixed, then anything which raises labour's cost of living has the same effect as a tariff on this input. To give a very Ricardian example, a tariff on corn will raise money wages and reduce effective protection for the labour-using industries. In fact, corn is an input into labour, and labour is an input into cloth, and a constant real wage is the equivalent of a constant effective protective rate for labour. A tariff on the input corn then requires a rise in the money wage—which is the equivalent of a compensating nominal tariff for labour—which in turn reduces effective protection for the labour-using industries. A more realistic contemporary example applying to many less developed countries is that an export tax on an agricultural product which is also consumed domestically by wage-earners reduces the domestic price of this product and so, with a given real wage, leads to a lower money wage than otherwise. This increases effective protection for manufacturing industry employing this labour. It is as if the agricultural product were a direct traded input into manufacturing. If it is the real wage after tax that is fixed, then an income tax levied on labour employed in industry reduces effective protection. On the other hand, state provision of urban facilities which raise the real value of a given money wage spent in the city increases the effective protective rate for the employing industries by reducing money wages.

The meaning of this approach of calculating effective rates in relation to some primary factors only must be considered

carefully.[12] It means that if labour is in infinitely elastic
supply, the supply responses of the other primary factors,
not of labour, determine the effects of the protective structure
on output. Let us interpret this approach in terms of Fig. 4.2.
The transformation curve in the south-western quadrant refers
now to value-added products produced by these other factors,
say capital and land. Labour services are the equivalent of
the imported input, and output per person employed—that
is the fixed input-output coefficient in each industry—is
indicated by the slope of GO and OG'. The price of labour
services must be fixed in terms of the given foreign free trade
prices of the final products (and any produced traded inputs).
If it were fixed in terms of domestic prices there would be an
index number problem. A change in the protective structure
will bring about a movement along the transformation curve
and so alter the relationship between the price of land and of
capital, depending on which is the land-intensive and which the
capital-intensive product. These factor intensities refer to the
relative land-capital ratios. If there were only one primary
factor beside labour, and assuming constant returns to scale
in both industries, the transformation curve would be a straight
line. Unless the country is very large, there would then be
complete specialization and hence the protective structure
would not affect the pattern of output. So we must assume at
least two primary factors, beside labour. These could of course
be two types of capital. Alternatively, unskilled labour might
be in infinitely elastic supply, in which case the primary factors
which determine the effects on the output pattern of a protective structure would consist of skilled labour, various kinds
of capital and of land.

In a general equilibrium model with mobile, malleable
factors one cannot describe such effective rates as giving
effective protection to, say, capital and land. This would be to
return to the partial equilibrium approach of input effective
rates. In general equilibrium terms, if industry A has a higher
effective rate in this sense than industry B, capital and land

---

[12] The concept of 'effective protective rates for capital' was first developed
in Corden, 'The Structure of a Tariff System and the Effective Protective Rate',
pp. 231–2, but the approach was essentially partial equilibrium. The remaining
discussion in this section improves this by putting it into a general equilibrium
framework.

will be drawn from B to A—the inducement for the resource movement is indeed that these factors are being more highly 'protected' in A than in B—but the factor prices of capital and land cannot both go up. If A is capital-intensive the rental on capital-goods will rise and the rent on land will fall, while if A is land-intensive it will be the other way round. Without knowing relative factor-intensities we cannot know which factor will gain.

One might also like to know what happens to the use of labour by the country as the result of a protective structure. The price of labour services is given (relative to the given prices of foreign goods) but the quantity of labour may change, so we might say that labour is 'protected' when extra foreign labour, or labour from the hinterland, is brought into the country. If in the hinterland the population increases in a Malthusian way so as to substitute for the labour that has moved into the economy then the new population has been 'protected', that is, brought into being. Whether a protective structure increases the economy's use of labour depends broadly on whether relatively higher effective rates in our special sense are being given to the industries with the relatively higher ratios of wages to value of gross output, the latter valued at world prices. In our model of Chapter 4, where the quantity of labour in the economy as a whole was fixed, protecting the labour-intensive industry increased the real wage; in the present model, where the real wage is fixed, it increases the supply of labour.

VI. *Capital in Infinitely Elastic Supply and the Treatment of Capital Cost*

The price of the services of capital might be given, or at least might be unresponsive to the country's demand for capital. One could then calculate effective rates which represent the increases in the prices of the value-added products when the latter are defined as embodying the contributions only of the other factors. Such calculations have been made by Basevi in his pioneering work.[13] Yet, for reasons given above, the results

[13] G. Basevi, 'The U.S. Tariff Structure: Estimate of Effective Rates of Protection of United States Industries and Industrial Labor', *Review of Economics and Statistics*, 48, May 1966, 147–60. Apart from his actual statistical

cannot be interpreted as yielding 'effective protection for labour'. In a three-factor model, the real wage will rise only if the industries with relatively high labour-land ratios obtain higher effective rates for 'labour plus land' than other industries. There are three other qualifications to such calculations. Firstly, it is necessary to assume that the structure of interest rates is given from outside the country. But one must have grave doubts about assuming that the supply of capital funds is perfectly elastic to all industries at a given interest rate. Secondly one must assume that all capital is malleable once installed; that is, reduced demand for capital in an industry will always lead to a supply reduction sufficient to keep its price constant. Thirdly, there is the problem of fitting tariffs on capital-goods as well as the use of non-traded capital-goods into the picture. This requires some further formal analysis.

If we are to avoid the substitution problem at this stage fixed physical capital-output ratios must be assumed just as fixed labour-output ratios were needed before. Now let b_k be the cost of the services of a unit of physical capital per annum to the users, just as the wage rate is the cost of the services of a unit of labour; thus, it is the 'rental' on capital-goods, or the equivalent of the price of a traded input. It is b_k which has to be constant, except when it is increased by tariffs or their equivalents. Now

$$b_k = (r+z)p_k, \tag{11}$$

where p_k is the price of capital goods, r is the relevant rate of interest facing the industry concerned and z is the annual rate of depreciation on capital. It follows that p_k, r, and z must all be constant in response to changes in demand for capital from protected industries. Now z can perhaps be regarded as a fixed coefficient, and r is constant if we assume that the interest rate is a given world market rate. But what about p_k? Extending our earlier analysis, this is given when the capital goods are traded and is not given when they are non-traded. Traded

---

work, Basevi's highly original contribution is this concept of the effective protective rate for labour. He does not deal with the difficulties discussed here —that is, he ignores tariffs on capital goods, the possibility of non-traded goods, and the general equilibrium implications.

capital goods with annual cost per unit of b_{kt} must really be distinguished from non-traded capital goods with annual cost per unit of b_{kh} where

$$b_{kt} = (r+z_t)p_{kt}, \qquad (11.1)$$

$$b_{kh} = (r+z_h)p_{kh} \qquad (11.2)$$

Only the annual service (or 'rental') of *traded* capital goods can be treated as a traded input, and only when it is legitimate to assume in addition a perfectly elastic supply of capital funds. The resulting effective rate will then be the protective rate for the value-added product defined in terms of labour, of non-traded inputs, whether capital goods or materials, and of land.

It seems obviously desirable to take into account tariffs on capital goods in the calculation of effective rates of other goods. The question arises whether this can be done even when it is *not* reasonable to assume a given interest rate. This point was not pursued in Chapter 4 since the simple assumption, characteristic of pure, static trade theory, was made implicitly that the capital stock inherited from the past was non-depreciating and that its cost in a previous period was irrelevant; all that mattered was its 'rental' in the current period. With non-depreciating capital, the relevance of tariffs on capital-goods is in altering the rate at which rentals on capital-goods—which result from the solution of the system—are translated into rates of financial return on capital—and in equilibrium this rate of return on capital is equal to the relevant rate of interest. Increases in tariffs on capital-goods will reduce rates of return on capital resulting from a given structure of tariffs, export subsidies, etc., on other goods (unless there is domestic production of capital-goods and these tend to be capital-intensive).

Tariffs on capital-goods also affect depreciation. The depreciation cost per unit is the physical rate of depreciation multiplied by the price of capital-goods. If one could assume a fixed capital-output ratio, and that all capital-goods are traded with a given world price, then one could treat depreciation per unit of product as just another input cost which is given to the industry, altered only by tariffs and other taxes or subsidies on capital-goods. The assumption of a fixed capital-output ratio is not really consistent with our general equilibrium model expounded in Chapter 4. Furthermore, some capital-goods are no doubt non-traded or contain a non-traded element. Nevertheless, it may be reasonable—if not an ideal solution—to treat the whole of depreciation as a cost, similar to the cost of a traded produced input, such as yarn, and hence to define the value-added product in *net* rather than *gross* terms. In the effective rate formula, a_{ij} would then include depreciation and the weighted average input tariff would take into account tariffs on capital goods.[14] Apart from the theoretical problems, which have not been entirely resolved here, there are also two measurement problems created by this approach. The first is that, since the detailed composition of depreciation is not usually known, rather rough estimates must be made of an appropriate average tariff on capital-goods. The second is that financial depreciation allowances often do not indicate correctly the cost of keeping capital intact, but may, for well-known reasons, overstate or understate this cost.

VII. *Small Country Assumption Removed for Final Goods*

The small country assumption that elasticities of import supply and export demand are all infinite has been immensely significant for our analysis so far. It has been at the heart of our distinction between traded and non-traded goods and has made possible crucial simplifications. This assumption must now be removed. We shall break the problem down into two elements, first non-infinite foreign elasticities for final goods, assuming infinite elasticities for their traded inputs, and then (in section VIII) non-infinite elasticities for inputs. Many goods are both inputs and final goods, and for them the two elements of the analysis must simply be combined.

In the first stage of our analysis in Chapter 3 the effect of a tariff structure on the pattern of production among traded goods depended only on the scale of effective rates and the production substitution elasticities. Thus it was possible to separate production from consumption effects. The two sides

---

[14] This is the method regarded by B. Balassa as most desirable, and is used in most of the studies in Balassa (ed.), op. cit. Balassa points out that as the share of depreciation in the value of production is generally low, in practice the differences between the estimates of effective protection on gross and on net value-added are rather small.

came together again once the need for supply and demand balance for non-traded goods was taken into account. But it was helpful to be able to start by analysing production effects separately. This simplification is lost when the small country assumption for final goods is removed.

This matter can be explained, at least initially, in partial equilibrium terms. If the foreign import price were given the increase in output of the industry would depend on its effective rate and on the elasticity of supply of the value-added product. But when there is an upward-sloping foreign import supply curve, while a given tariff rate does indeed raise the price received by domestic producers, the foreign supplier bears part of the incidence of the tariff. The lower the foreign import supply elasticity and the higher the elasticity of domestic demand for the importable product, the less the domestic price rises. If one means by *rate of protection* the proportional increase in the effective price that finally results, this will now be less than the effective rate when the latter is calculated in the usual way with given foreign prices. Thus the movement of resources into the industry depends not only on the effective rate and the domestic supply elasticity but also on (1) the foreign import supply elasticity, and (2) the nominal rate and the domestic demand elasticity. Similarly the extent of the fall in consumption depends not just on the nominal rate and the demand elasticity but also on the import supply elasticity, on the effective rate and on the domestic supply elasticity. Exactly the same analysis applies to the effects of an export subsidy or tax.

This approach can then be extended to the general equilibrium model, though with some difficulty. First, assume away demand effects. We start with a scale of effective rates, one which ideally takes account of the substitution effects in the production function of each final good discussed in the previous chapter. This scale indicates the general nature of the pulls on resources. Consider any pair of importable final products. As before the greater the elasticity of transformation between them the more resources will move from the product with the lower to the product with the higher effective rate. But in addition, for any given elasticity of substitution in production, resources will move more the greater the elasticity of import supply for the product with the higher effective rate relative to the import supply elasticity for the product with the lower effective rate. It is clear from Fig. 2.4 that the nominal rate expresses the proportional rise in the domestic price of the product only when the foreign price is given; when, as in Fig. 2.4, the price is not given the actual price rise that results depends also on the various elasticities. Similarly, the effective rate expresses only the proportional rise in the price of the value-added product when foreign prices are given. When they are not, then the actual relative price change between the two products depends also on the relative foreign import supply elasticities. *For a given effective rate the price of a product will rise less the lower the foreign supply elasticity.* Similarly, on the export side, a given export subsidy will have a lower protective effect on an industry the lower the relevant export demand elasticity.

It follows that the extent of the resource flows induced by a protective structure depends not only on the levels of effective rates and the transformation elasticities but also on the import supply and export demand elasticities. In general, relatively high foreign elasticities are protective and relatively low elasticities are anti-protective, or at least modify protective effects (and anti-protective effects) that would otherwise take place. And this—if one reflects on it—is just commonsense. If reduced imports resulting from a tariff lead mainly to a reduction of the foreign supply price, or if extra exports resulting from an export subsidy lead mainly to a reduction in the foreign price for exports, then there will not be much protection provided. Broadly, the scale of effective rates continues to play some role in determining the direction of resource flows induced by the protective structure, but the extent of the flows and the precise pattern of the flows depends now not only on the elasticities of the domestic production transformation curves—in partial equilibrium terms, the supply curves—but also on the foreign supply and demand curves. The same analysis could be carried out on the consumption side, assuming that the production substitution elasticities were zero. Consumption effects would be seen then to depend not only on the nominal scale and the consumption substitution elasticities, but also on the foreign trade elasticities.

The matter becomes really complicated once we allow for both consumption and production effects. Putting the workings of a system of simultaneous equations into words is never easy or particularly elegant, and just picking out a few equations is bound to be inadequate. But, to illustrate some possibilities, suppose that products X and Y are substitutes on the production side and products Y and Z are substitutes on the consumption side, and that the effective rate for Y is greater than that for X. All three goods are traded. So (other things being very much equal . . . and this means neglecting other production substitution effects) resources will tend to move from X to Y. How much they move will depend, among other things, on the extent to which the foreign price of Y rises as a result, and this depends (among other things) on the consumption effect for Y. But this depends not just on Y's nominal rate but also on the nominal rate for Z and on the consumption substitution elasticity of Y with Z, and on the production effect that the whole tariff structure has on industry Z. But this production effect on Z depends on Z's effective rate, its production substitution elasticity with other industries, and so on. And in addition, all these effects depend on the various foreign supply and demand elasticities. Everything does, regrettably, depend on everything else. But since, in particular real circumstances some things are rather obviously more related to *some* other things than to *other* other things, one need not perhaps despair in the application of this analysis to practical situations.[15]

The saving grace finally is that for many countries which depend significantly on protection, namely all or almost all of the less developed countries, and countries such as Canada, Australia and New Zealand, it is clearly reasonable to assume, at least for the longer-run analysis with which the theory of protection is usually concerned, that import supply elasticities for most products are infinite or close to infinite. The assumption is less reasonable for their primary export products, but here it is helpful that mostly the elasticities of substitution in domestic consumption, and quite often the elasticities of substitution with domestic import-competing production, and

[15] Another complication that arises when we remove the small country assumption is the possibility of the *Metzler paradox*, discussed in Appendix II.

sometimes even with each other, are very low. If these domestic elasticities are not low—and of course in the long-run they tend to be higher than in the short-run—then an analysis might usefully start by assuming all foreign trade elasticities infinite and then introduce particular qualifications on the lines of the discussion above, applying these directly to effects concerned with exports and those importables where substitution in production or consumption with exportables is believed to be fairly high.

VIII. *Small Country Assumption Removed for Inputs*

We shall now assume away the difficulties just discussed and suppose that the foreign prices of all final traded goods are given. But this time we assume that all imports of traded *inputs* are supplied along upward-sloping foreign supply curves while foreign demand curves for exportable inputs slope downwards.

The important distinction which has so far been made between traded and non-traded inputs, that the former are in infinitely elastic supply to the using industry while the latter are not, now disappears. Consider again the case where a final good j, which is an importable, is produced by a traded importable input i, a non-traded input h and the value-added product v. A tariff t_j will now lead to a rise in the price of each of the three. We saw above that the rise in the price of h brings about backward linkage towards h. But now the rise in the price of i will also produce backward linkage towards domestic producers of i. In partial equilibrium terms, we would now have three input effective rates, one each for i, h and v. The three supply elasticities would be ingredients in each of these rates. The relevant supply elasticity for i would not be the import supply elasticity but rather the elasticity of the total supply curve of i facing the industry, which is the horizontal addition of the domestic producer's supply curve and the import supply curve. If the input were an exportable then the supply curve to the using industry would be derived by horizontally subtracting the export demand curve from the domestic supply curve, the elasticity of the resultant net supply curve being then an ingredient in each of the three input effective rates. The objection to such input rates has already been stated. What then is the alternative? We might relate the rise in the price of j to (p_v+p_h), so obtaining $g_j = \mathrm{d}p_j/(p_v+p_h)$. This means that we would be calculating the effective rate on the ordinary basis and just ignoring the fact that the supply elasticity of i is less than infinite. We would then overstate the proportional increase in (p_v+p_h). Alternatively we might decide to lump together the three elements of v, i and h—so that $g_j = \mathrm{d}p_j/(p_v+p_h+p_i)$—on the grounds that the effects of them cannot really be separated. We would then end up with the nominal rate . . . and would be back where we started before the effective rate was invented.

The abandonment of the small country assumption for traded inputs has thus even more serious implications than the abandonment of this assumption for final goods. In the latter case the effective rate and a reasonably simple partial equilibrium analysis survive, though the general equilibrium analysis becomes much more complicated. But when the small country assumption for inputs is abandoned even the simple effective rate idea is thrown in doubt. For the partial analysis one might replace it with input effective rates, but for general equilibrium analysis the answer appears to be, in general, to confine the technique of analysis to countries where it is reasonable to assume that most import supply and export demand elasticities of inputs are at least in the long-run very high, introducing specific qualifications for particular known exceptions.

8

ON THE UNIFORMITY OF TARIFF STRUCTURES

So far the analysis has been wholly *positive* economics. Nothing has been said or implied about the gains or losses from tariffs or about an optimum protective structure. To pursue these matters one would not only have to specify exactly whose welfare we are concerned with but also to examine closely the various 'arguments for protection'. Since most arguments for tariffs and other trade interventions hinge on particular, but not inevitable, constraints, the constraints would have to be examined closely to see how the new multi-commodity approach to the theory of protection outlined in this book affects optimum protection policies. This will not be done here in any systematic way. But it can be noted that the new approach has not uncovered any essentially new arguments for or against protection. Its relevance is rather for spelling out the multi-commodity implications of well-known arguments. Here we shall depart from the positive economics emphasis of this book to discuss the *uniform tariff issue*—an issue of second-best welfare economics that is of practical importance in many industrializing countries and that two-sector theory, by its very nature, has ignored. The discussion of this issue probably brings out the main welfare aspects of the new approach.[1]

[1] Welfare implications of effective protection are discussed in B. Balassa and D. Schydlowsky, 'Effective Tariffs, Domestic Cost of Foreign Exchange, and the Equilibrium Exchange Rate', *Journal of Political Economy*, 76, May/June 1968, 348–60; H. G. Johnson, 'The Theory of Effective Protection and Preferences', *Economica*, 36, May 1969, 119–38; R. H. Snape, 'Sugar: Costs of Protection and Taxation', *Economica*, 36, Feb. 1969, 29–41; and R. J. Ruffin, 'Tariffs, Intermediate Goods, and Domestic Protection', *American Economic Review*, 59, June 1969, 261–9. Balassa and Schydlowsky have a model akin to that represented by Figure 8.2 of this chapter, Johnson and Snape relate effective protection to the partial equilibrium *cost of protection* concept, and Ruffin presents a second-best welfare analysis with some similarities to the basic analysis in this chapter.

I. *The Uniform Tariff Concept*

The uniform tariff issue can be put as follows. Given that a country wants to protect its import-competing industries, or just wants to reduce imports (perhaps to improve the balance of payments), and that there is no particular reason for fostering one type of industry more than another, what is the optimum tariff structure? It seems simplest to provide a uniform tariff. This would provide the same degree of protection for each industry and would leave it to the price mechanism to sort out the precise way in which import-competing industry would be expanded. One accepts the constraint that there shall be some protection but avoids the administrative complexities of differential protectionism and the opportunities for pressure-groups to manipulate the tariff system. The present author at one time suggested that Australia replace a complex system of quantitative import restrictions and tariffs with a uniform tariff, so 'cutting through the jungle with the price mechanism'.[2] The idea has also made its appearance in other countries.[3] Subject to various modifications it has considerable appeal— the appeal, above all, of simplicity. We begin here by developing the case for the uniform tariff approach. Qualifications will be developed in later sections. The discussion to follow should not be understood as economic advocacy. Many considerations, notably income distribution effects, are left out of account. Various assumptions are made that are clearly not realistic.

We assume to begin with that there are many importables though only one exportable. Protection is desired for either one of two reasons. The first is that it may be believed that the marginal private cost of all import-competing value-added exceeds the marginal social cost (measured in terms of exports) by a uniform percentage. The reason for the divergence between private and social cost may be that non-pecuniary external

---

[2] W. M. Corden, 'Import Restrictions and Tariffs: A New Look at Australian Policy', *Economic Record*, 34, Dec. 1958, 331–46. The proposal created a lot of controversy and eventually influenced Australian tariff policy through encouraging tariff simplification and some tendency towards uniformity. See W. M. Corden, 'Australian Economic Policy Discussion in the Post-War Period: A Survey', *American Economic Review*, 58, June 1968, 88–138.

[3] See especially S. Macario, 'Protectionism and Industrialization in Latin America', *Economic Bulletin for Latin America*, 9, March 1964, 61–101, where a case for uniform effective protection is made.

economies, whether static or dynamic, attach to all import-competing—which we can think of as manufacturing—production. Perhaps some kind of generalized infant industry argument for protection applying to all manufacturing production is accepted. It may be realized that the divergence is unlikely to be uniform, but in the absence of more detailed knowledge about the precise pattern of the divergences it may seem reasonable to form policies on the assumption of uniformity. Conceivably there may be a fixed target for total manufacturing production (in terms of value-added), but also indifference as to the precise pattern of the desired production. We are not concerned here with the validity or sensibleness of the relevant protection argument, but only with spelling out its implications. We could accept the proposition that, given certain assumptions, the first-best policy in such cases is to subsidize manufacturing production directly, or to tax exportable production, rather than using trade taxes,[4] but here direct production subsidies or taxes are ruled out and the only policy device available is the tariff. This may be a quite realistic way of presenting the problem, though the reader should never lose sight of the fact that in all the more complicated cases to be discussed below there are likely to be technically feasible alternative policies that would attain a higher level of welfare than the use of tariffs alone. The second possible reason for protection is that there are terms of trade effects on the export side, reduced exports leading to a higher world price of the export product. In this case first-best policy is to impose an optimum export tax, the optimum rate of tax being higher the lower the foreign elasticity of demand for exports (assuming no foreign retaliation). Again, we rule out this straightforward approach, perhaps because of adverse effects on the balance of payments, and assume that only tariffs can be used. We assume that the elasticity of supply of all imports is infinite, so that the terms of trade can be influenced only on the side of exports. We neglect income distribution and revenue considerations and assume

---

[4] See H. G. Johnson, 'Optimal Trade Intervention in the Presence of Domestic Distortions', in R. E. Baldwin et al., *Trade, Growth and the Balance of Payments* (Rand McNally, Chicago, 1965). The basic idea comes from J. E. Meade, *Trade and Welfare*, 1955, Ch. XIV. If the aim is to redistribute incomes away from the export sector, perhaps to reduce profits of foreign-owned enterprises, the first-best policy is the use of direct income taxes and subsidies.

that all production is and remains perfectly competitive.[5] We assume fixed input-output coefficients. Two more assumptions at this stage are vital. One is that there is no exportable content in importable production; this means that a uniform ad valorem nominal tariff on all imports will yield also a uniform rate of effective protection. The other is that all demand effects can be neglected because all elasticities of substitution in consumption are zero. Both assumptions will be removed later.

The case for a uniform tariff can now proceed as follows. Neither of the two arguments for protection (external economies, terms of trade) provides any justification for shifting the pattern of output from one importable activity to another. Thus, taking into account the production substitution effects *between* these activities, the case is clearly for a uniform degree of effective protection. Secondly, taking into account the substitution effects between the various importable industries on the one hand and the exportable industry on the other, there is no reason for giving more marginal encouragement for resources to move from exportables into one importable industry rather than into another. Thus, again, the case is for a uniform degree of effective protection. This argument will be given some geometric support below. The third step is simply that a uniform nominal tariff will yield the desired uniform effective tariff.

In Fig. 8.1a, SS' is the foreign supply curve of the importable product, bags, and VV' is the domestic supply curve. It is assumed for the moment that there are no produced inputs in bags. The supply curve refers to the supply of primary factors of production and the effective rate complication can be ignored. Free trade output is OB. The demand curve DD' has zero elasticity. Free trade imports are BD. Similarly Fig. 8.1b refers to another importable product, hats, the units

---

[5] Neglecting revenue considerations means that we assume that tariff revenue is redistributed to consumers and spent by the latter in accord with their demand patterns. Neglecting income distribution requires the assumption that the community actually redistributes incomes costlessly in accord with its (or 'the appropriate') social welfare function. Neither of these assumptions is, of course, realistic, and optimum tariff policy must obviously take into account revenue and income distribution considerations. Various references to subsidies being preferable to tariffs also imply neglect of revenue-raising costs.

being so chosen that the free trade price of a 'unit of hats' is equal to the free trade price of a 'unit of bags'.[6] The foreign supply curve is again SS', the domestic supply curve is $V_h V_h'$, the demand curve, again with zero elasticity, is $D_h D_h'$, free trade production is OH and free trade imports HD_h. In the background there is a third product, the exportable, which is the numeraire. The foreign supply curves, SS', show the

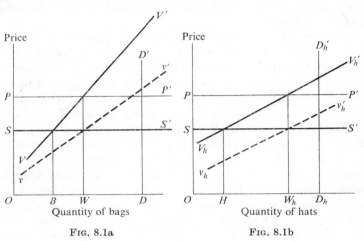

FIG. 8.1a   FIG. 8.1b

cost of imports in terms of exports. The domestic supply curves, VV' and $V_h V_h'$, show how outputs of bags and hats increase as their prices increase relative to the price of the exportable and trace out the marginal costs of the products in terms of the exportable. This exposition (though not the main argument) is essentially partial equilibrium because it assumes that the two supply curves, at least over the relevant ranges, are independent.[7]

If the elasticity of demand for exports is less than infinite

[6] If, at the duty-free c.i.f. import price, a dozen hats cost as much as five bags, our units could be 12 hats and 5 bags, or 24 hats and 10 bags, and so on.

[7] By assuming that the supply curves are independent of each other we are ignoring the general equilibrium complications of section VII of Chapter 4 (which suggest, for example, that a uniform tariff may lead to a decline in output of one of the protected industries), but these complications would not affect the main welfare arguments of the present chapter. Note also that drawing in fixed demand curves implies absence of income effects, but we need not have drawn in the demand curves at all.

the social return on a unit of exports is less than the private return; hence socially imports cost more in terms of exports than privately. This extra cost per unit at the optimum trade volume may be SP, so that the social import supply curve is PP' and optimum outputs will be OW and OW_h, where marginal cost of domestic production is just equal to the social cost of importing. A uniform tariff of SP/OS will achieve this. Alternatively, external economies of an equal degree may attach to production of bags and hats; in both cases the social supply curve of domestic output will then be less than the private one, namely vv' and $v_h v_h'$. Again output should go to OW and OW_h respectively, being the points where marginal social cost of domestic production is equal to the cost of importing the products; and a uniform tariff at the rate SP/OS will again achieve this. If the aim of the tariff is to achieve a 'target' increase in production of bags and hats combined, valued at free trade prices, it could be shown by using the usual technique of minimizing the fall in the sum of consumers' and producers' surpluses that a uniform tariff would attain the target at less cost than any differential tariff.

The effective rate complication can easily be allowed for. Assume now that there are produced traded inputs into bags or hats, but let the two diagrams refer to the value-added products in bag and hat production. The price shown is now the *effective price* and the supply curves refer to the supply only of value-added products. The free trade price OS is now the free trade effective price and the tariff SP/OS is an effective rate. The analysis can then proceed as before.

In one respect the uniform tariff is indiscriminate. It distributes surpluses to producers of importables indiscriminately; if the elasticity of supply is low more surplus will be handed out for any given increase in output than when the elasticity is high. If the elasticity of supply is zero no increase in output results at all; only extra surplus for the producers results. In another sense a uniform tariff is a very efficient discriminator. It discriminates on the basis of private marginal cost. It automatically ensures that, if the supply curves reflect private marginal costs and diverge uniformly from marginal social cost, that the social gain from the tariff structure is maximized, at least in the potential income sense.

The role of the uniform tariff as a device for efficient discrimination can be explained in terms of a special, but not unrealistic, model which is represented in Fig. 8.2. The horizontal axis shows units of various types of import-competing outputs (value-added products), actual and potential. Each number represents a different activity or industry. The units are so chosen that all the products have the same free trade effective price, namely OS. It is assumed that each value-added product is produced at constant cost (including normal profit), product 1 at cost OP_1, product 2 at OP_2 ($= OS$), and so on. The costs are assumed to be independent of each other, each industry drawing its resources from exportables, so that the method has again partial equilibrium elements; the simplicity of the diagram, though not the main argument, depends on this assumption. Alternatively, one might assume that the products are produced not at constant costs but at decreasing average costs, the costs shown in the diagram being average costs when the industry concerned supplies the whole domestic market. It is attractive to interpret the diagram in this way since decreasing costs are surely common.[8]

In Fig. 8.2 the horizontal distance for each value-added product shows its total output assuming that the whole or a specified proportion of the domestic market is met from domestic production. It can be seen that at free trade, products 1 and 2 will be produced, the former being intra-marginal and the latter marginal.

If a uniform effective tariff at the rate of the marginal divergence of SP_4/OS is imposed products 3 and 4 will start production. There will be an excess *private* production cost indicated by the shaded area; in the case of the marginal product 4, this may measure the external economies believed to exist. If the uniform effective tariff were raised more production would start, first 5, then 6, and so on. What the tariff does is to sort out the high-cost products from the low-cost ones. Thus a uniform tariff of SP_4/OS discriminates in favour

[8] The concept 'whole domestic market' presents some difficulties. The size of the domestic market for particular products and hence the costs shown in Fig. 8.2 may not be independent of the tariff structure and the total pattern of output because these will affect incomes and income distribution. Once consumption substitution effects are introduced the pattern of nominal rates will have additional effects on the sizes of the various markets.

of products 3 and 4, and discriminates against products 5, 6 and 7. If a given increase in importable value-added, from OR to OW is desired, a tariff of SP_4/OS will ensure that this is attained at least private cost, so that low-cost products 3 and 4 are produced before high-cost products 5, etc., are started. Provided the proportional marginal divergence between private and social cost is the same for each product it will be attained at least social cost or maximum social gain.

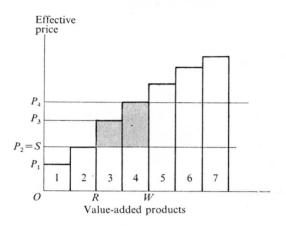

FIG. 8.2

The analysis could also be used to make a case for uniform, in preference to differential, effective export subsidies where it is desired to foster a broad category of goods, say all manufactures. A uniform rate of external economies (excess of private over social cost) may be believed to attach to all manufacturing value-added, whether for the home market or for export. Given our various assumptions and the same sort of analysis the case is then for a uniform effective tariff and export subsidy for manufactures. This is a very important consideration for some of the more advanced less developed countries (such as Brazil and Argentina) where there is scope for substantial exports of manufactures which are held back by tariffs unaccompanied by export subsidies.[9] If all production

---

[9] See I. Little, T. Scitovsky, and M. Scott, *Industry and Trade in Some Developing Countries*, 1970.

were vertically integrated, so that nominal and effective rates
were identical, the desired expansion of manufactures both for
the home market and for export could be achieved by a dual
exchange rate system.[10] The qualifications that will be developed
later to the uniform tariff idea will also apply to these devices,
though in the case of export subsidies there is likely to be the
additional complication of a financing constraint.

II. *Uniformity of Effective Rates and Non-uniformity of Nominal Rates*

Now let us introduce three realistic complications. The first
is that countries which import both raw materials and manufactures generally do not wish to protect domestic production
of the former, perhaps because external economies are believed
to attach only to manufacturing. The aim might then be to
have zero protection for materials and a uniform rate of
effective protection for manufactures. This leads to the complication that a uniform nominal tariff for all manufactures
will no longer yield uniform effective protection if the materials
are inputs into the protected manufactures in differing proportions. To obtain a given rate of effective protection, the
nominal rate must then be relatively high for those manufactures where the materials content is relatively low. Thus the
recommendation for uniform effective protection for a part
only of import-competing production is not a recommendation
for tariff simplicity. Secondly, there may be an exportable
content in protected import-competing production. Since
exportables are marketed domestically at world prices less
transport costs—that is, at frontier prices—a uniform nominal
tariff would not lead to a uniform effective one even if all
nominal tariffs *were* uniform. To obtain a given rate of effective
protection, manufactures with a relatively low exportables
content should obtain relatively high nominal rates. In fact
both complications introduce inputs into protected industries

[10] N. Kaldor, in 'Dual Exchange Rates and Economic Development', in
Economic Bulletin for Latin America, 9, Dec. 1964, 215–23, reprinted in N.
Kaldor, *Essays on Economic Policy*, *Vol.* 2 (Duckworth, London, 1964), suggested a dual exchange rate system of this type for less developed countries,
but did not allow for the effective rate complication, and hence that a dual
system in terms of nominal rates may yield a multi-rate system in terms of
effective rates.

obtained at free trade prices and so upset the simple result that a uniform nominal tariff for the protected sector leads to a uniform effective one.

The aim of obtaining a uniform effective tariff for the protected sector has now a horizontal and a vertical implication. The horizontal implication is that industries with low materials or exportables content require high nominal tariffs, and vice versa. The vertical implication is that, when raw cotton is obtained at world prices because it is a duty-free importable material or an exportable, and it is desired to create a uniform effective rate for the vertical chain of yarn, grey cloth, printed cloth, and clothing, it is necessary for the nominal tariffs to rise with the degree of processing (to 'escalate'); this was explained in section VII of Chapter 3. It follows thus, from both the horizontal and the vertical implication, that an extremely dispersed structure of nominal rates may be required to achieve the desired uniformity of effective rates.[11] The matter could be further complicated by reintroducing the possibility of manufactured exports and hence the aim of a uniform effective export subsidy at the same rate as the uniform effective tariff.

The third complication arises if there is an importable content in exportables. This means that tariffs yield negative effective protection for exportables so that the uniform effective rate for protected importables understates the price advantage which the tariff structure gives the protected industries relative to exportables. Assume for the moment that there is just one importable and one exportable. The price advantage (p) is the proportional increase in the effective price of the importable relative to the effective price of the exportable and can be expressed in terms of the nominal tariff rate (t_j) and the two input coefficients (a_j, the exportable content in the importable, and a_x, the importable content in the exportable), where g_j is the effective rate for the importable and g_x the effective rate for the exportable:

[11] The general policy recommendation of varying nominal rates so as to obtain equal effective rates for protected industries was made in a report of the Swedish Customs Tariff Commission, and the Swedish tariff was revised on this basis. See *Revision of the Swedish Customs Tariff* (Stockholm, 1957). A similar recommendation is made for Latin America in S. Macario, op. cit., pp. 83–90.

$$g_j = t_j/(1-a_j) \tag{1}$$

$$g_x = -t_j a_x/(1-a_x) \tag{2}$$

$$p = (g_j - g_x)/(1+g_x) \tag{3}$$

from (1), (2) and (3)

$$p = \frac{\dfrac{1}{1-a_j} + \dfrac{a_x}{1-a_x}}{\dfrac{1}{t_j} - \dfrac{a_x}{1-a_x}} \tag{4}$$

Say the exportable content in importables is 40 per cent and the importable content in exportables 52 per cent. If the nominal tariff is 12 per cent the effective rate for importables is 20 per cent and for exportables is — 13 per cent, yielding a price advantage of approximately 38 per cent. Now allow again for many importables, though still assuming that there is only one exportable. The recommendation for uniformity of effective rates is not affected, but the negative effective rate imposed on the exportable will now depend on the relative importance of different importables in the cost of the exportable. Nevertheless, given all the input coefficients, for every desired price advantage, there is always one uniform effective rate for importables, and hence a unique structure of nominal rates.

To conclude, the three complications introduced in this section have not affected the argument that given certain assumptions, effective rates for protected industries should be uniform. But they have deprived this policy of much of its simplicity.

III. *Qualifications to the Uniform Tariff Concept: Consumption Effects*

In this section and the next two we introduce complications which modify the simple idea that effective rates should be uniform. Here we introduce consumption effects and in section IV, more than one exportable. In each case we consider separately two cases, first where the motive for protection is to foster manufacturing value-added because of a uniform rate of external economies, and secondly where the motive is to reduce the volume of imports and hence exports so as to improve the terms of trade. In section V we assume that the motive is to improve the balance of payments.

Consumption effects require the uniform tariff idea to be seriously qualified. One may, of course, take the view that consumption effects 'don't matter', in which case the analysis in this section is irrelevant. The view is undoubtedly common, possibly because the concept of a 'consumption cost' resulting from a distortion in the pattern of consumption is rather difficult to explain in simple terms.[12] Consumption effects are of two types. First, the structure of nominal tariffs will affect the pattern of consumption *within* the protected import-competing sector, and secondly it will affect consumption of import-competing goods relative to exportables. If the nominal tariffs are uniform the first effect will not operate; the problems arise only when uniformity of effective rates requires *non-*uniformity of nominal rates. Given that the motive for tariffs provides no reason for seeking to encourage consumption of one type of importable at the expense of another the consumption effect induced by non-uniform nominal rates is an undesired distortion and hence inflicts a *consumption cost*. The policy prescription that seemed to emerge from the previous section—that nominal rates should be so varied as to yield uniform effective rates—turns out to be no longer valid. It would lead to a *production gain* (that is, a rise in real income resulting from equating for each product marginal social cost of production to the cost of imports), but also to a consumption cost. The problem arises because the use of tariffs is second-best in the circumstances. When the aim is to foster manufacturing production uniformly, the first-best policy is a direct subsidy to value-added. The second-best optimum tariff structure will now be one that involves some departure from uniformity of effective rates by adjusting nominal rates so as to bring the

---

[12] Johnson has suggested two reasons: 'the tendency of economists when confronted with policy problems to ignore the rather elusive principle of consumers' sovereignty and the historical emphasis in the theory of international trade on the real cost approach to economic welfare as contrasted with the opportunity cost approach, an emphasis ultimately derived from the labour theory of value'. (H. G. Johnson, 'Optimal Trade Intervention in the Presence of Domestic Distortions', op. cit., p. 31.)

nominal rates closer to uniformity. If nominal rates were uniform there would be no consumption cost but also no production gain; if the effective rates were uniform the production gain would be maximized but against this would have to be set the consumption cost. Hence we must trade-off production gain against consumption cost.[13]

But this is not all. The structure of nominal tariffs will also affect consumption of import-competing goods relative to exportables.[14] Let us now focus on this. It becomes important to distinguish the motives for protection. If the motive is to foster manufacturing value-added because of uniform external economies, it is not desired to shift consumption from manufacturing (importables) to exportables. First-best policy requires a production subsidy. But given that a tariff structure is used, the consumption cost can still be reduced by appropriate adjustment of the structure of nominal tariffs. The tariffs on those goods which are close consumption substitutes for exportables should be reduced relative to those goods which have a low elasticity of substitution with exportables. This will of course require departure from uniformity of effective rates; the less uniform the effective rates the less the production gain, and the more tariffs are raised relatively on inelastically demanded goods the less the consumption cost. Production and consumption effects must again be traded off.

Next, suppose that the motive for the tariff structure is not to foster import-competing *production*, but rather to reduce the volume of imports, the reduced import volume leading indirectly to reduced exports, and hence improved terms of trade. We continue to assume only one exportable. Now the marginal divergence in consumption of importables is the same for all products and hence optimum policy calls for a uniform nominal tariff. Since the marginal divergence is also the same for all importable production it also calls for a uniform effective tariff. If there is complete nominal tariff uniformity (with tariffs also on materials imports) and no exportable content in importables one is able to attain both uniformities, and thus

---

[13] The method of second-best welfare optimization as explained in J. E. Meade, *Trade and Welfare*, 1955, is being used here.

[14] See H. G. Johnson, 'Tariffs and Economic Development', *Journal of Development Studies*, 1, Oct. 1964, 3–30, for detailed exposition of the subsequent argument against tariff uniformity.

tariff policy can attain a first-best optimum. This is the situation that calls for an unqualified uniform tariff (which is symmetrical with the optimum export tax). A problem now arises only when there is an exportable content in importables or there are duty-free materials imports, so that one cannot have both uniform nominal and effective rates. Any departure from effective rate uniformity will then lead to a production cost (or forgoing a production gain) and any departure from nominal rate uniformity to a consumption cost. The second-best optimum will involve some departures in both directions. Irrespective of whether there is an exportable content in importables or any other complication, the direct approach is to impose an export tax at the appropriate rate. This must yield a first-best solution when the only reason for any intervention is a terms of trade effect on the export side.

IV. *Qualifications to the Uniform Tariff Concept: Many Exports*

Now we allow for many exportables, not just one. We shall assume that there is *no* exportable content in importables and that there are no materials imports which it is desired to import free of duty. Thus we now return to our simple model of section I where uniformity of nominal rates leads to uniformity of effective rates.

Assume first that the motive for tariffs is to foster import-competing production. We know then that the nominal tariff structure must be adjusted so as to reduce the adverse consumption effects. The fact that there are many different exportables towards which consumption can shift does not alter the argument. But a complication arises when there is an importable content in exportables. There is no reason to foster production of one exportable relative to another; all we want to do is to set up a price advantage in favour of importables relative to all exportables which should ideally be uniform. When there are many exportables, and given for the moment also a uniform nominal tariff, the negative effective protection which the tariff structure yields for exportables will vary according to whether the importable content in exportables is high or low. A uniform tariff thus sets up an undesirable non-uniformity. The structure of nominal rates must then be modified so that tariffs on those goods which are important inputs into exportables are reduced relative to those which are unimportant in this regard. An export drawback system would be a partial solution to this problem with respect to the production effects (aside from the administrative complications). It would avoid negative effective protection for exports, but not for exportable production for the home market. Production of exportables would then be determined by their free trade effective prices. But the system may go contrary to the desired protection of domestic producers of the importable inputs, at least if exporters were their main potential customers. Furthermore, since the drawback would not apply to home market sales, domestic consumption of exportables would be discouraged differentially, producers of exportables switching from selling on the home market to selling for export. The direct approach, avoiding this and all other second-best problems, is to subsidize importable value-added directly, allowing importables to be sold at world prices both to final consumers and to users, such as exporters.

If the motive for protection is to improve the terms of trade on the export side, the first-best policy requires a set of export taxes, the rates of tax being higher in those cases where the foreign elasticities are lower. Anything else is bound to be second-best. We have now two complications to consider, not, as in the previous case, just one. First, there may be importable content in the exportables creating different degrees of negative effective protection. The particular discrimination that results is unlikely to coincide with the discrimination required by the terms of trade argument. Hence an adjustment to the tariff structure, or alternatively offsetting subsidies, may be required as in the previous case. To isolate the terms of trade consideration assume now that there is no importable content in exportables. Some importables are closer substitutes for some exportables rather than others. If differential export taxes cannot be imposed, then the tariff structure (both nominal and effective) needs to be differential so that it will have the effect of reducing more those exports which have a low elasticity of foreign demand rather than those with a high elasticity. For example, suppose that the elasticity of demand for jute exports is low and for cotton high and that jute is grown in province J and cotton in province C. Import-competing industry M_1 is mainly in province J and industry M_2 in province C. Labour is fairly specific to each province. There may then be a second-best case for putting a higher effective tariff on M_1 than on M_2.

v. *Qualifications to the Uniform Tariff Concept: Tariffs to Improve the Balance of Payments*

A balance of payments argument might also plausibly give rise to a uniform tariff. The currency may be overvalued and for some reason the exchange rate cannot be altered. Thus the aim is to increase foreign exchange earnings. We assume here (as in Chapter 5 and elsewhere) that domestic absorption of goods and services is adjusted so as to maintain internal balance. This also means that the reduction in absorption which is required to attain a balance of payments improvement starting in internal balance is assumed to take place automatically; we are concerned with the problem that this be accompanied by the appropriate 'switching' policy. The first-best switching policy is devaluation, and the next-best is a combination of tariffs and export subsidies (applying also to invisibles). But again, only tariffs can be used, export subsidies being ruled out, perhaps because of a financing problem. The social cost of imports exceeds the private cost and there is no reason to increase one type of import-competing production, or reduce consumption of one type of imports, more than another. Does the third-best optimum call for a uniform tariff?

To deal with this case, assume now that there is only one exportable. One effect of a uniform tariff will be desirable. Resources will move out of the non-traded sector into importables and consumption will move the other way. These production and consumption effects between the importable and the non-traded sector will improve the balance of payments, and it is correct that uniform incentives be provided. But there are two other effects. Firstly, resources will also be drawn from exportables to importables and consumption the other way, these movements being quite unnecessary from a balance of payments point of view; imports may indeed be reduced, but this will be only at the cost of exports. The second-best optimum tariff structure cannot avoid such distortions, but it can reduce them. With regard to the production effect, it is necessary to reduce effective rates in those cases where the elasticity of transformation is much higher relative to exportables than to non-traded goods. Uniformity must also be departed from with respect to nominal rates if consumption substitution elasticities relative to exportables differ. The second effect to consider arises when there is an importable content in exportables. Any tariff on a product used by the exportable industry will yield negative effective protection for the latter and so will discourage exports, leading to an undesirable movement of resources out of exportables. It is then necessary to reduce, and perhaps sometimes avoid completely, nominal tariffs on importables which are important inputs into exportables (possibly through a drawback system). When we considered this complication in relation to the other reasons for tariffs we saw that the main aim was to avoid *non-uniformity* of negative effective protection, a problem that did not arise when only one exportable was assumed. But now the aim is additionally to minimize the degree of negative effective protection for exportables. We wish to improve the balance of payments, and to put a tariff on an input into the exportables, so giving the latter negative effective protection, is quite likely to worsen the balance of payments.

In section I we developed an argument for uniform tariffs simple in principle and simple in practice. In section II we introduced realistic complications which kept the simple principle of uniform effective rates but destroyed the simple practice of uniform nominal rates. Have we now (in sections III, IV and V) destroyed also the simple principle? It is of course a matter of practical judgement in each particular case as to how one should approach this problem. One must inevitably start with a simplification. Which simplification should one start with? Perhaps the simplification of uniform effective rates is quite a useful starting-point, given that one of the *general* arguments for tariff protection really applies. One can then modify the tariff structure that will emerge to take into account the complications of sections III, IV and V. These may be briefly summarized as follows:

(1) If the reason for tariffs is to foster import-competing production then (a) nominal tariffs should be discriminatory

on the basis of consumption substitution elasticities with exportables, and (b) there should be no discrimination between different exportables. But (i) the nominal tariff structure resulting from uniform effective rates is likely to be quite different from the one required from the point of view of (a), so that it must be adapted somewhat in the direction of (a), and (ii) the negative effective rates for exportables resulting from the tariff structure may be non-uniform, which is undesirable from the point of view of (b), so that the tariff structure must be adapted to reduce this non-uniformity.

(2) If the reason for tariffs is to improve the terms of trade on the side of exports, then (a) nominal tariffs should be discriminatory on the basis of consumption substitution elasticities with different exportables, the appropriate pattern depending on relative foreign demand elasticities, and (b) effective tariffs should discriminate in a similar way. But (i) the nominal tariff structure resulting from uniform effective rates is likely to be quite different from that required by (a), so that it must be adapted, and (ii) the negative effective rates for exportables will be non-uniform, while effective rates for importables are uniform, so that non-uniform price disadvantages for different exportables will result; again, this non-uniformity is not likely to coincide with that required by (b), so that the tariff structure must again be appropriately adapted.

(3) If the purpose of tariffs is to improve the balance of payments, then (a) nominal tariffs should be relatively lower where the closer consumption substitutes are exportables, (b) nominal tariffs should be relatively lower also where the importables are significant inputs into exportables, and (c) effective rates should be relatively lower where the products are close substitutes on the production side for exportables. But, again, the structure of nominal tariffs that yields uniform effective rates will not have the discriminatory pattern required by (a) and (b), and so must be modified, while some discrimination in effective rates on the lines of (c) must be introduced.

Finally, it must be stressed that all the complications arise because we have assumed that only tariffs can be used. Even in the simple case of section II, with no consumption effects and only one exportable, we found that uniformity of effective rates may require a complicated set of nominal rates. If the motive is to foster domestic import-competing production, *and if revenue-raising problems could be ignored*, it would obviously be simpler to have a uniform subsidy on import-competing value-added. This is even truer once we allow for consumption effects and many exportables. If the motive is to improve the terms of trade on the export side, *and if balance of payments effects could be ignored*, it would be simpler to have appropriate export taxes, while the exchange rate is clearly the proper balance of payments instrument, in association, of course, with appropriate aggregate expenditure adjustment. It is because the alternative policies are not always feasible politically or have costs of their own, such as the distortion and administrative costs in financing subsidies, that the uniform tariff analysis is of interest.

9

IMPORT QUOTAS: PARTIAL
EQUILIBRIUM ANALYSIS

QUANTITATIVE restrictions or quotas are widely used in less developed countries, and are particularly important in India and Pakistan, where they are probably the main channel through which the government influences the allocation of resources.[1] In the nineteen-thirties and the immediate post-war period they were also prevalent in Europe, though in recent years the only developed country with a wide-ranging quota system has been New Zealand.[2] Hence no adequate theory of protection can be limited to price mechanism devices, and we must examine how quantitative restrictions can be related to the preceding analysis in this book. A central aim will be to see to what extent the various conclusions derived with respect to tariffs apply when imports are restricted instead by quotas. The analysis can also be applied to export quotas, but this can be left to the reader. This chapter parallels the partial equilibrium positive analysis of tariffs in Chapters 2 and 3, though considerable attention will be given to effects on the profits of traders, a matter which is not of such importance in the

[1] See J. Bhagwati and P. Desai, *India: Planning for Industrialisation* (Oxford University Press, London, 1970); S. R. Lewis, *Pakistan: Industrialisation and Trade Policies* (Oxford University Press, London, 1970); S. R. Lewis and S. E. Guisinger, 'The Structure of Protection in Pakistan', in B. Balassa (ed.), *The Structure of Protection in Developing Countries*, 1971, and also many articles in the *Pakistan Development Review*. In Latin America, of the main countries, only Mexico now uses quantitative restrictions as the chief instrument of protection, but until the mid-1950s import and exchange controls were prevalent throughout Latin America. See S. Macario, 'Protectionism and Industrialization in Latin America', *Economic Bulletin for Latin America*, 9, March 1964, 61–101.

[2] Many developed countries still have quotas for particular products, notably textiles, petroleum, coal, and agricultural products. See R. E. Baldwin, *Nontariff Distortions of International Trade* (Brookings, Washington, 1970).

case of tariffs. The next chapter will deal with general equilibrium.[3]

I. *The Partial Equilibrium Foundations*

The familiar partial equilibrium analysis of quantitative import restrictions runs as follows. The domestic consumers of the product concerned, the domestic producers, the traders who bring it into the country and the foreign suppliers are

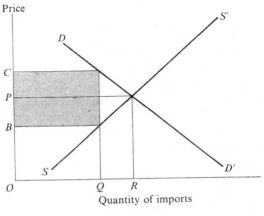

FIG. 9.1

all assumed to be competitive. We refer to Fig. 9.1, with DD' the import demand curve and SS' the foreign import supply curve. In free trade the quantity of imports is OR and the price OP. Let imports be restricted to an amount OQ, with import licences to this amount awarded to the domestic traders and prices freely flexible in the market. So the price of the product to consumers rises to OC, the price paid to foreign suppliers falls to OB, and the traders obtain a margin above

[3] The standard reference on the partial equilibrium analysis of quotas is H. Heuser, *Control of International Trade* (George Routledge and Sons, London, 1939). See also J. E. Meade, *The Balance of Payments* (Oxford University Press, London, 1951), Ch. XXI, and L. B. Yeager, *International Monetary Relations* (Harper and Row, New York, 1966), Ch. 7. Heuser, op. cit., describes the use of quotas in Europe pre-war. Two detailed case-studies are G. G. Moffatt, *Import Control and Industrialization: A Study of the Australian Experience* (Melbourne University Press, Melbourne, 1970), and Bhagwati and Desai, op. cit.

their normal profits of BC per unit. This margin spread over imports OQ yields total quota profits shown by the shaded area. These profits reflect the scarcity value of the quota licences; thus they are rents. The value of imports falls by a greater percentage than the quantity because not only the quantity but also the price has fallen. If the world price of the product had been given the value of imports would have fallen by the same proportion as the quantity and the quota margin per unit would have been equal to the rise in the domestic price. The quota could have been fixed in the first place as a value quota rather than a volume quota. If fixed so as to yield the same value of imports as the volume quota it would have had the same effect in every respect. For a given volume quota the margin between demand price and supply price will be the greater the lower the elasticities of demand and supply.

This familiar analysis then goes on to point out that a tariff at the rate of BC/OB would have achieved the same result as the quota, except that the quota yields quota profits to the traders who obtained the licences while the tariff would yield customs revenue. Furthermore, a quota might be combined with a tariff. If the margin between demand price and supply price produced by the quota is greater than the tariff then it is the quota that sets the internal price, and if the tariff is higher, it sets the price. A tariff which is redundant from the point of view of the domestic price and the volume of imports may still have a purpose since it transfers part of the quota profits from traders to government revenue while a redundant quota may have a purpose in ensuring that imports are reduced at least to a certain amount in case the tariff turns out to be inadequate.

This simple approach ignores the interesting possibility that the total profits of traders—normal profits combined with quota profits—may fall, and that this may cause imports to cease.[4] In fact it assumes that import licences are transferable between firms and there is a market in licences. When imports decline the demand for traders' services must decline, and so the number of trading firms is likely to decline. The remaining firms will continue to receive their normal profits, but total normal profits will decline simply because there are fewer

---

[4] J. E. Meade, *The Balance of Payments*, op. cit., p. 278 (footnote).

firms. In addition to this, there will be quota profits which will go to all the firms that received the licences, the firms that went out of business selling their licences to the remaining firms.

But in fact the market for licences may be very imperfect. Thus the transfer of licences may be illegal and may only be able to proceed through various devious ways.[5] Suppose that the licences are not at all transferable between firms, that all the original firms receive licences in proportion to their original imports, and that they all have the same average cost curve, all producing at the point of minimum average costs. The import quota will force each firm to move back up its cost curve. Hence the average costs of all the firms will increase because of the diseconomies of reducing scale. This will be, at least in part, because a given amount of normal profit must be spread over a smaller output. At the same time, as before, the price received for traders' services will rise since there is also a movement backwards up the demand curve. On balance the price may have risen more than average costs, so that some profit above normal profit may still emerge. But it is also possible that profits disappear entirely and indeed that a loss is made. In the short-term the firms may survive, to be saved in time by the removal of the import restrictions. Or they might amalgamate into a smaller number of firms, so in fact achieving the same result as a transfer of licences. But one can conceive of various obstacles to this, in particular the diseconomies from amalgamating their other activities outside this particular importing business. Finally, as an extreme case, all the firms might leave the industry, the licences all becoming unused. It is, of course, more likely that the cost curves of the various firms differ so that only some of them go out of business.

II. *Trader's or Producer's Monopoly*

So far we have assumed competition among domestic traders and domestic producers. We will continue to assume that licences are distributed to domestic traders and allow separately for (a) a trader's monopoly and (b) a domestic import-competing producer's monopoly. In both cases there are two possibilities: the monopoly existed even before the quota was imposed, and

[5] See section II of Chapter 10.

the monopoly resulted from the quota. Thus there are four cases, and in three of them interesting results, substantially different from those of the simple model, ensue.

The least interesting case is where there is a single monopoly trader even under free trade. The result of an import quota is then almost exactly the same as in our simple model: the domestic price rises, so that there is a protective effect, the foreign price falls, and the value of imports declines. The difference only is this: the trader's profits must fall. He was previously maximizing profits; now a new constraint in the form of the quota is imposed on him, and he is forced to move from his original profit maximization point. If he is moving along the rising part of his average cost curve, so that the reduction in imports lowers his unit costs, profits per unit of imports must rise and, as long as the quota is positive, total profits cannot actually fall to zero. Note that the reduced profits he is making depend on his quota. If he had to buy the quota he would be prepared to pay the amount of these profits less normal profits. Thus what were monopoly profits become quota profits. If he has been producing at the point of minimum average costs or on the falling part of his average cost curve, so that his unit costs, including normal profits, rise as a result of the quota, his profits could disappear and he could run into a loss.

The next case is where a group of competitive traders is turned into a monopoly or cartel as a result of the imposition of import quotas. This would be likely when the restrictions set up a barrier to new entrants by confining the quotas mainly to existing firms, and when the main obstacle to the establishment of a monopoly under free trade had been the freedom of entry. The establishment of the monopoly might make no difference at all. The result might be the same as if there had been competition with licence transferability—our simple case. This would be so if the import volume which would maximize profits in the absence of a quota were greater than the quota level. Then the newly formed monopoly could not attain the profit-maximizing imports but would just have to settle for the import level set by the quota. The value of imports, domestic and foreign prices, and so on, would all then be set by the quota, as in the competitive case. But if profit-maximizing imports are *less* than the quota level imports will fall to a level below the quota and some licences will remain unused. The fall in imports has then two elements: first the fall imposed directly by the quota, and second the fall imposed indirectly by the quota through its creation of a traders' monopoly. Compared with the situation before the quota, profits will increase in both these cases where a monopoly has been created. And in both cases the continuance of the profits is dependent on the quota, which thus has a value to the monopolist equal to the profits.

It has been the general conclusion so far that import quotas will raise the domestic price of the import. Normally one would expect this to have a protective effect on domestic import-competing producers, stimulating them to replace imports. This will indeed be the result if the domestic producers are competitive. But it can be shown that if there is a domestic producer's monopoly, domestic import-competing output may actually fall.[6] While the price to the producer will still go up, he may reduce his output. This result should not surprise since it parallels that of a prohibitive tariff which allows a domestic producer to exploit his monopoly power.[7] To avoid situations of bilateral monopoly it will be assumed that the traders, exporters and consumers are and remain competitive. We continue to assume that the traders receive the licences. The quota has now two effects. First, by restricting imports it increases the demand for the product of the domestic producer, so inducing him to raise output and replace imports. This is the normal import-replacing effect which is the only effect when the domestic producers are competitive. Secondly it reduces the elasticity of the demand curve facing the producer. This elasticity has as one element the elasticity of import supply, and beyond a certain point it now becomes zero. And with a lower elasticity of demand the producer's monopoly power is increased, so that he is induced to restrict production. Thus on balance his output may rise or fall.

Fig. 9.2 illustrates this argument for the simple case where the elasticity of supply of imports (as well as of traders' services)

---

[6] Heuser, op. cit., pp. 163–7. Heuser acknowledges an article by P. Fontigny in the *Bulletin de l'Institut des Sciences Economiques*, May 1936.

[7] See section VI of Chapter 2.

is infinite, so that under free trade the producer could not exercise any monopoly power. The horizontal axis shows the *importable*, whether imported or home-produced. The import supply curve is SS', the domestic demand curve is DD' and the domestic producer's marginal cost curve is CC'. In free trade the demand curve facing the domestic producer is the composite curve SLD'. Free trade output is OR, consumption

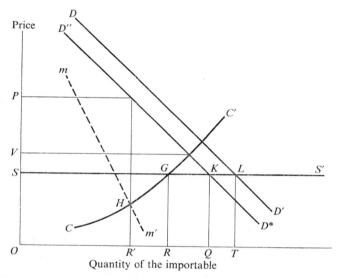

FIG. 9.2

is OT and imports are RT. A quota is imposed limiting imports to QT ($= KL$). Draw a curve $D''D^*$ parallel to DD', being to the left of DD' by a distance QT at all prices. The new quota-distorted demand curve facing the domestic producer is the composite curve $D''KLD'$. For our discussion only the stretch $D''K$ is relevant. From this demand curve can be derived a marginal revenue curve. The relevant segment of such a curve, mm', is shown. It is drawn as intersecting CC' at H, below the point G where the SS' curve intersected CC'. The price rises to OP. Thus, as drawn, output would decline to OR'. But the marginal revenue curve might have intersected CC' above G, in which case output would have risen. The smaller the quota, the more the $D''D^*$ curve and the mm' curve are to the right, and hence the more likely it is that output increases. On the other hand, the lower the elasticity of total demand (the DD' curve), the more the marginal revenue curve is below the average revenue ($D''D^*$) curve at any given output, and hence the more likely it is that output falls. The elasticity of DD' has only become relevant for determining the volume of domestic output because there is a quota. It is interesting to note that if the quota equalled the original imports ($= RT$) the import substitution effect would disappear and only the monopoly-creating effect would be left, so that domestic output would be bound to fall. A little geometric manipulation will confirm this. The case where the domestic producer was able to exploit his monopoly position even before the quota was imposed, so that the foreign import supply curve (or the supply curve of traders' services) must have been rising, is more complicated to illustrate, but the same considerations apply.

III. *Licence Profits go to Exporters, Government or Users*

The foreign exporters may do their own importing, so that there are no separate trading firms, and may thus receive the import licences. The domestic price will then rise as before, with the same effects on domestic production and consumption, but quota profits will go to the exporters, and not domestic traders, and the terms of trade will deteriorate. We assume at this stage competition all round. In Fig. 9.1 the new price of imports would be OC. If the quota were a volume one and the elasticity of demand were less than unity the value of imports would actually rise. Of course if it were a value quota the value of imports would have to fall. In that case, if the elasticity of demand is initially less than unity a restriction in volume designed to reduce the value of imports to the value permitted by the quota would *at first* raise the value of imports. But the reduction in volume would continue. Eventually the elasticity of demand would become unity and then more than unity, and from then on further volume restrictions would lead to a fall in the value of imports. The analysis also applies when the traders are domestic but the licences are nevertheless awarded to the foreign suppliers directly or through the intermediation of foreign governments.[8] This may be because the motive for import restriction is protection, not balance of payments or terms of trade improvement, this being a way of achieving the desired result without incurring the same degree of foreign criticism. It may also be convenient to pass the responsibility for administering the quota system on to foreign governments. An important case is where the licences are awarded to foreign-owned trading firms operating domestically. The quota profits would then go abroad, or at least be credited to foreigners, just as if the licences had been awarded to exporters. In fact, the quota profits would take the form of invisible instead of visible imports; our basic analysis also stands.

If an exporter's monopoly exists to begin with exports will initially have been restricted to the profit-maximizing point, a point at which the elasticity of demand must be greater than unity. Thus the imposition of a volume quota cannot raise the value of exports. But provided the exporter's supply curve is rising, the effects otherwise are the same as when the exporters were competitive and received the licences. There is now a possibility that the exporter was operating on the falling section of his average cost curve; the quota would then raise his average costs, and his profits might disappear entirely so that he would cease exporting to the country concerned. If the quotas create an exporter's monopoly for the first time the new profit-maximizing equilibrium may involve imports below the permitted quota level, so that some licences remain unused. This is the same possibility which arose earlier when a trader's monopoly was created by the quotas. An exporter's monopoly could result from a quota system in two ways. First, the licences may be awarded to existing exporters only, and they may be able to combine because the quotas have set up a barrier to new entrants. This is the same story as in the case of domestic traders. Secondly, the licences may be awarded to domestic traders but separate licences may be issued for many different sources or countries of supply, so that the suppliers become fragmented and prevented from competing with each other.

---

[8] Pre-war examples are in Heuser, op. cit. The United States and the United Kingdom restrictions on cotton textile imports from less developed countries involve the latters' governments allocating the national quotas among their own exporters.

Thus a set of export monopolies would be created; each of these monopolies would then be in a position to force a rise in the export price so as to transfer the quota profits from the domestic traders to themselves.

The licence profits may go neither to traders nor to foreign exporters but to the government, to civil servants in the form of bribes, to consumers or users, or to third parties. These are practically important cases, though we shall discuss them very briefly here. The government could charge a fee for the licences, perhaps varying the fee until all licences are taken up and excess demand is absent. Assuming the traders are competitive it could have a completely flexible price, that is, it could auction the licences.[9] The income distribution effect is then the same as that of a tariff. The difference is only that the size of the fall in the volume or value of imports (whichever form the licences take) can be known in advance in the case of auctioned licences but not in the case of a tariff. If there is a monopoly trader or cartel there are complications. An import fee varying with the amount of imports will affect the monopolist's marginal costs and hence his trading equilibrium. To ensure that imports are at the desired quota level the fee should be no higher than is necessary to raise the trader's marginal costs so as to make them equal to marginal revenue at this import level. If the fee were higher the trader would choose to import less than the quota. But such an import fee may not absorb the whole of the monopoly profits. This would definitely be so if the trader were operating at constant costs or the rising part of his cost curve. For price will be greater than marginal revenue, marginal cost is made equal to the latter by the import fee, and average cost is equal to marginal cost (if costs are constant) or less than marginal costs (if on the rising part of the average cost curve). Hence price must be greater than average cost (including normal profits); so some monopoly or quota profits must remain. If it were desired to absorb the whole of the profits it would be necessary to have a lump-sum fee, independent of import volume.

---

[9] J. E. Meade, *The Balance of Payments*, op. cit., p. 286. Brazil auctioned some part of her foreign exchange from 1953–61, with separate auctions for various categories. See A. Kafka, 'The Brazilian Exchange Auction System', *Review of Economics and Statistics*, 38, Aug. 1956, 308–22.

The auctioning system clearly breaks down when there is a monopoly buyer or the likelihood of a buyer's cartel developing. The situation would be one of bilateral monopoly. If the government wishes to appropriate to itself some of the quota profits it should then fix an arbitrary and perhaps variable licence fee which the monopolist has to regard as a constraint. If part or all of the quota profits go to civil servants in the form of bribes one could argue that indirectly the bribes go to the government since relevant civil service salaries can be lower than otherwise. But there is liable to be a somewhat random and unpredictable element in the distribution of the bribes among civil servants! So appropriate salary adjustment may be difficult.

Price control may prevent the price of an import on which a quota restriction has been imposed from rising.[10] With a given foreign supply price there will then be no quota profits. If traders' average costs rise as a result of the contraction in imports they will of course be in difficulties, and imports might even cease. But let us assume here that their costs do not rise or that a rise in price sufficient to maintain their normal profits is permitted. In a notional sense one might now say that the quota profits have gone to consumers. Nevertheless, on balance consumers will be worse off (since their choices have been restricted) though not as badly off as they would have been if the quota profits had gone to traders, exporters or the government. Note that if the price-control applied also to domestic producers the quota would not be protective. It is also possible that the domestic price fails to rise because of some form of price rigidity, rather than price-control, perhaps because traders wish to maintain goodwill and expect the restrictions to be temporary.

An interesting and practically very common case is where the restricted import is an input into another product and the producers of this other product—the users—are the importers and receive the import licences. The licences may also go to the users when they are not the actual importers. Sometimes

[10] Prices as well as imports were controlled in many advanced countries (e.g., United Kingdom and Australia) during and after the Second World War. In less developed countries price-control is less likely to be effective, and this analysis is not relevant to any current situation.

this is called an *import entitlement scheme*, domestic producers getting 'entitlements' to imports on the basis of their own production or capacity. Thus they will receive the notional quota profits. The profits will again be purely notional because there will not be any actual rise in price of the input. In fact, if the foreign suppliers are competitive and supplying along an upward-sloping supply curve the price will fall. But let us assume a given foreign price. Let us also assume that there is no domestic production of the input so that we can ignore income redistribution as between domestic producers of the input and its users. If the user is a monopolist he will have been maximizing his profits initially. The quota imposes a new constraint on him and so reduces his profits, even though it is true that if the quota profits had gone to traders his fall in profit would have been greater. If he was operating on the falling part of his cost curve his profits may disappear and he may go out of business. Similarly profits will fall if the users are competitive and face a perfectly elastic demand curve for their product. But this conclusion does not necessarily apply if the using industry is competitive and faces a demand curve which is less than infinitely elastic. Now the reduction in its output enforced by the quota restriction on the input may bring it closer to the output level which the industry would choose if it were monopolized. In this case its profits may rise. Furthermore, the quota restriction on the input imposes an entry barrier, so that the using industry may turn into a monopoly and might choose an output level less than that indicated by the import quota, so that some licences will remain unused. The effect when the licences go to users depends in fact on much the same considerations as when they go to traders.

Finally, the quota profits may go to none of the parties directly concerned with the production, consumption or import of the product. The licences may simply be given to persons or institutions whom the government or its officials wish to benefit financially, whether relatives of politicians or officials, contributors to the governing party's funds or the party itself, army officers whose guns keep the government in power or the army as a corporate body. If these beneficiaries become nominal traders but in fact sell the licences or the use of their names to traditional traders who continue to do the work of importing

then they are *briefcase importers*.[11] Some or all import licences
may be issued to the country's own exporters who can then sell
them to importers. This is an *export bonus scheme*. Many
varieties of such schemes are, or have been, used in various
countries.[12] A rubber exporter may receive licences (*bonus
vouchers*) to import manufactured goods as part-payment for
the dollars he has earned through his exports. These licences
he may sell on a market with a fluctuating or a fixed price to
traders who will then import the manufactured goods in the
usual way. Thus the net result is to subsidize exports and tax
imports; it is rather like a partial devaluation and is best
regarded as part of a multiple exchange rate system. In any
case, it is a way of encouraging exports and linking expenditure
on imports to foreign currency receipts from exports. Usually
it is a supplement to exporters when their earnings have to be
converted at an unfavourable exchange rate.

IV. *Effects of an Import Quota: Summary*

Let us now summarize the effects of an import quota (unaccompanied by a tariff) as it emerges from our partial equilibrium analysis so far. In the simple model described at the
beginning of section I and in Fig. 9.1 the conclusions listed in
column 1 of this table applied. Column 2 shows for each of these
conclusions the qualifications which have emerged.

(1) A quota causes imports to
fall to the level set by the
quota.

(a) The profits of traders, exporters or users may disappear if their average costs
rise because of the quota
restriction. In that case imports may cease or fall below the quota level.

(b) A monopoly of traders, exporters or users may be

---

[11] The term comes from Indonesia. The firms that result have been called
Ali-Baba firms—Ali, the Malay-Indonesian gets the licences and carries the
briefcase, and Baba, the Chinese, does the trading.

[12] Indonesia has made much use of export bonus schemes. See W. M. Corden
and J. A. C. Mackie, 'The Development of the Indonesian Exchange Rate
System', *Malayan Economic Review*, 7, April 1962, 37–60. The best-known
export bonus scheme is that of Pakistan, and there is an extensive literature
on it; see S. R. Lewis and S. E. Guisinger, op. cit., and references cited by them.

(2) A price margin develops between the domestic price and the import price, the domestic price rising and the import price possibly falling.

newly created, and the profit-maximizing import volume may be below the quota volume, so that imports would fall by more than indicated by the quota.

(a) Exporters may get the licence profits, so that there is no distinction between the import supply price and the domestic price; both rise.

(b) Users are the importers; again, there is no distinction between supply price and domestic price.

(c) There is price-control or price rigidity.

(3) A volume quota causes a fall in the value of imports.

The value of imports will rise if exporters get the licence profits and the elasticity of demand for imports is less than unity.

(4) Output of domestic import-competing production rises.

(a) If there is a monopoly in domestic import-competing production, output may fall.

(b) If price-control applies to domestic production as well as to imports domestic output will not rise.

(5) If the licences go to traders quota profits emerge or monopoly profits rise.

(a) Profits may fall or disappear entirely if average costs rise sufficiently; if traders are competitive this is possible only if licences are not freely transferable between firms.

(b) Profits will fall if there is initially a trader's monopoly.

v. *The Equivalence Between Quotas and Tariffs*

In the simple model represented by Fig. 9.1 it is possible to choose a single tariff rate which would have the same effect as an import quota on the volume and value of imports, on the domestic and foreign price, and on the volume of domestic output. This may be described as the *implicit tariff rate*. The only difference would be that with the tariff traders would only earn the normal profits appropriate to the restricted volume of imports while with the quota they also earn quota profits.

In most of our other cases a single tariff rate that achieves *all* these equivalences does not exist. For a given quota one tariff rate would achieve the same import volume, perhaps another the same import value, another the same domestic price and yet another the same domestic output. To make a comparison between tariffs and quotas we must fix one of these equivalences and see in which direction the other effects of the resultant tariff differ from the effects of the given quota. While the choice is arbitrary and the analysis could proceed in any number of ways it seems at least reasonable to fix the import volume. We shall call the tariff rate that achieves the same import volume as a quota the *comparable* tariff. By reviewing the various cases that have been discussed in this chapter so far the following results emerge.[13]

Firstly, in certain circumstances a comparable tariff may not exist. This possibility arises when the trader, exporter or user is a monopolist operating on the declining part of his cost curve so that his average costs rise as a result of the restriction of imports. The point is most easily made by considering the case of a monopoly trader whose average costs, including normal profits, have risen as the result of a quota to the same extent as his price, so that his quota profits (or monopoly profits) are zero. In the absence of the quota he would of course have chosen a higher import volume at which there would have been positive monopoly profits. If a tariff were imposed, and hence his costs were raised, and he operated at the quota import level he would make a loss, so no tariff could induce him to import at this point. To proceed further, let us assume that a comparable tariff exists.

[13] The general subject of the equivalence between tariffs and quotas was first opened up by J. Bhagwati in 'On the equivalence of tariffs and quotas', in R. E. Baldwin, et al., *Trade, Growth and the Balance of Payments* (Rand McNally, Chicago, 1965), but his definitions and approach are *not* followed here. See also, H. Shibata, 'A Note on the Equivalence of Tariffs and Quotas', *American Economic Review*, 58, March 1968, 137–42; J. Bhagwati, 'More on the Equivalence of Tariffs and Quotas', *American Economic Review*, 58, March 1968, 142–6; G. J. Yadav, 'A Note on the Equivalence of Tariffs and Quotas', *Canadian Journal of Economics*, 1, Feb. 1968, 105–10.

Secondly, a comparable tariff will lead to the same import value and *foreign* price in all cases except where exporters obtain the quota profits. In that case, the quota worsens the terms of trade while a tariff may improve them; hence a comparable tariff would lead to a larger reduction in the value of imports than the quota, and indeed—as we saw earlier—the quota may not lead to a reduction at all.

Thirdly, a comparable tariff will lead to the same domestic price in all cases but three. If we give the term *implicit tariff rate* the narrow meaning of *the rate of tariff that will bring about the same domestic price increase as the quota* then in all but three cases the *comparable* tariff (same import volume) is also the *implicit* tariff (same price effect).[14] This is a particularly important equivalence as it also means that, provided domestic production is competitive, it would have the same protective effect. It is worth noting that this equivalence exists even when there is a trader's monopoly to begin with or such a monopoly has been created by the quota. If there is a trader's monopoly to begin with (and thus also would exist with the tariff) the proportional increase in the price brought about by the tariff will not necessarily be identical with the tariff rate. More important, if a newly created monopoly restricts imports below the level set by the quota the comparable tariff rate is that which attains not the level of imports permitted by the quota but rather the lower actual level.

Now consider the three exceptions to this equivalence between the *comparable* and the *implicit* tariff. First, if there is price control or inflexibility the tariff will raise the price by more than the quota. Advocates of quotas in preference to tariffs who argue that tariffs are 'inflationary', meaning simply that they raise prices directly on the restricted imports, usually imply price inflexibility. Secondly, and rather trivially, if the users of the restricted imports obtain the licences then they are

---

[14] Bhagwati, in 'On the equivalence of tariffs and quotas', op. cit., defined the *implicit tariff rate* as the proportional discrepancy the quota creates between the price paid by domestic consumers and the foreign supply price, and defined equivalence as the equality between (his) implicit tariff rate and (what we call) the comparable tariff. But this approach leads to difficulties which he recognizes in *American Economic Review*, March 1968. His revised definition of equivalence is in terms of the comparable tariff leading to the same domestic production. Shibata, op. cit., defines equivalence in terms of the domestic price effect, as in our paragraph here.

unlikely to raise the prices to themselves; a tariff will of course raise the prices of their imported inputs. But, provided the users stay in business at all, the effect on the production and prices of their own goods will be the same. The third exception arises when there is a potential domestic producer's monopoly. We will consider the small country case here. A non-prohibitive tariff does not, in that case, have the monopoly-creating effect of a quota, but shares with it the import-replacing effect. A given reduction in imports when achieved by a tariff will be associated with a greater rise in domestic output than when achieved by a quota (in which case there might actually be a fall in domestic output). Hence it must be achieved with a lesser fall in domestic consumption compared with a quota, and to induce the lesser fall in consumption a lesser rise in the domestic price is required. In Fig. 9.2 the comparable tariff rate (which achieves the same import reduction as the quota) is SV/OS (reducing imports to QT), while the implicit tariff rate (which achieves the same rise in the domestic price as the quota) is SP/OS.

Finally we might compare the effects of a quota and the comparable tariff on traders' profits. When traders obtain the quota profits there is obviously not equivalence. If there is monopoly both with the tariff and with the quota both will lead to a fall in traders' profits but the tariff will lead to a greater fall. A more interesting elaboration is that in the case where traders are competitive but licences are not transferable one can get the surprising result that traders' profits might be greater with a tariff than with a quota. The quotas compel all the individual firms to contract in size and so to reduce the scales of their individual imports, thus raising their average costs. On the other hand a tariff allows the number of firms to decline while the remaining firms maintain their operations, so that their costs need not rise.

VI. *Quotas on Input and Final Good, and Effective Protection*

So far we have been concerned with input quotas for a single good. Now we consider the imposition at the same time of import quotas on a final good and on the produced input into this final good. The aim is to show how the two quotas are interrelated. We shall assume perfect competition among

producers and traders, that quota profits go to traders, that
world prices are given, that coefficients are fixed, and that
imports of each good remain after quotas have been imposed.
We shall use Fig. 9.3, which is the same diagram as Fig. 3.1,

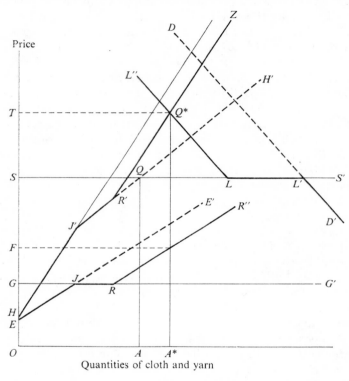

Fig. 9.3

showing quantities of cloth and of yarn along the horizontal
axis. The free trade price of cloth is OS, the free trade price of
yarn is OG, the cloth demand curve is DD', and the domestic
yarn supply curve is EE'. As was shown in Chapter 3, in free
trade the cloth producers are faced with a supply curve of
yarn, EJG', which is made up of a segment of the domestic
yarn producers' supply curve EE' and a segment of the foreign
yarn supply curve. When the supply curve of their value-added
product is added on to this we obtain the total supply curve

of domestic cloth producers, $HJ'H'$. At the same time they are faced by a demand curve for their cloth $SL'D'$ made up of a segment of the domestic consumers' demand curve DD' and a segment of the foreign cloth supply curve. The intersection at Q of these two composite curves $HJ'H'$ and $SL'D'$ yields free trade cloth output OA.

A technique can be devised to show the effects of the two quotas and changes in their sizes. A quota on cloth shifts the demand curve facing the domestic cloth producers. Suppose that the quota is LL' and that $L''L$ is parallel to DL'. Then $L''LL'D'$ is the *quota-distorted demand curve* facing producers. It shows that if domestic supply is less than SL the price will have to be above the import price; extra imports cannot replace domestic output because of the quota. Next consider a quota on yarn of JR. This will shift the yarn supply curve facing cloth producers; if they wish to purchase more yarn than GR they have to pay a price higher than the import price in order to induce extra domestic yarn production. The yarn quota makes extra yarn imports impossible. Hence the *quota-distorted yarn supply curve* is $EJRR''$ (RR'' being parallel to JE'). By adding on to it the supply curve of the value-added product we obtain $HJ'R'Z$, the *quota-distorted cloth supply curve*. The intersection of the *quota-distorted cloth demand curve* facing cloth producers with the *quota-distorted cloth supply curve* is Q^* and yields cloth output OA^*, resulting thus from the two quotas combined. It can readily be seen that this output could be greater or less than free trade output OA (which resulted from the equilibrium point Q), depending on the sizes of the two quotas. The cloth price will rise to OT, the implicit cloth tariff being ST/OS. The yarn price will rise to OF, the implicit yarn tariff being GF/OG. It would be possible to show consumption of cloth, production of yarn, and imports of both, as well as traders' profits on both, but this would clutter up the diagram. The technique can be used to show what happens when either of the two quotas is varied in size. For example, enlarging the yarn quota will lower the implicit nominal tariff for cloth, raise the implicit effective tariff for cloth (hence leading to greater cloth output) and lower yarn output. It can also be shown that the effect of imposing one of the quotas depends on the size of the other quota.

Can the concept of the effective protective rate be applied when protection is by import quotas?[15] Clearly in the simple case represented by Fig. 9.3 it can. A quota brings about a given increase in the domestic price; this represents the quota profit per unit and is measured by the excess of the domestic price over the import price. Expressed in relation to the import price it is the implicit tariff rate that can be fed into the effective rate formula. Thus in Fig. 9.3, for the case where there are quotas on both cloth and yarn, the implicit nominal tariff rate for cloth is ST/OS and for yarn GF/OG, while the effective rate for cloth is $(ST - GF)/GS$. If there are costs and normal profits of traders the exercise is in practice more difficult since these must be separated from the quota profit element, as the implicit tariff will be equal only to the quota profit per unit. But in principle there is still an un-ambiguous implicit effective rate. If the foreign supply curve is upward sloping, so that the foreign price falls owing to the quota, the implicit tariff is greater than the rise in the domestic price. But it is still equal to the quota profit per unit and (insofar as the concept of the effective rate is compatible with a rising foreign supply curve) an effective rate can in principle be calculated.

The effective rate concept gets into difficulties once we allow for the various complications that have been discussed in this chapter. If comparable tariffs for the input and the output exist then a *comparable effective rate* exists. But this will not necessarily lead to the same changes in domestic prices or in domestic outputs. It will lead only to the same import volumes and (if world prices are given) the same import values. Altern-atively one could try to calculate for every set of input and final good quotas the nominal rates that would yield the same domestic price changes. These would yield the *implicit effective rates*. These may not always exist, but if they do they will not necessarily lead to the same import quantities and hence will differ from the *comparable effective rates*. If there is price-control on the restricted imports or some degree of price inflexibility there will be a comparable effective rate which has an equivalent effect on import volume and value and on

---

[15] See Bhagwati and Desai, op. cit., and various contributions in B. Balassa (ed.), *The Structure of Protection in Developing Countries*, 1971, for calculations of effective rates taking into account quotas.

domestic output, but it will not be possible to calculate such a rate from price observations, since actual prices do not reflect equilibrium prices.

The case where the users of a product are its importers and obtain the licences is of particular interest as it is common in practice. Let us assume that the foreign supply price is given, that there is no domestic production of the input, and that no quota or tariff on the product of the using industry has been imposed. The price of the input will then not reflect its equilibrium price. A calculation using actual prices might then suggest that the effective protective rate is zero.[16] But the comparable tariff on the input would yield a negative effective rate for the using industry. And there is indeed negative effective protection, for the quota on the input will have compelled the using industry to reduce its output. The point is that the shadow price for the input which the using industry ought to have charged to itself is the one which should be used for calculating the comparable tariff rate. This does not mean, of course, that the effects of the quota and the comparable tariff are identical in all respects. The tariff leads to a transfer from producers' surplus in the using industry to government revenue on the imports that remain, while the quota does not. If the quotas had been allocated to independent traders and they had extracted their quota profits the transfer would be from producers' surplus to these quota profits. The problem seems to disappear when there is domestic production of the input, provided the producers of the inputs are competitive and quite separate from the producers in the using industry. The quota on the input will then raise the price of competing domestic output, and this rise in the price, represented by the excess of the unit cost of domestic production over the import price, measures the comparable tariff on the input. This comparable tariff can then be used to calculate the comparable effective rate on the product of the using industry.[17] The

[16] This is the method used in Bhagwati and Desai, op. cit., Ch. 17. An additional complication in India and Pakistan has been that in some industries some firms receive quotas for their inputs while others have to buy inputs on the market, or firms receive licences for a part of their inputs, buying the remainder on the market.

[17] This case must be distinguished from the *contents protection scheme* of section V, Chapter 3. In that case duty-free imports of inputs were *linked* to

practical method of calculation that this approach seems to suggest is that all inputs of a given homogeneous product should be treated in the same way in the effective rate calculation, irrespective of who obtains the licences and what price the using industry actually pays for the inputs. Yet this approach is not entirely satisfactory, since it ignores the difference in the income distribution effect which, in a more complicated case (downward-sloping average cost curves for the using firms, or monopoly) might affect output.

---

purchases from domestic input producers, so that the cost to the using industry of increments of inputs was a weighted *average* of the cost of imports and of domestic production. The implicit tariff on the output—required for the calculation of effective protection for the using industry—was thus the proportional excess of this weighted average input cost over the cost of duty-free imports. In the present case the cost of an increment of input once the import quota has been filled is simply the marginal cost of domestic production.

10

IMPORT QUOTAS: GENERAL
EQUILIBRIUM ANALYSIS

We now move beyond the one-product model, or the one-final-good, one-input model, in the analysis of import restrictions. Sections I and II deal with two important aspects of import quotas that have not received much attention in the literature while section III parallels the general equilibrium analysis of tariffs in Chapter 4. Section IV deals briefly with some aspects of the second-best welfare economics of import restrictions (parallel to Chapter 8). But no attempt is made to present a comprehensive welfare analysis on which a judgement about the appropriateness of the use of quotas in particular situations could be based.

1. *The Interchange of Licences Between Products*

Some import licences may be issued for the import of hats and others for the import of bags, and the licences for one may not be used for importing the other. Licences are then not interchangeable between the two products. But this raises the question of the definition of a product. Any import licensing system must contain some element of interchangeability. If a product group were narrowly defined as 'straw hats' there would be interchangeability between straw hats of various sizes. In addition, clearly distinct products may be grouped into categories and interchangeability may be permitted between licences within each category but not across categories. In setting up the detailed import licensing structure this issue of interchangeability is crucial.

Consider then two homogeneous products, hats and bags, assuming to begin with that licences for hats and bags are *not* interchangeable. But the licences can be bought and sold among firms, there being a perfect market for each of the two

categories of licences. There is competition all round. For
each product separately a quota profit margin and hence an
implicit tariff rate will emerge. This will depend on the relative
import cut imposed by the quota, on the elasticity of import
demand and also on whether the demand curve has shifted.

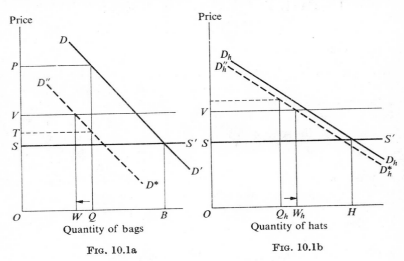

Fig. 10.1a   Fig. 10.1b

The two implicit tariff rates that result may differ from each
other. Next imagine that interchangeability of licences is
permitted. The implicit tariff rates will then become equalized,
imports of one product rising and the other falling. Hence
interchangeability has the same effect on import volume and
value, and on domestic prices, as replacing a differential tariff
with a uniform nominal tariff.

This is only one aspect of interchangeability, but before
going on, let us spell it out a little more rigorously. In Fig. 10.1a
the import supply curve of bags is SS', the import demand curve
is DD' and free trade bag imports are OB. Traders' costs and
normal profits can be assumed to have been deducted from
import demand to obtain DD'. The import quota is OQ, the
domestic price rises to OP and the quota profit margin is SP.
The lower the elasticity of demand for a given quota the greater
this margin. All this is familiar. In due course the demand for
bags may decline owing to a change in tastes, the new demand

curve being $D''D^*$. The quota profit margin then declines to ST. Fig. 10.1b refers to imports of hats. Units are so chosen that the free trade price of a 'unit of hats' is equal to the free trade price of 'a unit of bags'. The diagram is the same as for hats, the demand curve also having shifted to the left after a quota was imposed. Whether the quota profit margin for hats or for bags is greater clearly depends on three ratios: the ratio between the two proportional quota cuts, the ratio between the two demand elasticities, and the ratio between the two proportional leftward shifts of the demand curves. If all the ratios were unity the two profit margins that would emerge would be the same. In the diagrams the proportional quota cuts are the same, the bag elasticity over the relevant range is lower than that for hats, which in itself would cause the price of bags to rise more than that of hats, but the leftward shift of the demand curve for bags has been relatively so great that on balance the price of bags has risen less than that of hats.

Now introduce interchangeability of bag and hat licences. Before interchange a licence for a given value of imports when used for hats yields a higher profit than when used for bags. So there will be a transfer of licences. The profit margin on bag imports will rise and on hat imports will fall until they are equalized. The new equilibrium yields a margin of SV for both products, with imports of OW of bags and OW_h of hats. Total imports have remained unchanged, since $OW+OW_h = OQ+OQ_h$. The general point is clear. If there is complete interchange of licences between a group of products, a free and perfect market in licences and competition generally, then the results will be the same as that brought about by a uniform nominal tariff within the group. The price mechanism reallocates the licences among products. Of course the profits will go to traders and not the government, and this can have further repercussions which are neglected here. It is possible that in the absence of interchangeability some licences remain unused because the demand curve for a product has shifted so far to the left that free trade imports after this shift are below the import level permitted by the quota. Interchangeability will then enable the holders of these unused licences to sell them to other importers or to use them themselves to import other products; it will thus bring licences out of retirement and so increase combined imports.

How are the combined quota profits affected by the interchangeability of licences? This is an important question because it is widely believed that the transfer of licences raises profits, especially when it takes place through a market. It is also important since it might be an object of policy to minimize quota profits when constructing an import licensing system. If we continue to assume competition all round the general answer is that interchangeability may raise or lower total profits. From each import demand (average revenue) curve can be derived a marginal revenue curve, and total profits will be maximized when the marginal revenues per unit are equal for the two products. This is profit maximization subject to the constraint that the total volume of imports measured at free trade (foreign supply) prices is fixed by the total quotas. Interchangeability of licences yields the uniform tariff result and so brings about price or *average* revenue equalization. But will it bring the system closer towards or further away from *marginal* revenue equalization? If the proportional quota cuts are identical, the demand curves have not shifted, and movements along the curves do not reverse the relationships between the elasticities, the price of the good with the lower elasticity will have risen more than that of the good with the higher elasticity. Interchangeability may then raise or lower profits. It would lower it if by chance the quota had initially attained the profit maximization point for both products. This is perfectly possible since it is a property of the profit maximization situation that the price of the lower elasticity good is higher. But the price discrepancy appropriate to profit maximization may be less than that which actually resulted from the quotas before interchangeability; hence interchangeability could raise profits. In our diagrams the price of the good with the lower elasticity (bags) has risen less than the price of the good with the higher elasticity (hats). But profit maximization requires the price relationship to be the opposite. Thus the price equalization which will result from interchangeability must bring the system closer to profit maximization.

Now let us allow for monopoly. If there is initially a separate monopoly for each product, with two products there would be bilateral monopoly in the licence market while with a few products there would be oligopoly. Here it will be assumed either that there is initially a single trader's monopoly covering all the products or that the separate monopolists maximize joint profits. But the following results would also apply if there were many products and thus many monopolists, so that the licence market were competitive. If the only constraint were the total volume of imports, measured at foreign supply prices, then the monopolist or group of monopolists would maximize profits by allocating licences among products so that the marginal revenues were equal for all imports. If the demand elasticities among the imports differed this would mean varying price margins, relatively higher for the low elasticity goods. The monopolist would discriminate. But if interchangeability had not been permitted he would not necessarily have been able to equate marginal revenues; being subject to an additional constraint his profits would be lower, other than in the special case where the imposition of the quotas by chance brought him to the point where marginal revenues were equal even in the absence of interchangeability. Apart from this case, interchangeability, by removing a constraint, will thus raise profits above what they would otherwise be. Whether it would bring the result closer to or further away from the uniform tariff solution—that is towards or away from price equalization—could be determined from the previous analysis. There it was shown that with competition interchangeability would lead to price equalization but might raise or lower total profits. In the present case, with monopoly, it would lead to an increase in profits, but could lead towards or away from price equalization. Of course, only if the elasticities for the two goods were the same would it actually lead to price equalization.

An important effect of interchangeability of licences may be to prevent the formation of trader's monopolies. An import quota with licences limited to existing traders imposes a barrier on new entrants and thus may encourage the formation of monopoly or a cartel. But if licences for one product can be used to import another this barrier disappears. The market is no longer fragmented. The hat importers can no longer form a cartel with the sense of security that no one else can import hats. If there is interchangeability only between bag and hat licences the cartel could still be effective if it embraced both bag and hat importers, but the more extensive the area within which licences are interchangeable the more difficult it is to form a monopoly or cartel and hence the weaker the barrier to entry. It remains true of course that the imposition of quotas and the allocation of licences to a limited number of traders, whether existing traders or a fixed group of newcomers, does impose a barrier on general entry into the importing business even when there is complete interchangeability; so, compared with free trade or with tariffs, the possibility of monopoly or the formation of a cartel is somewhat increased.

Finally, it was shown in Chapter 9 that if there is a single domestic producer of an import-competing product and the foreign import price is given, and in the absence of interchangeability, a quota will offer him the opportunity for the first time to exercise monopoly power. But if there is interchangeability of licences this will no longer be so. The result will be the same as with a tariff. A quota margin will be established in the licence market which will raise the price which the producer can charge, but (in the small country case) the elasticity of the demand curve facing him will continue to be infinite over the relevant range.

ii. *The Market for Licences*

The market for import licences is the mechanism through which import licences are transferred between firms. This must be distinguished from interchangeability of licences between products. It is possible to have licence transfers between firms without product interchange. The implications of a licence market within one product category were discussed in Chapter 9. Similarly it is possible to have product interchange without licence transfers between firms. This simply requires multi-product importing firms. But generally the interchange of licences between products is likely to involve the transfer of licences between firms or at least would set up incentives for such transfers. This is true insofar as trading firms are to some extent specialized or at least 'intensive' in the import of particular products and would be able to move into unfamiliar fields only at significant cost.

Let us then consider two questions. First, what determines

the formation and turnover of a market in licences? Secondly, what are the consequences of such a market compared with its absence?[1]

The perfection and turnover of a licence market depends first of all on whether the buying and selling of licences between firms is legal. In the import licensing systems of many countries it is not. It has to be remembered here that, apart from direct evasion of the law, there are various ways of circumventing a prohibition.[2] A sale of licences by firm A to firm B may take place indirectly through B paying a commission to A to import a product when in fact the actual work is done by B and A is only lending its name for the transaction. Or firm A may allocate its licences to a subsidiary firm which is then sold to firm B, with a value placed on goodwill that embodies expected quota profits. Secondly, the turnover in the market will be the greater, the greater the desire for licence interchange among products, that is, the greater the price divergences set up by import quotas in the first place. If an equal proportional import cut is imposed in the first instance on all imports, and the demand elasticities between different imports differ greatly, the market will be more active than when the elasticities do not differ so much. Thirdly, the wider the permissible field of product interchange, that is the wider the possible market, the more active will be the actual market. Fourthly, the more firms tend to specialize in the import of particular products and prefer to continue specializing in this way, the greater the market turnover. Finally, the market turnover depends on geographic and institutional characteristics; in geographically fragmented countries or those where market institutions are generally imperfect, the licence market, like other markets, will be imperfect.

The consequences of a licence market can be considered under four headings. First, firms can avoid part or all of the increase in average costs that would otherwise be associated with a declining scale of imports. The point was made in Chapter 9

---

[1] For some earlier discussion, see H. Heuser, *Control of International Trade* (George Routledge and Sons, London, 1939), p. 158 and pp. 233–35.

[2] See G. G. Moffatt, *Import Control and Industrialization: A Study of the Australian Experience* (Melbourne University Press, Melbourne, 1970), pp. 118–24, for description of such evasion in Australia (though in fact it was very limited).

with respect to the market in licences for one product, but it also applies when the market involves trading in licences by firms specializing in different products. Imports by some firms can cease, so freeing licences for other firms which can then attain an adequate scale of imports. Secondly, it makes product interchange easier and hence more likely and thus has all the consequences of product interchange discussed above. Thirdly, a market reduces the incentive for trading firms to amalgamate; the absence of such a market puts a premium on multi-product firms and more generally puts the smaller more specialized traders at a disadvantage. Fourthly, it makes it more obvious that profits are to be derived from obtaining licences. This may have no effect on the reality of profit-taking. Indeed, as we have seen, in certain circumstances when the market encourages product interchange it may actually lead to a decline in total profits. Furthermore it will reduce the likelihood of a monopoly or cartel being formed. But it is also possible that, quite apart from the considerations already discussed, it raises profits through increasing price flexibility and profit-taking. Traders may not always exploit their opportunities to take quota profits when this is at the expense of regular customers. They may trade both in local products and in imports and charge a price for the two which averages their costs. But an open market in licences may be an invitation to them to take profits, even if this is indirectly at the expense of their regular customers who will have to buy the higher-priced local product or to buy imports from a trader who has had to purchase his licences. To what extent profit-taking would be affected by a licence market is of course an empirical question, but the fact that a market makes profit-taking more obvious may lie behind the frequent reluctance of governments to allow the transfer of licences between firms. And the fact that product interchangeability increases the pressure for, and scope of, a market may then, in turn, lead them to limit interchangeability.

III. *The General Equilibrium Resource Allocation Effects of Import Restrictions*

If a structure of import restrictions is imposed to remedy a balance of payments deficit, and is combined with appropriate fiscal or monetary measures to maintain internal balance, a certain allocation of resources will result. One might compare this with the resource allocation that would have resulted if devaluation combined with the same fiscal and monetary measures had been used instead to attain external and internal balance. A similar question was asked with respect to a structure of tariffs and other taxes and subsidies in Chapter 4.

Many of the same complications enter the analysis. It is similarly difficult to arrive at general conclusions unless one makes rather drastic simplifying assumptions. Here we shall focus on certain ways in which the answer is likely to differ from the earlier case. Again, we begin with a simple case, making the following assumptions. World prices of imports are given (small country assumption). Some imports of each restricted good remain after restrictions have been imposed. Both these assumptions are convenient, and will be maintained consistently, but are not essential to the argument. All consumption substitution elasticities are zero; so we can focus on production effects. All products are vertically integrated; so we can ignore the effective rate complication. Producers and traders are competitive. A quota genuinely limits the imports of the good to which it applies and cannot be exceeded by using licences issued for other products; thus there is no interchangeability of licences between 'products' however the latter are defined in the system. Finally, there are no controls on domestic production or investment; the only controls are on imports. The latter five assumptions will be removed in due course.

If there were no income effects the third assumption would fix the demand for each product. Because of income effects, demand for each product for which there is a positive income elasticity will fall (assuming the quota system lowers real income and ignoring shifts in demand owing to income redistribution). Taking this fall in demand as given, an import quota will determine the new level of output of the import-competing product. Output will increase by the enforced reduction in imports less the fall in demand owing to the income effect. The lower the quota for any particular product the greater the rise in domestic production of it. The elasticity of supply of domestic production plays no part in this effect. Nor does it seem to be relevant what the level of the implicit tariff rate is. There may be quotas on products X and Y and the two import-competing industries may compete with each other for factors, so that the quota on Y shifts the domestic supply curve of X upwards. Nevertheless this shift in the supply conditions for X will not affect the change in its output resulting from its quota (other than through a possible income effect). Thus, in spite of the interconnections through substitutability in production, one can apparently look at the effects of each quota separately. Yet this is not wholly true even given our limiting assumptions. The precise pattern of reallocation of factors between industries will still depend on the relationships between the quotas. If factors could come into X from Y or from Z, they are more likely to come from Y if there is a tight quota restriction on Z and no quota limitation on Y.

Suppose we start in the quota situation, knowing the outputs and import volumes appropriate to that situation. We want to know what resource allocation would have been in the absence of quotas and with the exchange rate appropriately adjusted. Assuming that we do not actually have recent experience of the free trade alternative the problem then is to know what import cuts have really been imposed by the quotas and how they have caused resources to move. The approach must be essentially the same as in the case of the tariff structure. First one must calculate the implicit tariff rates and so obtain a scale of implicit rates, and then one must guess at the relevant production substitution relationships to see how resources must have moved. The analysis is in principle much the same as when we study the effects of a tariff structure, aside from the immense practical difficulties in obtaining the basic data, namely the implicit tariff rates.[3] The qualifications in interpreting the significance of a scale of effective rates are the same as

---

[3] Implicit tariff rates must be calculated from comparisons between prices of domestically produced goods and prices of similar imported goods. Product differentiation presents a major problem here. Calculations have been made for Pakistan, India and Mexico. See S. R. Lewis, 'Effects of Trade Policy on Domestic Relative Prices: Pakistan, 1951–64', *American Economic Review*, 58, March 1968, 60–78; S. R. Lewis and S. E. Guisinger, 'Measuring Protection in a Developing Country: the Case of Pakistan', *Journal of Political Economy*, 76, Nov./Dec. 1968, 1170–98; J. Bhagwati and P. Desai, *India: Planning for Industrialisation*, 1970; G. Bueno, 'The Structure of Protection in Mexico', in B. Balassa (ed.), *The Structure of Protection in Developing Countries*, 1971.

before. The difference is that the scale of implicit tariff rates cannot be said now to determine or even influence the general equilibrium resource allocation effects of the protective structure; rather, it reveals after the event, and of course only to a limited extent, what these effects must have been.

With the introduction of consumption effects it ceases to be true that the supply elasticities play no part in determining the effects of a quota system on the pattern of output. In this exposition we will now ignore income effects. With zero consumption effects the increase in domestic production is equal to the enforced fall in imports in the case of each product concerned. But when consumption effects are positive the import cut will lead to *both* an increase in domestic import-competing output and a reduction in domestic consumption. How it is split up between these two effects will depend on the supply and the demand elasticities, on the initial ratio of domestic production to consumption and on the shifts in supply and demand curves determined by quotas on other products. But it remains true that the process of deducing what the free trade alternative would look like must start with a calculation of implicit tariff rates; but this time, to obtain a vision of the alternative one must guess not only at the production substitution relationships but also at the substitution relationships on the consumption side.

Introducing vertical relationships and hence the effective rate complication means, of course, that one must calculate separately implicit nominal and effective rates, obtain two scales, and use the effective rate scale as a guide to assessing what the resource allocation effects must have been. There is nothing new here in principle. But an additional point is that, even with no consumption substitution effects and with the usual fixed coefficient assumption, the resource allocation effects of a quota on product X will now depend on quotas firstly on those other products which contain X as an input and secondly those products which are inputs into X; furthermore, the interrelationships between the quotas will depend on the relevant supply elasticities. All this emerged from section VI of Chapter 9 and Fig. 9.3. In fact, input-output relationships, even with fixed coefficients, have the same sort of effects on the general equilibrium analysis as allowing for consumption effects.

Monopoly complicates this story in the following ways. First, domestic producer's monopoly has introduced the possibility that an import quota leads to lower domestic production even though the domestic price rises. Insofar as this is of significance, it means that the change in relative prices as indicated by the scale of implicit effective rates does not necessarily indicate the direction in which resources have moved.[4] It raises the important question as to whether—when there is a producer's monopoly and monopoly profits are made as a result of the quota—the implicit rate should not ideally be defined and measured as the proportional excess of the producer's *marginal costs* over the import price rather than the proportional excess of the *price* he charges to consumers (all this in effective terms, of course) since it is movements along marginal cost curves that determine output responses. Secondly, if a domestic trader's monopoly is newly created by a quota and if imports as a result fall by more than is required by the import quota then the general equilibrium resource allocation effects will of course depend on the actual import level that has resulted and not on the higher level permitted by the quota. The implicit tariff rate that results from the actual imports is the relevant one for the scale of implicit rates. Thirdly, if there was a pre-existing trader's monopoly and hence monopoly profits even under free trade it is not the implicit tariff rate (the tariff rate that would attain the same domestic price increase as the quota) but rather the *actual* proportional price increase that must be put on the scale.[5]

So far we have assumed that there are a number of distinct products with no licence interchangeability between them. Assuming competition in trading, the effects of interchangeability are quite simple to incorporate into the analysis. Interchangeability introduces flat stretches into the scale of implicit nominal rates. The wider the range over which licences can be

[4] For the reasons given in section VII of Chapter 4 the scale may not do so in any case; in fact, we have here an additional reason for the possibility of perverse resource flows.

[5] In partial equilibrium terms, the implicit tariff rate is equal to the proportional increase in *marginal* revenue over the relevant range (moving backwards along the curve) while the rate required is the proportional increase in *average* revenue. In general one cannot say which would be greater, but if the import demand (average revenue) curve were a straight line, the implicit tariff rate would be.

interchanged or—what is the same thing—the wider the definition of a 'product' for licensing purposes—the longer these flat stretches where the nominal rates are the same. If all products were allocated among, say, three categories and interchange were allowed within each category but not across category boundaries, then the nominal scale would simply consist of three rates. The resource allocation implications then follow naturally. If uniformity of nominal rates made for uniformity of effective rates one could conclude that resource shifts as between the relevant import-competing industries would be reduced or eliminated. But of course, as emerged from Chapter 8, the matter is not so simple. The conclusion becomes even less certain once we allow for traders' monopoly. In that case interchangeability could conceivably increase the price divergences and so, instead of flattening out the scale of nominal rates, could increase its variations.

Finally, we might allow for controls on domestic production or investment. This is of interest since one of the main countries where quantitative restrictions are wide-ranging and important, namely India, also has controls on investment.[6] If investment into import-competing industries is controlled, quotas, and for that matter, tariffs, may not have the usual effects on production and one cannot make many or any deductions about the resource allocation effects of a scale of effective rates. In the extreme case all investment designed to expand import-competing production may be prevented by controls, so that quotas and tariffs affect only demand, apart from possible indirect effects on export production. A more interesting point concerns the interpretation of implicit tariff rates in such a case. We know that, for given domestic supply and demand elasticities, the smaller the import quota the higher the implicit tariff and (apart from the monopoly case) the more resources are likely to move into the domestic industry. Thus there is some basis for saying that resources are likely to move into industries with relatively high implicit tariffs. But now we must introduce an additional variable, namely investment controls that reduce the domestic supply elasticity. One can see by simple manipulation of the partial equilibrium diagram that, for a given quota, the lower the domestic supply elasticity

[6] Bhagwati and Desai, op. cit., pp. 341–3.

the higher the implicit tariff rate and the lower the increase in import-competing output; the lower this supply elasticity the more of the reduction in imports will be borne by a reduction in demand, rather than increase in supply. This means that relatively high implicit tariff rates go with relatively low increases in output. If then we are considering the joint effects of a regime of import controls and investment controls we cannot deduce much from a scale of implicit tariff rates, at least not from a resource allocation point of view, though it will still be significant as a guide to the effects of a quota system on the pattern of consumption.

IV. *The Optimum Structure of a Quantitative Import Restriction System*

A country has a balance of payments deficit. Perhaps there is even a crisis. For one reason or another, whether sound or not, it is decided to use quantitative restrictions to cope with the problem. Fiscal and monetary policies will concurrently ensure the appropriate disabsorption. Many choices will have to be made. By how much are different products to be restricted? How large should the product categories be and to what extent should licences be interchangeable between products? Is a market in licences to be permitted or even encouraged? In fact, what is the optimum structure of a quantitative import restriction system? The problem is a second-best one, since devaluation or tariffs, or some combination of them, may be preferable; but for various reasons which will not concern us here these instruments are not used. The question posed is similar to that posed in Chapter 8 for the case where the motive for tariffs was to improve the balance of payments.

Let us first set out a simple answer by making the following assumptions: (1) Traders and producers are competitive. (2) There are no domestic distortions of any kind and relative product and factor prices are completely flexible. Of course the exchange rate and the general level of money factor incomes are not flexible, for otherwise there would be no balance of payments problem. (3) There is only one exportable, it does not use importables as inputs and is not itself an input into exportables. (4) Income distribution effects 'don't matter'. These assumptions mean that if tariffs were to be used to improve the balance of payments, the optimum structure would be a uniform *ad valorem* nominal tariff, bringing about in this case also a uniform effective tariff.[7]

The answer to our problem is now simple. The system of quantitative restrictions should aim to reproduce the uniform tariff solution. Since income distribution does not matter, it does not matter who gets the licences. They can be distributed to anyone, they should be completely interchangeable between products and the buying and selling of licences on a market should be permitted and indeed encouraged. The results will be identical with those of a uniform tariff, except that quota profits will have replaced revenue to the Treasury and— given that the licences are for imports fixed in *value* terms— the total value of imports can be known in advance. This *uniform tariff equivalent* solution means that imports of those goods where the domestic demand and supply elasticities are relatively high will fall proportionately more than imports of goods with low elasticities.

Let us suppose for a moment that interchangeability of licences between products or categories of products is *not* permitted. It would still be possible, in theory, to reproduce something like the uniform tariff equivalent solution. The proportional reduction in imports of those products where the domestic elasticities are low would be less than those where the elasticities are high. This time quotas have to be carefully determined for each category, the size of the quotas depending on the estimate of the domestic elasticities. The obvious limitation of this approach is that the elasticities are not known. Furthermore, as tastes or domestic production conditions change the quotas would have to be altered so as to maintain a uniform tariff result. By contrast, the simple approach with product interchangeability would continuously maintain a uniform tariff solution, even though the level of the *uniform tariff equivalent* would vary if domestic conditions changed while the total quota value stayed constant. But we can recognize in this more complex approach one element in a

---

[7] This conclusion also requires either the small country assumption or the assumption that an optimum structure of tariffs and export taxes (to allow for terms of trade effects) is being imposed consistently and quite independently of tariffs and quotas designed to improve the balance of payments.

popular logic—the logic of imposing smaller quotas on imports of 'inessentials' than on imports of 'essentials'. Inessentials might be regarded as imports which consumers or users can readily do without—that is, where demand elasticities and import-competing supply elasticities are relatively high. It was pointed out in Chapter 8 that the uniform tariff solution is an efficient system of discrimination. This comes out very clearly when it is attained or approximated by quantitative restrictions without interchangeability between products or categories. The discrimination is in favour of essentials against inessentials, defining the latter in terms of relative domestic demand and supply elasticities.[8]

Let us now remove some of our assumptions. The uniform tariff solution will then no longer be optimum, so that the simple approach of allowing complete product interchangeability may no longer be satisfactory. This problem is best expounded by imagining that we start with a quota structure that simulates the effects of the uniform tariff solution—that is, tight restrictions on high elasticity goods and lesser import cuts for low elasticity ones, with no interchangeability of licences between products. The general principle is that quotas should be expanded in all those cases where in the optimum tariff structure nominal tariffs would be below the average (uniform equivalent) level, and quotas should be contracted where nominal tariffs would be above the average. We shall look at two particular, but practically important cases, the first concerned with exports and the second with employment. First, suppose that some importables are inputs into exportables; we know then from Chapter 8 that a departure from tariff uniformity is called for: the tariff on such goods should be relatively lower than otherwise. With a quota system it means that quotas available for imports that are inputs into exportables should be relatively higher than otherwise, and not interchangeable. This is in practice a common reason why

---

[8] There are two elements in the popular use of the 'essentiality' term, the *price* elasticity element being one. The other is in terms of *income* elasticities, 'inessential' goods being those consumed relatively more by the rich. It is often thought that mainly the rich should bear the aggregate real income fall needed to allow the balance of payments to improve; so quotas for 'inessentials' defined in income elasticity terms should be relatively low and licences not interchangeable.

interchangeability is not permitted; it is argued—in principle correctly—that exporters should not have to pay increased prices for their inputs to the same extent as domestic consumers. Secondly, suppose that certain importable intermediate goods are used in fixed proportions with labour in some industries, and that the labour concerned is specific to these industries. If the relative money wage of this labour were flexible there would be no need for departure from our simple uniform-tariff-equivalent principle. First a quota on the importable inputs is imposed; this would create unemployment in the using industries in the first instance. So money wages would fall and the using industry could pay more for the imported raw material. Quota profits will then result. With product interchangeability this would attract licences from other products. Imports of the raw material will increase and so the unemployment will disappear. The crucial assumption is localized factor-price flexibility. If there had been no product interchangeability but wages had fallen because of unemployment caused by the import restrictions the quota profits would simply have increased and stayed high. This would have been an example of a low elasticity of demand for the controlled import—in fact, an 'essential' good. Now suppose that the money wage does *not* fall when there is unemployment. So quota profits would not rise in the first instance and product interchangeability would not attract licences from other products. Rather, unemployment would remain and might even increase as licences originally issued for the raw material concerned were used for other products. It is then necessary to allocate an especially large quota for the product sufficient to ensure full employment in the using industry, and not allow the licences to be used for importing any other product. This is in fact the practice in most import licensing systems. The aim is to avoid unemployment caused by shortage of imported raw materials. Yet there is a problem in this approach. Given that there has to be a certain total reduction in imports, the reduction will be mainly in imports of final goods rather than intermediate goods. Consumers will then be compelled to reduce consumption of imported final goods rather than of those final goods that contain some imported inputs but also have a domestic value added content. Yet from the point of view of *their* demand elasticities, the latter goods might well be less essential than the former. An undue relative encouragement is given to goods which happen to have some domestic value added content.[9]

Finally, it should be borne in mind that the more complicated an import restriction system is, the more costly it is in its demands on administrative skills and the more inefficient it is likely to be in attaining its objectives. The administrative costs are borne by the civil service and by traders and others involved. These are real economic costs which must enter any economic calculus. They have been much discussed and are clearly likely to be greater in a country where administrative skills are scarce.[10] It would hardly be appropriate in many— if not most—countries to attempt fine-tuning of an import licensing system designed to take into account all the considerations suggested by our formal analysis. Furthermore, bribery of officials may not only have an income distribution effect, as mentioned earlier, but may also make it more difficult to bring about a desired discrimination in the quota structure since it may affect not only who gets the profits from given quotas but also the actual sizes of the quotas themselves. The greater the problem of administration the stronger the case for allocating licences for long periods at a time, and for allowing wide product interchangeability and a market for licences.

---

[9] An additional disadvantage arises if the imported materials or components are allocated to firms not on the basis of their planned or actual production but on the basis of manufacturing capacity (as has been the case in India and Pakistan). There is then an incentive to expand capacity so as to obtain more inputs; the creation of excess capacity is built into the system. See I. Little, T. Scitovsky and M. Scott, *Industry and Trade in Some Developing Countries*, 1970, pp. 225–6.

[10] See Little, Scitovsky and Scott, op. cit; and Bhagwati and Desai, op. cit.

11

CONCLUSION

W H A T does the new theory of protective structure as expounded in Chapters 3 to 7 'boil down' to? At the core there is a rather simple model, one resting on three assumptions, namely (1) fixed input-output coefficients, (2) parametric domestic nominal prices of traded goods, and (3) a sole non-traded good, the price of which is the numeraire.[1] With these assumptions one can produce a fairly clear and neat model for analysing the resource allocation (and consumption pattern) effects of a protective structure. We have no substitution problem, no terms of trade effects, no redundant tariffs, no trade reversals and no indirect protection. Furthermore, the awkward problem posed by non-traded inputs into traded goods can be dealt with by the *Scott* method.[2] Even with these assumptions there are problems. It is not possible solely from the scale of effective rates to predict resource movements within the traded goods sector. Certain paradoxes are conceivable. This was stressed in Chapter 4. In addition, the crucial problem remains that one needs to guess at the devaluation rate, at least if the non-traded good is important, and this again requires knowledge of all relevant elasticities. Removing the three assumptions makes everything more complicated and predictions more difficult. The details of the difficulties that result—the meaning of the rate of protection, the substitution problem, non-traded inputs, indirect protection, and so on—need not be repeated. Indeed it may appear that much of this book has been concerned not with *building up* the theory of effective protection and tariff structure but with *pulling it down*, at least by implication.[3]

[1] This is the model of Chapters 4 and 5, except that non-traded goods are only introduced in section VIII of Chapter 4, and there, as well as in section V of Chapter 4, we have more than one non-traded good.
[2] See section II of Chapter 7.
[3] A number of writers would be sympathetic to such an act of destruction; see especially W. P. Travis, 'The Effective Rate of Protection and the Question

Nevertheless it is arguable that something important has been achieved. We have broken out of the straight-jacket of the orthodox two-sector general equilibrium model which has dominated trade theory for so long, and are beginning to face the complications and difficulties of the world of many commodities and of input-output interrelationships. This is not to say that there have never been any multi-commodity models in trade theory.[4] But it cannot be said that there has been a systematic and usable multi-commodity theory of protection. The simplest version of our model with its three crucial assumptions seems to focus on the relevant issues, though even with these assumptions it does not give complete answers. But the business of exploring the implications of removing these assumptions has brought out new and relevant issues that have not emerged from two-sector theory or from mathematical general equilibrium theory.

Leaving aside technicalities, there seem to be three main lines of criticism of the whole approach, the first two resting on the belief (which I share) that at least some of the difficulties discussed may be empirically relevant.[5] The first is that the approach obtains its neat results only when it stays very simple and ignores all the important complications. My defence is that the model which is at the core of the new approach is at least *less* simple than the orthodox two-sector model. We have managed to obtain many useful insights from manipulating the two-sector model—partly because of its basic simplicity— and the same is true of the new approach. But it is of course only a staging-post on the road.

The second criticism is concerned with empirical practicability rather than heuristic value. It can be put as follows.

---

of Labor Protection in the United States', *Journal of Political Economy*, 76, May/June 1968, 443–61; and V. K. Ramaswami and T. N. Srinivasan, 'Tariff Structure and Resource Allocation in the Presence of Factor Substitution', in J. N. Bhagwati, et al. (eds.), *Trade, Balance of Payments and Growth: Essays in Honor of C. P. Kindleberger* (M.I.T. Press, Cambridge, 1970).

[4] See especially F. Graham, *The Theory of International Values* (Princeton University Press, Princeton, 1948); and more generally J. S. Chipman, 'A Survey of the Theory of International Trade' (in three parts), *Econometrica*, July 1965, 477–519, Oct. 1965, 685–760, and Jan. 1966, 18–76.

[5] Apart from the critics listed in footnote 3, systematic criticisms have not at the time of writing yet found their way into print. I have in mind criticisms made verbally.

If one wants to know how a complicated protective structure will affect resource allocation and factor prices there is no point in pausing half-way to the complete answer. One needs to know, or estimate, the relevant elasticities, production functions, demand functions and so on, and by use of programming techniques, linear or non-linear, one can then work out how changes in any of the parameters, such as nominal tariffs, affect the whole solution. One should feed in as parameters the original data, not the derived, calculated data, such as effective rates. After all, what is the point of calculating these rates and obtaining a 'scale' of them when this will not show in any definite way how resources or factor prices will have moved? The answer is that effective rates *actually* can be and have been calculated, that they tell us something *more* than formal or nominal rates, and that the data for complete general equilibrium programming exercises do not normally exist for those countries where the analysis of protective structures is particularly important. The desirability of the more ambitious exercises, if practicable, and bearing in mind their cost, need not be denied. But something is better than nothing.

A third criticism is that the whole approach is quite irrelevant from a welfare or policy point of view.[6] It has become the conventional wisdom of recent trade theory that in the small country case trade taxes and subsidies are never first-best policies. The correctness of this view for any particular case hinges on various assumptions; one man's constraint is another man's removable political folly. But if we accept this view then tariffs and similar devices do indeed not matter for the study of first-best policies. Does this then mean that one should only be concerned with working out the package of direct subsidies, taxes and other interventions that will attain the first-best optimum? One answer is that, given the follies of our rulers, we actually *have* tariffs and other trade interventions, so that there is something to analyse as a simple positive economics exercise. The other answer is that there is a role for suggesting optimum policies subject to various constraints; and for this type of second-best analysis, as shown in Chapter 8, the new concepts are certainly relevant.

[6] See Ramaswami and Srinivasan, op. cit.

More empirical work is required to establish the practical relevance of some of the complications and hence of the criticisms. It is already established that non-traded inputs into traded inputs can be important, and their treatment can make a big difference to the results of effective rate calculations.[7] This might be pursued further to see how far non-traded inputs can be decomposed so that they reveal a large traded input content. 'Empirical' work on the substitution problem has not gone much further than experimenting with plausible production functions and elasticities of substitution—and such experimentation has suggested that there may not be a great problem. But it is not difficult to think of particular instances where there might be a problem. And this is generally true of the various difficulties discussed in this book. The most important and worrying limitation of the analysis, in my view, is its heavy dependence on the small country assumption. I do not think that one must necessarily conclude that effective rates are meaningless for any country which has any influence at all on its terms of trade, but a serious question-mark hangs over the relevance of the approach when applied to countries which face steeply sloping foreign supply and demand curves.

In conclusion the reader might recall the story of consumers' surplus. Here was a simple intuitively appealing idea, discovered by Dupuit, rediscovered and developed by Marshall, revived by Hicks, and obviously useful. Upon careful examination it turned out to require many assumptions for its validity, and to have several possible meanings. The purists convinced themselves it was unnecessary for dealing with any relevant problem. It was a 'totally useless theoretical toy'.[8] Officially, one might say, it died. And yet it would not stay in its grave. It has such a strong intuitive appeal, and there is nothing better available, so people keep on measuring it. Indeed, with the overwhelming belief, characteristic of modern computer-age

---

[7] See the references in footnote 9, Chapter 7.

[8] The purists: P. A. Samuelson, *Foundations of Economic Analysis* (Harvard University Press, Cambridge, 1947), Ch. VIII; I. M. D. Little, *A Critique of Welfare Economics* (Clarendon Press, Oxford, 2nd ed. 1957), Ch. X; J. de V. Graaff, *Theoretical Welfare Economics* (Cambridge University Press, Cambridge, 1957), Ch. VII. The quotation is from Little, but it has not stopped him from using consumers' surplus in a rough sort of way in empirical work, and the quotation no longer represents his view.

economics, in measurement as the proper activity of econo-mists, it has had a revival. One suspects that the perfectionist theorists gave up too quickly. They forgot that theory should be the handmaiden of applied economics. Theorists should provide some useful concepts that their practical colleagues, or they themselves, can test and use. They should certainly help to explain the limitations and necessary qualifications of the concepts. But theory does not have to be contrary to common-sense and the qualifications to a theory need not necessarily overwhelm its simple message; rather, they should be regarded as signposts to further development.

APPENDIX I

EFFECTIVE PROTECTION:
SOME HISTORY

BUSINESSMEN, tariff-making authorities and even economists have usually realized that a tariff on an intermediate input reduces protection for the using industry; one can find many references in the international trade literature to this rather obvious effect. The idea of a *compensating tariff* is very old. Taussig's *Tariff History of the United States*[1] has much discussion of the relationship between the tariff on wool and the tariff on woollen goods. The United States tariff on woollen goods contained two elements, a specific duty compensating for the duty on wool and an *ad valorem* duty that represented the net protection for woollen manufacture. In a footnote Taussig presented an arithmetic example showing that the net result of increases in the tariffs on wool and on woollen goods in 1824 was to keep what he called *net protection*—and we call the *adjusted nominal rate*—almost constant.[2] Much later, Haberler, in his classic *Theory of International Trade*, discussed 'import duties on means of production'.[3] He pointed out that tariffs on inputs may reduce exports, or increase imports of products competing with using industries, and that, as a result, the input tariff may not affect the balance of payments. It would be tiresome to seek out or list numerous examples from many countries, and numerous casual references in the economic literature, to show that tariff-making authorities and economists have been aware of the obvious effects that tariffs on inputs have on using industries.[4] The universally used system of export drawbacks shows that there has been an awareness of the potentially adverse effects of input tariffs upon exports.

The simple idea of effective protection as expounded in Chapter 3

---

[1] F. W. Taussig, *The Tariff History of the United States* (G. P. Putnam's, New York, 8th ed., 1931; also Capricorn Books, New York, 1964). (This book was first published in 1888.)

[2] Taussig, op. cit. (Capricorn Books edition), p. 75.

[3] G. v. Haberler, *The Theory of International Trade* (W. Hodge & Co., London, 1936), pp. 235–6.

[4] For example, see J. Viner, *The Customs Union Issue* (Carnegie Endowment for International Peace, New York, 1950), pp. 47–8.

involves two considerations when compared with the concept of nominal protection: first, that tariffs on inputs negatively affect protection for the using industry, and secondly that the net protective margin should be expressed not in relation to the free trade nominal price (which would yield the adjusted nominal rate) but in relation to the free trade effective price. This simple calculation Taussig never made: he mostly told his story in terms of nominal rates, and occasionally in adjusted nominal rates. The idea of the effective rate does not appear in Haberler's book, and is not so easy to find in the literature. Lary[5] has uncovered one early reference (though no doubt there are others to be found): the Austrian economist Schüller presented in 1905 a clear arithmetic example of the effective rate resulting from tariffs on a final good and its input.[6] Moving on to recent years, the major work on the theory of protection is Meade's *Trade and Welfare*. Meade shows clear awareness of the effective protection idea at two points, and produces the appropriate arithmetic.[7] He stresses that rates of protection should always be interpreted in these terms, but does not refer to this complication elsewhere in his volume.

One has to explain why the idea of effective protection was not systematically incorporated into the international trade literature until the late nineteen sixties. Various suggestions can be made. Insofar as the effect of input tariffs was noted, the concept of net protection—our adjusted nominal rate—seemed adequate. The reason was that perhaps writers on tariffs did not think systematically in general equilibrium terms. It was pointed out in Chapter 3 that in partial equilibrium terms one might just as well use the adjusted nominal rate. The concept of the effective rate only acquires its real significance in a general equilibrium context. Why, then, did it not find a place in general equilibrium international trade theory as it has been developed over the years? The answer here may be that this theory has, for ease of exposition, been dominated by the two-commodity model; furthermore, it has focused on the free trade versus protection issue and the exploration of 'arguments for protection'. As pointed out in Chapter 8, effective protection is relevant for second-best tariff-making, but the development of the concept has not uncovered any new first-best arguments for or against tariffs, and the idea of second-best tariff-making is relatively

[5] H. B. Lary, *Imports of Manufactures from Less Developed Countries* (National Bureau of Economic Research and Columbia University Press, New York, 1968), p. 119.

[6] R. Schüller, *Schutzzoll und Freihandel* (Vienna and Leipzig, 1905), pp. 149–50.

[7] J. E. Meade, *Trade and Welfare*, 1955, p. 157, pp. 162–3.

new. An additional consideration is that, until Leontief, economists did not think systematically in input-output terms. Essentially the theory of effective protection is the application of the elementary Leontief innovation of inter-industry economics to trade theory; this application has taken place with a lag because the importance of tariffs, and hence academic interest in them, has revived only since the mid nineteen fifties. If we ask why the idea of effective protection did not find a systematic place in the writings of Viner, Ohlin, Haberler and Meade, we might just as well ask why one had to wait for Leontief to give us systematic input-output economics. A final consideration is that the theory of effective protection appears to hinge on, or at least is only comfortable with, the small country assumption, one which would not be appropriate for many of the countries where modern economics has been mainly developed. It is not surprising that some of the main developments have come from Canadians, Australians and Swedes, and that the effective protection idea is a familiar one to Israeli economists.

The first systematic discussion of the concept, and its application to problems of policy, was in an article by Barber on Canadian tariff policy.[8] As for contributions since then, there is little point in assigning 'priority', nor is it always clear to what extent various authors thought up ideas independently and to what extent they were influenced by others. The general idea developed about the same time in many places because it was a natural next step in the development of tariff theory, and because there was a revival of interest in tariffs owing to the dismantling of quantitative restrictions in the developed countries and the pursuit of deliberate protectionist policies in newly independent less developed countries.

The 1956 report of the Swedish customs tariff commission[9] proposed a revision of the Swedish tariff on the basis of (what we would now call) uniform effective protection. This report does not seem to have had any impact elsewhere, except for its influence on Macario,[10] who made a similar proposal in 1964 in a thorough discussion of Latin American protectionist experience.

The idea of rates of protection in relation to value-added, especially as a method of comparing rates of export subsidization, was widely current in Israel in the nineteen fifties, and a number of

[8] C. L. Barber, 'Canadian Tariff Policy', *Canadian Journal of Economics and Political Science*, 21, Nov. 1955, 513–30.
[9] Swedish Customs Tariff Commission, *Revision of the Swedish Customs Tariff* (Stockholm, 1957).
[10] S. Macario, 'Protectionism and Industrialization in Latin America', *Economic Bulletin for Latin America*, 9, March 1964, 61–101.

publications in Hebrew during the early nineteen sixties used the basic idea of effective protection.[11]

The concept of effective protection became current in Australia in the nineteen sixties, mainly through the work of the present author.[12] The Vernon committee of enquiry on the Australian economy[13] took it up, stressed its importance for assessing the height of protective levels, and made comprehensive calculations. Under the influence of this report the concept was taken over by the Tariff Board, which proposed tariff policy reforms expressed in terms of effective rates. As a result, the concept of the effective rate, and the idea of some sort of upper limit to new tariffs expressed in terms of effective rates, became a matter of public controversy. Only in Australia does the concept have wide currency outside academic economics. Needless to say, since its use by the Tariff Board was combined with an attempt to limit the level of protection it has met some hostility from protectionist interests, who have not been slow to stress the measurement problems.

Humphrey discussed 'some neglected aspects of tariffs' in a book on the United States and the Common Market in 1962[14] and clearly explored many implications of what we now call effective protection.

The first serious theoretical exploration of effective protection was by Johnson in 1965,[15] the first two large-scale empirical studies were by Balassa[16] and Basevi,[17] negative value-added was 'discovered' by Soligo and Stern working on Pakistan in 1965,[18] and the present

[11] See the survey of the Israeli literature in N. Halevi, 'Economic Policy Discussion and Research in Israel', *American Economic Review*, 59, Sept. 1969, 92–5. The main references (in Hebrew) on effective protection are D. Pines, *Direct Export Premiums in Israel:* 1952–58 (Jerusalem, 1963); and M. Michaely, *Israel's Foreign Exchange Rate System* (Jerusalem, 1968).

[12] W. M. Corden, 'The Tariff' in A. Hunter (ed.), *The Economics of Australian Industry* (Melbourne University Press, Melbourne, 1963).

[13] J. Vernon, et al., *Report of the Committee of Economic Enquiry* (Commonwealth of Australia, Canberra, 1965), Chapter 13 and Appendix L (iv).

[14] D. Humphrey, *The United States and the Common Market* (Praeger, New York, 1962), pp. 61–3.

[15] H. G. Johnson, 'The Theory of Tariff Structure with Special Reference to World Trade and Development', in H. G. Johnson and P. B. Kenen, *Trade and Development* (Geneva, 1965).

[16] B. Balassa, 'Tariff Protection in Industrial Countries: An Evaluation', *Journal of Political Economy*, 73, Dec. 1965, 573–94.

[17] G. Basevi, 'The United States Tariff Structure: Estimates of Effective Rates of Protection of United States Industries and Industrial Labor', *Review of Economics and Statistics*, 48, May 1966, 147–60.

[18] R. Soligo and J. J. Stern, 'Tariff Protection, Import Substitution and Investment Efficiency', *Pakistan Development Review*, 5, Summer 1965, 249–69.

author's 1966 theoretical paper[19] was the first attempt to explore complications such as non-traded goods, the substitution problem and the relationship to the exchange rate, and to put effective rates into some sort of general equilibrium context. The numerous theoretical papers on the subject that have appeared in print from 1964 to 1970 are listed in the bibliography. Empirical work has been proceeding on many countries, and full scale studies have been completed on a number of developed countries, including the United States and Canada,[20] on India,[21] and on seven countries— Brazil, Chile, Mexico, Malaysia, Pakistan, Philippines and Norway —in the study initiated by Balassa under the auspices of the World Bank.[22] Calculations are under way in various other countries.

[19] W. M. Corden, 'The Structure of a Tariff System and the Effective Protective Rate', *Journal of Political Economy*, 74, June 1966, 221–37.

[20] Balassa, op. cit.; Basevi, op. cit.; J. R. Melvin and B. W. Wilkinson, *Effective Protection in the Canadian Economy* (Economic Council of Canada, Ottawa, 1968); R. E. Baldwin, *Nontariff Distortions of International Trade* (Brookings Institution, Washington, 1970). Baldwin's figures for the United States allow not only for tariffs but also for import quotas and various other non-tariff distortions.

[21] J. Bhagwati and P. Desai, *India: Planning for Industrialisation*, 1970.

[22] B. Balassa (ed.), *The Structure of Protection in Developing Countries*, 1971.

APPENDIX II

THE METZLER PARADOX

IF one defines the rate or degree of protection as the proportional increase in the domestic effective price that finally results from a tariff,[1] then partial equilibrium analysis suggests that the degree of protection will be lower the lower the foreign elasticity of supply. If the latter were zero, so that a tariff would lead to a fall in the foreign price equal to the tariff, there would be no rise in the domestic price and hence the tariff would provide no protection. But it also suggests that this terms of trade effect, while it modifies and may even eliminate the protective effect of a tariff, cannot possibly reverse it. Surprisingly, in the general equilibrium model it may do so. This is the famous Metzler paradox.[2] It is familiar from international trade theory and is in no sense peculiar to the theory of effective protection. But it is very relevant to the question which is the central theme of this book, namely how tariffs affect resource allocation. The exposition here is meant to explain the commonsense of the paradox, a matter that does not emerge clearly from the usual expositions. The explicit introduction of the exchange rate is meant to help in this respect.

Consider a three-good model, with an importable, an exportable and a non-traded good. For simplicity assume that the elasticity of supply of imports is infinite, though this is not essential for the argument. A tariff is imposed, providing positive nominal and effective protection and improving the balance of payments. The exchange rate is then appreciated (or the money price of the non-traded good is increased) to restore external balance. Now introduce the crucial assumption that the elasticity of demand for exports is less than unity so that the appreciation actually raises the value of exports in terms of foreign currency. It is necessary to assume also that the foreign exchange market is stable; hence an appreciation

---

[1] See section VI of Chapter 2.

[2] L. A. Metzler, 'Tariffs, the Terms of Trade and the Distribution of National Income', *Journal of Political Economy*, 57, Feb. 1949, 1–29, reprinted in R. E. Caves and H. G. Johnson (eds.), *Readings in International Economics* (Richard D. Irwin, Homewood, 1968).

does reduce the surplus in the balance of payments, the value of imports in foreign currency rising by more than the value of exports. The appreciation might go so far as to restore the value of imports in foreign currency terms to the pre-tariff position, in which case the price of imports would be back to its free trade position and there would have been zero *net* protection. But since it will have raised the value of exports this would leave the country with a surplus. So the appreciation must go further; in the final situation the value of exports *and imports* will be higher than they were in free trade, and the domestic price of importables will be lower. In terms of the analysis of Chapter 5, the ordinary effective rate is positive but, because of the large exchange rate adjustment, the *net* effective rate for the importable is actually negative. This account has neglected income effects. Real income for the country will be higher since a greater amount of imports is being obtained with less resources expended on producing for export. If the extra income were spent mainly on importables it would help to reduce the initial payments surplus, so that less exchange rate appreciation would be needed and the paradoxical result would be less likely, while if it were spent mainly on exportables it would increase the surplus further by reducing the supply of exports, hence making necessary a greater appreciation.

This paradox could also be shown to be possible in a model with many traded goods. The general point is simply that if the elasticity of demand for some exports is less than unity the net result of a tariff may be to increase rather than decrease imports, and hence to be anti-protective rather than protective for some or all import-competing industries. Exactly the same argument applies to an export tax, in which case it is indeed more obvious. Given the elasticity assumption, an export tax would raise the value of exports and thus make possible extra imports.

The exposition here has concentrated on the change in the price relationship between the importable and the non-traded good, as expressed by the net protective rate. Looking at the change (from free trade to the final situation) in the price relationship between the importable and the exportable, the domestic prices of both have fallen because of the appreciation, but the price fall for the importable has been modified by the tariff and for the exportable by the rise in the foreign price of exports. It is perfectly possible that on balance the price of importables has fallen more, so that resources have moved out of importables into exportables.

This is an intuitive (and not formally complete) explanation in terms of our three-good model of a proposition originally proven by

17

Metzler in terms of the orthodox two-sector model.[3] Metzler showed that in this model the precise condition required for the paradox is that the sum of the marginal propensity to spend on importables and the elasticity of foreign reciprocal demand (expressed as a demand elasticity) is less than unity.[4] A necessary, though not sufficient condition is that the export demand elasticity is less than unity (unless importables are inferior goods). The proof is given by Metzler, there are geometric or mathematical proofs in various books[5] and Meade explains the result verbally in four close pages.[6]

---

[3] A more rigorous mathematical analysis of the Metzler paradox in this three-good model is in I. A. McDougall, 'Tariffs and Relative Prices', *Economic Record*, 42, June 1966, 219–43; see also I. A. McDougall, 'Non-Traded Commodities and the Pure Theory of International Trade', in I. A. McDougall and R. H. Snape (eds.), *Studies in International Economics* (North-Holland, Amsterdam, 1970).

[4] On the basis of available data about propensities and elasticities it appears improbable that this condition is often fulfilled. See I. A. McDougall, 'A Note on "Tariffs, the Terms of Trade, and the Distribution of the National Income",' *Journal of Political Economy*, 70, Aug. 1962, 393–9.

[5] J. E. Meade, *A Geometry of International Trade* (Allen and Unwin, London, 1952), pp. 71–5; and M. C. Kemp, *The Pure Theory of International Trades* 1964, pp. 72–5.

[6] J. E, Meade, *Trade and Welfare*, 1955, pp. 292–5.

APPENDIX III

BIBLIOGRAPHY ON EFFECTIVE PROTECTION

THE following comprehensive bibliography lists books and articles on effective protection, including many not referred to in this book. It excludes items that refer to the new concept only briefly or incidentally. It is not a general bibliography on protection.

ANDERSON, J. and NAYA, S., 'Substitution and Two Concepts of Effective Rate of Protection', *American Economic Review*, **59**, Sept. 1969, 607–612; and 'Reply', **60**, Dec. 1970, 1005–7.

ANDERSON, J. E., 'General Equilibrium and the Effective Rate of Protection', *Journal of Political Economy*, **78**, July/Aug. 1970, 717–24.

BALASSA, B., 'Tariff Protection in Industrial Countries: An Evaluation', *Journal of Political Economy*, **73**, Dec. 1965, 573–94.

BALASSA, B., 'The Impact of the Industrial Countries' Tariff Structure on their Imports of Manufactures from Less Developed Countries', *Economica*, **34**, Nov. 1967, 372–83; and 'Reply', **37**, Aug. 1970, 316–20.

BALASSA, B. and SCHYDLOWSKY, D. M., 'Effective Tariffs, Domestic Cost of Foreign Exchange, and the Equilibrium Exchange Rate', *Journal of Political Economy*, **76**, May/June 1968, 348–60.

BALASSA, B., 'Tariff Protection in Industrial Nations and its Effects on the Exports of Processed Goods from Developing Countries', *Canadian Journal of Economics*, **1**, Aug. 1968, 583–94.

BALASSA, B., GUISINGER, S., and SCHYDLOWSKY, D., 'The Effective Rates of Protection and the Question of Labor Protection in the United States: A Comment', *Journal of Political Economy*, **78**, Sept./Oct. 1970, 1150–62.

BALASSA, B., 'Tariffs, Intermediate Goods, and Domestic Protection: Comment and Further Comment', *American Economic Review*, **60**, Dec. 1970, 959–63 and 968–9.

BALASSA, B., et al., *The Structure of Protection in Developing Countries* (Johns Hopkins University Press, Baltimore, 1971).

BALASSA, B., 'Effective Protection in Developing Countries', in BHAGWATI, J. N., et al. (eds), *Trade, Balance of Payments and Growth: Papers in International Economics in Honor of Charles P. Kindleberger* North-Holland, Amsterdam, 1971).

BALDWIN, R. E., *Nontariff Distortions of International Trade* (Brookings Institution, Washington, 1970).

BARBER, C. L., 'Canadian Tariff Policy', *Canadian Journal of Economics and Political Science*, 21, Nov. 1955, 513–30.

BASEVI, G., *International Trade Restrictions and Resource Allocation in the United States* (unpublished doctoral dissertation, University of Chicago, 1965).

BASEVI, G., 'The United States Tariff Structure: Estimates of Effective Rates of Protection of United States Industries and Industrial Labor', *Review of Economics and Statistics*, 48, May 1966, 147–60.

BHAGWATI, J. and DESAI, P., *India: Planning for Industrialisation* (Oxford University Press, London, 1970).

CHARLES, D. T., *Effective Protection, Resource Allocation and the Protective Structure: A Study with Special Reference to Australia* (unpublished doctoral dissertation, London School of Economics, 1970).

COHEN, B. I., 'The Use of Effective Tariffs', *Yale University Economic Growth Center Discussion Paper* No. 62, 1969.

CORDEN, W. M., 'The Tariff', in A. HUNTER, ed., *The Economics of Australian Industry* (Melbourne University Press, Melbourne, 1963).

CORDEN, W. M., 'Protection', *Economic Record*, 42, March 1966, 129–48.

CORDEN, W. M., 'The Structure of a Tariff System and the Effective Protective Rate', *Journal of Political Economy*, 74, June 1966, 221–37.

CORDEN, W. M., 'The Effective Protective Rate, the Uniform Tariff Equivalent and the Average Tariff', *Economic Record*, 42, June 1966, 200–16.

CORDEN, W. M., 'Effective Protective Rates in the General Equilibrium Model: A Geometric Note', *Oxford Economic Papers*, 21, July 1969, 135–41.

DIAMOND, P. A., 'Effective Protection of the East African Transfer Taxes', *East African Economic Review*, 4, Dec. 1968, 37–48.

ELLSWORTH, P. T., 'Import Substitution in Pakistan—Some Comments', *Pakistan Development Review*, 6, Autumn 1966, 395–407.

EVANS, H. D., *A General Equilibrium Analysis of Protection: The Effects of Protection in Australia* (unpublished doctoral dissertation, Harvard University, 1968).

EVANS, H. D., 'A Programming Model of Trade and Protection', in McDOUGALL, I. A. and SNAPE, R. H. (eds.), *Studies in International Economics* (North-Holland, Amsterdam, 1970).

FINDLAY, R., 'Comparative Advantage, Effective Protection and the Domestic Resource Cost of Foreign Exchange', *Journal of International Economics*, **1**, 1971.

FINGER, J. M., 'Substitution and the Effective Rate of Protection', *Journal of Political Economy*, **77**, Nov./Dec. 1969, 972–5.

GAMIR, L., 'La medición del proteccionismo arance lario español: El análisis de los aranceles nominales y la teoría de la protección efectiva', *Moneda y Credito, Revista de Economia*, March 1970, 3–46.

GUISINGER, S. E., 'Negative Value Added and the Theory of Effective Protection', *Quarterly Journal of Economics*, **83**, Aug. 1969, 415–33.

GRUBEL, H. G. and JOHNSON, H. G., 'Nominal Tariffs, Indirect Taxes and Effective Rates of Protection: The Common Market Countries 1959', *Economic Journal*, **77**, Dec. 1967, 761–76.

GRUBEL, H. G., JOHNSON, H. G., and RAPP, W. V., 'Excise Taxes and Effective Protection: A Note', *Economic Journal*, **79**, Sept. 1969, 674–5.

GRUBEL, H. G. and LLOYD, P. J., 'Factor Substitution and Effective Tariff Rates', *Review of Economic Studies*, Jan. 1971.

GRUBEL, H. G. and LLOYD, P. J., 'Substitution and Two Concepts of Effective Rate of Protection: Comment', *American Economic Review*, **60**, Dec. 1970, 1003–4.

HUMPHREY, D. B., 'Measuring the Effective Rate of Protection: Direct and Indirect Effects', *Journal of Political Economy*, **77**, Sept./Oct. 1969, 834–44.

HUMPHREY, D. B., 'Demand Inflation and Effective Protection', *Southern Economic Journal*, 37, Oct. 1970, 144–150.

HUMPHREY, D. D., *The United States and the Common Market* (Praeger, New York, 1962).

HUMPHREY, D. B. and TSUKAHARA, T., 'On Substitution and the Effective Rate of Protection', *International Economic Review*, **11**, 1970.

JOHNSON, H. G., 'Tariffs and Economic Development: Some Theoretical Issues', *Journal of Development Studies*, **1**, Oct. 1964, 3–30.

JOHNSON, H. G., 'The Theory of Tariff Structure, with Special Reference to World Trade and Development', in JOHNSON, H. G. and KENEN, P. B., *Trade and Development* (Librairie Droz, Geneva, 1965).

JOHNSON, H. G., 'A Model of Protection and the Exchange Rate', *Review of Economic Studies*, **33**, April 1966, 159–63.

JOHNSON, H. G., 'The Theory of Effective Protection and Preferences', *Economica*, **36**, May 1969, 119–38.

JOHNSON, H. G., 'Effective Protection and General Equilibrium Theory', in JOHNSON H. G., *Aspects of the Theory of Tariffs* (Allen and Unwin, London, 1971).

JONES, R. W., 'Effective Protection and Substitution', *Journal of International Economics*, **1**, 1971.

LEITH, J. C., *Effective Rates of Protection: Analysis and an Empirical Test* (unpublished doctoral dissertation, University of Wisconsin, 1967).

LEITH, J. C., 'Substitution and Supply Elasticities in Calculating the Effective Protective Rate', *Quarterly Journal of Economics*, **82**, Nov. 1968, 588–601; and 'Reply', **84**, Feb. 1970, 158–60.

LEITH, J. C., 'Across-the-Board Nominal Tariff Changes and the Effective Rate of Protection', *Economic Journal*, **78**, Dec. 1968, 982–4.

LEITH, J. C. and REUBER, G. L., 'The Impact of the Industrial Countries' Tariff Structure on their Imports of Manufactures from Less-Developed Countries: A Comment', *Economica*, **36**, Feb. 1969, 75–80.

LEITH, J. C., 'The Effect of Tariffs on Production, Consumption, and Trade: A Revised Analysis', *American Economic Review*, **61**, March 1971.

LEWIS, S. R. and GUISINGER, S. E., 'Measuring Protection in a Developing Country: The Case of Pakistan', *Journal of Political Economy*, **76**, Nov./Dec. 1968, 1170–98.

LITTLE, I., SCITOVSKY, T., and SCOTT, M., *Industry and Trade in Some Developing Countries* (Oxford University Press, London, 1970).

LLOYD, P. J., 'Effective Protection: A Different View', *Economic Record*, **46**, Sept. 1970, 329–40.

KESSEL, D., 'Effective Protection of Industry in Tanzania', *East African Economic Review*, **4**, June 1968, 1–13.

KRUEGER, A. O., 'Some Economic Costs of Exchange Control: The Turkish Case', *Journal of Political Economy*, **74**, Oct. 1966, 466–80.

KRUEGER, A. O., 'Evaluating the Effects of Restrictionist Trade Regimes: Theory and Measurement', *Journal of Political Economy*, 1971.

MACARIO, S., 'Protectionism and Industrialization in Latin America', *Economic Bulletin for Latin America*, **9**, March 1964, 61–101.

McKinnon, R. I., 'Intermediate Products and Differential Tariffs: A Generalization of Lerner's Symmetry Theorem', *Quarterly Journal of Economics*, **80**, Nov. 1966, 584–615.

Massell, B. F., 'The Resource-Allocative Effects of a Tariff and the Effective Protection of Individual Inputs', *Economic Record*, **44**, Sept. 1968, 369–76.

Melvin, J. and Wilkinson, B. W., *Effective Protection in the Canadian Economy* (Economic Council of Canada, Ottawa, 1968).

Michaely, M., *Israel's Foreign Exchange Rate System* (Maurice Falk Institute for Economic Research in Israel, Jerusalem, 1968) [in Hebrew; English translation forthcoming].

Niculescu, B. M., 'Protection and the Tariff', *Economic Record*, **39**, Dec. 1963, 413–27.

Power, J. H., 'Import Substitution as an Industrialization Strategy', *Philippine Economic Journal*, **5**, 1966, 167–204.

Power, J., Sicat, G., and Hsing, M-H., *Philippines and Taiwan: Industrialization and Trade Policies* (Oxford University Press, London, 1970).

Ramaswami, V. K., and Srinivasan, T. N., 'Tariff Structure and Resource Allocation in the Presence of Factor Substitution', in Bhagwati, J. N., *et al.* (eds.), *Trade, Balance of Payments and Growth: Papers in International Economics in Honor of Charles P. Kindleberger* (North-Holland, Amsterdam, 1971).

Reimer, R., 'Effective Rates of Protection in East Africa', *Staff Papers No. 50* of the Institute for Development Studies, University College, Nairobi, Nov. 1969.

Ruffin, R. J., 'Tariffs, Intermediate Goods, and Domestic Protection', *American Economic Review*, **59**, June 1969, 261–9; and 'Reply', **60**, Dec. 1970, 964–7.

Snape, R. H., 'Sugar: Costs of Protection and Taxation', *Economica*, **36**, Feb. 1969, 29–41.

Soligo, R. and Stern, J. J., 'Tariff Protection, Import Substitution and Investment Efficiency', *Pakistan Development Review*, **5**, Summer 1965, 249–69.

Swedish Customs Tariff Commission, *Revision of the Swedish Customs Tariff* (Stockholm, 1957).

Tan, A. H. H., *Differential Protection, Economic Indices and Optimal Trade Policies* (unpublished doctoral dissertation, Stanford University, 1968).

Tan, A. H. H., 'Differential Tariffs, Negative Value-Added and the Theory of Effective Protection', *American Economic Review*, **60**, March 1970, 107–16.

TAN, A. H. H., 'More on the Interpretation of Negative Value-Added in Effective Tariff Rate Calculations', *Malayan Economic Review*, **15**, April 1970, 10–16.

TARIFF BOARD, *Annual Reports for Year 1966–67 and Year 1969–70* (Commonwealth of Australia, Canberra, 1967 and 1970).

TRAVIS, W. P., *On the Theory of Commercial Policy* (unpublished doctoral dissertation, Harvard University, 1961).

TRAVIS, W. P., *The Theory of Trade and Protection* (Harvard University Press, Cambridge, 1964).

TRAVIS, W. P., 'The Effective Rate of Protection and the Question of Labor Protection in the United States', *Journal of Political Economy*, **76**, May/June 1968, 433–61.

VERNON, J., *et al.*, *Report of the Committee of Economic Enquiry*, Vol. II, Appendix L (Commonwealth of Australia, Canberra, 1965).

WOOD, G. D., 'Substitution and Supply Elasticities in Calculating the Effective Protective Rate: Comment', *Quarterly Journal of Economics*, **84**, Feb. 1970, 154–7.

AUTHOR INDEX

SUBJECT INDEX